DATE DUE

DISCARD

The Library Trustee

The Library Trustee

A Practical Guidebook
fifth edition

by

Virginia G. Young

AMERICAN LIBRARY ASSOCIATION

Chicago and London, 1995

Project editor: Kathryn Solt

Cover design: Rich~~mond Jones~~

Composition: Precision T~~ypographers, Inc.~~
   in Century Schoolbook
   on a Miles 33 International composition system.

Printed on 50-pound Glatfelter,
   a pH-neutral stock, and bound in
   Hollistor Roxite B cloth by
   Edwards Brothers, Inc.

The paper used in this publication meets the minimum
requirements of American National Standard for Information
Sciences—Permanence of Paper for Printed Library
Materials, ANSI Z39.48-1992 ∞

Library of Congress Cataloging-in-Publication Data

The library trustee : a practical guidebook / [edited] by Virginia G.
   Young. — 5th ed.
      p.   cm.
   Includes bibliographical references and index.
   ISBN 0-8389-0659-1
      1. Library trustees—United States—Handbooks, manuals, etc.
   2. Public libraries—United States—Administration—Handbooks,
   manuals, etc. I. Young, Virginia G.
   Z681.7.U5L53   1995
   021.8'2—dc20   95-20766

Contents

Preface

In a world dependent upon communication for its survival, the role of the library assumes an importance even greater than its past significance. Language, both spoken and written, is the channel by which civilization moves among people.

Improvement and expansion of library service present ever-changing challenges to professional librarians and library trustees. Meeting these challenges calls for vision, energy, intellectual curiosity, and dedication on the part of trustees in their cooperation with professional librarians toward the goal of better library service.

This fifth edition of THE LIBRARY TRUSTEE: A PRACTICAL GUIDEBOOK is offered to library trustees to help them achieve that goal. It is designed for newcomers and old-timers. It is for trustees in small communities, urban communities, as well as in large systems. The new chapters and revisions are written to assist the trustees with today's problems and give them a look to the future. Certain helpful specifics are included in the appendixes. Further readings are provided, where they exist, at the end of the chapters.

Much gratitude is due the talented contributors who have written chapters in this edition. They graciously agreed to share their knowledge and experience in specialized areas of trusteeship and library work.

Appreciation is also expressed to those trustees, librarians, Friends of the Library, and educators who have come forward with helpful suggestions for this new edition. Special recognition goes to Mary Lee Sebastian, Gene Martin, and Linda L'Hote. The lively response of the readership of the last edition called for some new answers to old problems.

To all of these contributors, direct and indirect, go the sincere thanks of the editor for the new, updated, and revised material included in this edition. There is also the renewed hope that this book will be useful to trustees in fulfilling their public trust.

Virginia G. Young
Editor

1

The Trustee in Today's World

F. William Summers

ommunities in America believe in the public library board. They provide great trust in their fellow citizens to maintain this significant institution on their behalf, and they are very reluctant to turn it over to professional administrators, be they public administrators, or library professionals. Whether the public library is, as it has been called, the *people's* university may be arguable, but it is very definitely the *people's* and they seem determined to keep it so.

If the role of library trustee is so fundamental, then we may well ask what it is that these people hold in trust for their fellow citizens. Milton once observed that the greatest monument to vain hopes is a public library. Certainly Milton cannot be correct or the sixty thousand people who serve as public library trustees would not spend their time keeping the institution not only alive but advancing. Nor would a public library be an early item on any developing community's agenda of civic improvements. If Milton were correct, great cities that already have monumental public library edifices—San Francisco, Chicago, Atlanta, San Antonio—would not be spending millions of dollars to create modern functional library buildings to house expanded programs. If the current prevailing wisdom that local community decision making is always more accurate than centralized decision making is true, then we must conclude that Milton is not correct.

The public library may be the repository of public hopes but clearly those hopes are not vain. They represent the very basic principle of a

F. William Summers is professor and dean emeritus of the School of Library and Information Studies, Florida State University, Tallahassee, Florida.

democracy, that a free people, given the opportunity to inform themselves, will inevitably make the right decisions. The library trustee then is not just the caretaker of buildings and books but the preserver of the community's testament of its own view of culture and of its intellectual aspirations. In an otherwise not very remarkable novel entitled *Colonel Effingham's Raid*, a group of community leaders is discussing how to use a windfall gift that may come to the town. One of them observes that the money should go to improve the local library because "A library is a chock block under the wheel of progress, you can't slip back so easy if you've got a library behind you."[1]

Leading into the Future

The public library today is facing a major transformation in its basic business. The changes in information technology in the last thirty years have been very dramatic. The library of today acquires much of the information its users need in electronic rather than printed form. It also acquires this information from a wide variety of sources. A major shift is that the library must now participate in many networks, consortia, and similar organizations to obtain needed resources. The gain from this change is that the library is no longer limited to the information in its own collection but can call upon data in very remote locations to obtain needed information very quickly.

Many libraries are also using electronic technology to improve their own operations, including electronic catalogs and other data bases which users can consult without coming to the library. The developing "information superhighway" has also offered many libraries new avenues of service. Many public libraries are either serving as hosts or collaborating in the creation of community "freenet" services that provide local citizens electronic access to information of all kinds.

These new developments will certainly change the nature of the library and the nature of service on the community's library board as well. The board will need new kinds of talents and ideas from its board members.

How does it happen then that some communities have outstanding library boards and library programs, and in other cases both the board and the institution labor along, never attracting either much support or much opposition, much community concern or community awareness?

1. Fleming, Berry, *Colonel Effingham's Raid.* (New York: Duell, Sloan & Pearce, 1943), 197.

Having observed many libraries and their boards over a forty-year period, I see clearly that most library boards get the community they deserve and vice versa. The same can be said of the library boards and library directors—library boards get the library directors they deserve and vice versa.

Great communities do not get inferior public libraries. It also does not occur that highly effective library boards get inadequate libraries. Where the board is effective in its operations, addresses itself to the right questions, and interprets the library—its program and its needs—clearly to the community, the people respond. Effective library boards do not find it difficult to attract a quorum to conduct their business, nor do these boards find it difficult to find people willing to serve as their officers. Effective library boards make their fundamental decisions in such a way that the library program is enhanced and advanced. They make these decisions with an orientation to the future and to standards of enduring quality. What then are these fundamental decisions which differentiate excellent library boards from mediocre ones?

Validating Decisions

Fundamentally library boards are involved with the process of decision making. They make decisions for their fellow citizens about their public library, and these decisions determine whether the library will grow and flourish or wither and mold. It is the quality of these decisions which validate the service of the board.

1. *Membership of the Board.* The board must truly represent the community in the sense that the entire community must have confidence and trust in the board. The board cannot and should not at any one moment reflect the community in some direct fractional quota sense, but it should be observed, at least over time, that people from all parts of the community—geographical, ethnic, economic—are members of the board. In addition, whatever the composition of the board at any one point, its members should be people whose talents and contributions will be readily apparent to all.

   It will be argued that in some instances, the board is selected by persons outside the library. However, that does not relieve the board of the responsibility of ensuring that its membership reflects the community. If those with the appointing authority do not make appropriate decisions, then the board must be willing to take their case directly to the people. The library board cannot become the platform of those with axes to grind or laurels to burnish.

The board needs to address several issues about its own organization very directly. The most fundamental of these is what has in other aspects of public life come to be called *term limits.* All too many library boards are still characterized by very long tenure for members. These policies inevitably deprive the board of the opportunity for diversity in membership which any community merits. Neither the ability nor willingness to be continually reappointed to a library board makes any statement about the quality of one's service. Boards that directly set reasonable limits for board service tend, over time, to be much healthier and better regarded by their community than those which do not.

Another issue with which a healthy board will grapple directly is that of lack of attendance and participation by members. It is not an issue that arises often, but when it does the board will be well served by a set of policies and procedures developed in advance rather than having to make an ad hoc decision involving an individual. Most library boards are not and should not be so large that frequent or continued absence by a member does not diminish the effectiveness of the board. Boards should expect regular attendance and have mechanisms for informing the appointing authority when a vacancy has occurred because of absence and a lack of interest. To do less deprives the community of a voice on its board.

2. *Selection and Evaluation of a Library Director.* The selection and periodic evaluation of a library director has been described as the most crucial decision that a library board makes. Certainly these matters have far-reaching consequences for the library program. Whether the board is an administrative one or an advisory board, it should expect and insist on being fully and directly involved in the selection of a library director and in the periodic evaluation of that person's performance, regardless of where the responsibility for actual appointment may lie. If the board is not directly and fully involved in these key actions, the director will correctly conclude that the board is not of major importance in decision making.

The periodic evaluation of the director is also critical to reflecting the community's expectations into the operation of the library. The board that does not evaluate the director has no way to tell that person what the community really thinks about his or her administration of the library either positively or negatively. The city council and city manager may have different expectations of the library director than those of the community. The ability to keep the powers at city hall content may be a valuable skill, but it may or may not coincide with the ability to deliver the program of library services which the community needs and wants, and the board is uniquely qualified to address these matters. It is probably accurate to observe that in today's local politics the board that is willing to be shunted aside in these crucial matters is also very likely to be ignored on other matters of significance as well.

3. *Developing and Approving the Operating Policies.* From the community's point of view, the most crucial policies of the library are those which relate to the selection of materials and those relating to the rules and regulations for using the library and its facilities. The board must insist that there be written policies spelling out who is entitled to use the library and under what conditions. The authority of the library staff to restrain or prohibit use must be defined and those affected must be afforded access to the board for appeal of these decisions. Policies on such matters as length of loans, overdue fines, limits on the amount of materials that may be borrowed, and amount and kind of reference work to be done may seem mundane or pro forma. However, they are of critical importance to those citizens who will or will not use the library because of them. Boards, acting for the community, should seek to make these policies as broad as possible, and before accepting restrictions to be placed on their fellow citizens, should require hard evidence rather than opinion that these policies are necessary and equitable.

Many libraries have policies that have never been legally scrutinized, and some policies that have never been properly promulgated. A policy developed by a staff member twenty years ago to serve a particular problem, and assiduously followed since, does not achieve standing simply because of longevity. All library policies relating to users and to use need to be reviewed periodically, at least every five years. Materials change, circumstances change, and the community changes. A policy restricting the number of books a user may borrow might have made sense when the library was young and small, but it is probably unnecessary when the library is twenty years older and much larger.

If the library has meeting rooms that it intends to make available to community groups, policies will have to be carefully crafted to assure equity in affording all groups access to these spaces. Access to library meeting room space has been a matter of contention in some communities. Some groups and individuals interpret access to the library meeting room as a form of endorsement or encouragement of a group or its purposes and have not wished the library to grant access to groups with which they disagree.

4. *Selection and Retention of Materials.* Of all the areas of policy with which a board needs to deal, it is those relating to which materials are to be added to or retained in the library collection that are most likely to be challenged in a very public and controversial manner. Most often challenges will arise over material that is already in the library and which an individual and/or group seeks to have removed or restricted. Less frequently, but also troublesome, are challenges about materials that are not included in the library.

As will be detailed elsewhere in this volume, the effective board will have in place policies to deal with such matters. All too often boards regard these policies in much the same way a homeowner regards a fire extinguisher—something to be acquired, put in a safe place, and not noticed again until needed. As with fire extinguishers such a procedure is a recipe for disaster. The materials selection policy must be reexamined periodically. The board should receive regular reports from the director on the operation of the policy, and there should be periodic intervals at which the policy is reconsidered.

It also should not be assumed that challenges to the materials policy will be left solely to the library board. Even if the board has the operating authority to approve the policies, it would be well advised to periodically brief the county or city council on the operations of its collection development policies, so that challengers will not find "end runs" around the board to be a fruitful avenue.

The board also needs to spend sufficient time in developing and discussing these policies that it develops a genuine consensus and commitment to them. In the heat of a censorship conflict is not the place to find that several board members have reservations about the policies or that the board has an inconsistent understanding of their meaning.

5. *Financial Support of the Library Program.* Next to the selection of the library director, the board's most critical functions are in

the area of obtaining an adequate base of financial support for the library program. All too often boards are willing to leave this critical area to the director and staff because they are the most knowledgeable about the needs of the library and the translation of those needs into costs. However, one of the chief questions that the board is appointed to answer is "What should be the level of the community's investment in the library?" The appropriating authorities want to hear the answers to that question from the citizens whom they have appointed to oversee the library. The library director and staff can provide technical details on the preparation of the budget, but the board must demonstrate that it understands and supports the budget being requested. To do less will result in an eroding of support for both the budget and the board on the part of elected officials.

Library board members also need to remember that holding down the local level of public expenditure is not the function for which they are appointed. Most communities already have a more than adequate number of individuals and groups fulfilling that role. The role of the library board is to put forth a program of library service to meet the needs of their fellow citizens.

Conclusion

The above list is not a catalog of all the decisions the library board makes nor is it intended to be. Boards vary a great deal in their responsibilities and in the procedures of local government. These decisions are, however, among those which appear to be most critical in determining the success of the library program. Put another way, if these five areas are dealt with properly, most of the other decisions will also fall into place.

From all that is happening in our society, clearly the public library of the year 2010 may be a very different institution from that which most of us have known and cherished. Some of these differences have very serious consequences for library boards. The public library of the future will be:

1. Highly electronic in the information it offers and in the access to that information.
2. Very diverse in its staff and its user population. Different people now use the library for different reasons, and those differences will be magnified. Differences in ethnicity, gender, age, language, etc., will be a major characteristic of community life.

3. Utilized remotely as much or more than it is used in person. This change will have profound impacts upon the staff, services and roles that the library plays in the community.

The call to join the library board may not be viewed as the most glamorous or prestigious an individual can receive. It is an invitation to join in a long tradition of fundamental public service in governing, preserving, and improving a very significant part of the community's intellectual and cultural life. The library board is a quintessential democratic institution, and the person who serves well gives testament to the highest ideals of our country. Accept the call with enthusiasm and alacrity. You will enter upon important work, deal with critical issues and ideas emerging in our society, and meet an amazing variety of interesting people. What more can one ask of public service?

2 Duties and Responsibilities of Trustees

Virginia G. Young

oday's library trustee has undertaken responsibility for a changing and complex institution. There is a vast difference between a modern library with its many services and the mausoleum for books which prevailed many years ago. As great a difference has taken place in the implications of trusteeship. Any archaic misconception of the library trustee should be classed with the outdated cryptlike gloom of yesterday's library. These unrealistic images, together with the stock caricature labeled *librarian* (she of the repressive glare and the finger on the lip), should be firmly retired from cliché to oblivion.

There are differences in the establishment of library boards in that some are appointed, others are elected; some are governing boards, others are advisory; some state statutes and municipal ordinances have detailed rules for trustees, others are broad, but all library boards are responsible for the library.

Responsibility for control of the library, vested in the library board, makes heavy demands upon the time and thought of the library trustee. Services undreamed of a few years ago are now part of every library program. Modern educational methods, new technical aids, the general and specialized needs of the public, all require versatility and know-how in the board members charged with responsibility for the library.

Moreover, the public library today does not stand alone. Through li-

Virginia G. Young is a trustee and president of the Columbia (Missouri) Library board, past chairperson of the Missouri Coordinating Board for Higher Education and the Missouri State Library Board, and former president of the American Library Trustee Association.

brary networks and automated systems, the public library is an integral part of the whole of all types of libraries. These libraries are associated together to provide access to the total library and informational resources of the country regardless of the individual's location or station in life.

The public library is also currently much more involved with other institutions in the community. All of these cooperative efforts, which are designed to provide increased services to every individual, place even greater responsibilities on library trustees.

Purpose of the Library Board

Trusteeship by definition is the agency of a person (or persons) designated to act as governor or protector over property belonging to another. Since a public library belongs to its entire community, library boards have been created by law to act as citizen control or governing body of the library. Library trustees accordingly are public officials and servants of the public, and the powers delegated to library boards are a public trust.

Duties and responsibilities inherent in this public trust may be loosely classified as being of two kinds: the legal responsibilities specifically enjoined upon the board by statute, and the practical responsibilities dealing with day-to-day operation of the library.

The statutory board powers, such as fiduciary responsibility, handling of buildings and real estate belonging to the library, and control of library finances, are clearly defined in the state and municipal laws affecting libraries. These legal responsibilities are discussed in detail in other chapters in relation both to law and to finances. Boards, a creation of law, are responsible under the law for the actions they take.

Duties of Board and Librarian Are Different

The board's multiple responsibilities covering the actual operation of the library bear directly upon every aspect of its program. This has often led to the mistaken belief that the board's duties and responsibilities overlap those of the librarian, a misconception which can lead to endless confusion and misunderstanding.

It cannot be too firmly emphasized that the library board represents overall citizen control of the library, whereas the librarian's training and experience have been in administration of the library. A clear-cut definition of the duties of each is shown in the chart included in this chapter.

Although duties of the librarian and the library board fall into roughly parallel areas, the obligations and responsibilities of each are entirely separate. The board may properly expect the technical work for a number of their duties to be done by the librarian and staff. Also, the trustees will want to consult with the librarian and staff in fulfilling many of their duties even though the final determination rests with the board.

Properly comprehended and performed, these parallel duties will strengthen and complement each other without risk of competitive or divided authority.

Duties and Responsibilities[1]

Of the Library Board

1. Employ a competent and qualified librarian
2. Determine and adopt written policies to govern the operation and program of the library
3. Determine the purposes of the library and secure adequate funds to carry on the library's program
4. Know the program and needs of the library in relation to the community; keep abreast of standards and library trends; cooperate with the librarian in planning the library program, and support the librarian and staff in carrying it out
5. Establish, support, and participate in a planned public relations program
6. Assist in the preparation of the annual budget
7. Know local and state laws; actively support library legislation in the state and nation
8. Establish among the library policies those dealing with book and material selection
9. Attend all board meetings and see that accurate records are kept on file at the library
10. Attend regional, state, and national trustee meetings and workshops, and affiliate with the appropriate professional organizations
11. Be aware of the services of the state library
12. Report regularly to the governing officials and the general public

Of the Librarian

1. Act as technical advisor to the board; recommend needed policies for board action; recommend employment of all personnel and supervise their work
2. Carry out the policies of the library as adopted by the board
3. Suggest and carry out plans for extending library services
4. Prepare regular reports embodying the library's current progress and future needs; cooperate with the board to plan and carry out the library program
5. Maintain an active program of public relations
6. Prepare an annual budget for the library in consultation with the board and give a current report of expenditures against the budget at each meeting
7. Know local and state laws; actively support library legislation in the state and nation
8. Select and order all books and other library materials
9. Attend all board meetings other than those in which the librarian's salary or tenure are under discussion; may serve as secretary of the board
10. Affiliate with the state and national professional organizations and attend professional meetings and workshops
11. Make use of the services and consultants of the state library
12. Report regularly to the library board, to the officials of local government, and to the general public

1. Virginia G. Young, *The Trustee of a Small Public Library*, 2d ed., LAMA Small Libraries Publication, no. 1 (Chicago: ALA, 1992).

The Board's Duties

Although the twelve specific duties of the library board shown in the foregoing chart are not necessarily listed in the order of their importance, the first and second named are literally paramount. Employment of a librarian and making of library policy are two functions of the board which must be carried out before a workable program for the library can be formulated. These, together with most of the other responsibilities listed, merit chapters of their own, and are discussed at length elsewhere in this book.

The Board's Role in the Community

The duty listed as to "know the program and needs of the library in relation to the community; keep abreast of standards and library trends; plan and carry out the library program," covers the trustee's obligation not only to know the library but to interpret the library to the community. This liaison role, as interpreter between library and community, is an important part of the public trust assumed by service on a library board.

It devolves upon the trustee, as layperson and as community representative on the library governing board, to bring the public's point of view and the community needs into plans for the library program. As a public official charged with control of the library, it is also part of the trustee's liaison work to make the community aware of the library's need for financial and moral support, and of the plans and programs for development of better library service. Effective library service is that which meets, so far as possible, the needs of the total community, placing the library in its proper relationship of service in the community picture. Only the library trustee is in the unique position of forming a link between the public and the professional library world, through firsthand knowledge and experience in both areas.

The Trustee's Obligation to Know

Obviously this important liaison work, so necessary to building a favorable climate for the library's progress, cannot be carried out unless the library board knows its library. Indeed, the alert trustee should realize the need for knowing libraries as a whole—other public libraries, school libraries, college, and university libraries. What are the problems of libraries? How are the problems being met? What is the basic philosophy of good library service? How does the trustee's own library fit into the overall picture? What is the library profession as a whole thinking and talking about? What are the comparative values of new trends in library techniques, and how do they fit into the needs of the community for total library service?

The Board's Duty to Plan

The trustee's duties include the obligation to plan for the library's future growth and development—to think creatively. Channels for learning about the library are plentiful. Study of the library literature, observant visits to other libraries, consultation with the librarian, advice from the state library, all offer education to the trustee who honestly desires to learn.

Every trustee who enters upon service to the library has a choice to make: to be indifferent, acquiescent, and ineffectual, or to learn everything possible about the responsibilities of trusteeship and so fulfill the public trust.

The Public Trust

The ultimate purpose of a library program must be to meet the needs of the community and the individuals in it. These individuals form the public which in turn looks to the library board as its deputies to carry out a library program which satisfactorily provides this important community service.

Responsibilities of library board members are both tangible and intangible. Some are of immediate and practical effect; others have a far-reaching influence on the library's future.

The dedicated trustee accepts them all as part of faithfully rendered service to the library. These responsibilities constitute the board member's public trust.

3 Qualifications and Appointment of Trustees

Virginia G. Young

 ood library trustees are neither born nor made; they create themselves through inner growth of education and experience in trusteeship, built upon personal background and attributes. Individual backgrounds and characteristics may vary, but good library trustees have certain qualifications in common.

Desirable Qualifications for a Trustee

Surveys of the library literature and lists compiled by trustee organizations agree on the following qualifications for effective trusteeship:

1. Interest in the library, in the community, and in the library's relationship to the community.
2. Readiness to devote time and effort to carrying out the duties of trusteeship.
3. Recognition of the library's importance as a center of information, of community culture, recreation, and continuing education.
4. Close acquaintance with community social and economic conditions, and with groups within the community.
5. Ability to work well with others: board members, librarian and staff members, and the public served by the library.
6. An open mind, intellectual curiosity, and respect for the opinions of others.

7. Initiative and ability to establish policies for successful operation of the library and impartial service to all its patrons.
8. Courage to plan creatively, to carry out plans effectively, and to withstand pressures, prejudices, and provincialism.
9. Ability to envision library development to include internal improvement and external expansion.
10. Devotion to the library, its welfare and progress.

To this list of attributes held in common by all good trustees, every individual board member brings personal experiences and skills which may serve the library well. Professional experience in law, architecture, education, and accounting, for example, can be very valuable to a board member. Practical business experience, executive ability, management skills, and plain common sense are useful contributions. Often the library board has cause to be grateful to board members with political know-how.

The qualities listed are of nearly equal importance, although one has frequently been overlooked as essential. No library trustee can give full measure of service without willingness to give time and effort to the duties of trusteeship. The most brilliantly endowed trustee who does not attend board meetings will not render as much real service to the library as one less gifted who is faithful and diligent in performance.

Devotion to the library's welfare and progress is perhaps the most important single qualification, for all others stem from it. It would be better for the trustee who lacks this devotion not to be on the board at all, for as Barrie's Maggie Shand said of charm, "If you don't have it, it doesn't much matter what else you have."

The Board Should Represent Total Community

For many years, whether by accident of by design, library boards were invariably drawn from groups of similar background and experience. Today's library has a new and increasing importance to the total community, and a well-balanced board should represent a cross section of the community.

The outmoded notion that trustee appointments should be made only in a small class of "cultured" persons is disproved today by the very real interest in libraries evidenced by business, industry, and labor. Every segment of today's society has a stake in the library. The needs and desires of every segment of society, including adequate recognition of all minority groups, should be represented in the library program. It is important for trustees to reach their own group in the community;

collect their views, and speak to and for them. The resulting broad diversity of viewpoints will be not only democratic but conducive to a healthy and vital relationship between library and community.

Appointment or Election of Trustees

Library trustees usually serve by appointment, although in several states trustees are elected by the voters and must campaign for the office and take their chances at the polls as do other elected officials. In some instances, the appointing body requests the citizens to apply for appointment to the library board.

Trustees serve without compensation under appointment from the public official or governing body in charge of the political division in which the library is located. Governors, county judges, mayors, city managers, city councils, and boards of commissioners are all appointing bodies for their various library boards. Terms of office may vary in different localities.

Unless the appointing official is aware of the importance of choosing a trustee who has desirable qualifications, it is only natural that such appointments may often be left to chance or political patronage. It is only fair to state here, however, that in many cases trustees who have come onto library boards in this manner have felt the influence and appeal of the library to such an extent that they have proved to be excellent trustees. These trustees may or may not be the exceptions, but certainly the welfare of the library is too important for service on its board to be considered merely in the light of a status symbol.

The solution has frequently been to communicate with the appointing official, setting out qualifications necessary for a good library trustee, and stressing the importance of such appointments. This communication may well be carried through by the state trustee organization, although it is entirely ethical for a library board to lay these facts before their own appointing officials. When a vacancy occurs, the communication may be accompanied by a list suggesting names of individuals who would be valuable library trustees. The list of desirable qualifications is comprehensive enough to allow appointing officials wide latitude of choice. There are instances where appointing officials have set up procedures which provide for applications by citizens for appointments to boards and commissions.

When library trustees are elected, it is incumbent upon the local library board to encourage good and qualified candidates to run for the office. Since the board members are themselves elected public officials, it is perhaps best that the board take no official part in the campaign.

Individual board members are of course free to back a candidate of their choice by aiding in specific campaigns and helping to get the vote out on election day.

Tenure of Service

Even in cases where the trustee's term is defined by law, tenure of service may be drawn out to indefinite length by reappointment. Where trustees are elected, a trustee deeply interested in the library may run for the office again and again. So frequently has this been done and so lengthy has the tenure become in such cases, that a natural question arises: would it be better to have someone else serve who might bring new ideas and varied viewpoints?

Continuity of service, it may be argued, makes up in valuable experience and education in trusteeship what may be lost by absence of new blood on the board. The trustee who has devoted time and effort to learning as much as possible about the duties and responsibilities of board membership is without doubt valuable to the library. But it may be argued on the other hand that when the service of even a valuable trustee is terminated, the library still has a staunch, well-informed friend in the former trustee, and has at the same time the advantage of new faces and fresh thinking on the board.

Certainly a self-perpetuating board is much like closed-circuit television: the image reaches only the favored few. Having the best interests of the library at heart, the good library trustee would rather step down than see the library program stagnate. This question of voluntary termination by resignation or refusal of reappointment or reelection is one which requires honest self-appraisal. Perhaps the criterion by which to decide is simply to assess one's value to the library now, and to weigh that value against the benefits to be derived from thoughts and energies of new board members.

One workable solution to the dilemma has been found in staggered board terms, so that at all times senior board members are balanced by newcomers in trusteeship. Another solution has been statutory prohibition of self-succession, allowing for a certain period of time to elapse before a trustee is reappointed or reelected.

In the final analysis, the problem is best solved by the trustee's own attitude. A sincere devotion to the progress and welfare of the library means giving to it lifelong service, whether on or off the board.

4 Organization of the Library Board

Minnie-Lou Lynch

very board of directors meeting has three essentials: a quorum of its members, a well-prepared agenda, and an alert and informed chairperson presiding. Effective library board meetings need more: every board member should attend, if the community's image is to be faithfully reflected in the board's actions. Since the well-balanced board represents a cross section of the community, it should be taken for granted that each member will be at meetings. Willingness to attend board meetings is a primary responsibility of trusteeship. There are no proxies in fulfilling the public trust.

Provision for regularly scheduled meetings of the board should be written into the bylaws, and minutes of each meeting should be kept. These written records constitute a history of the library and of the board's actions, invaluable for future reference and consultation.

Individual library boards should settle upon dates, times, and frequency of meetings. The bylaws should cover these points, as well as establishment of a quorum, procedure on special or called meetings of the board, appointment of special committees, and amendments to the bylaws. A library's business is public business, and all library board meetings should be announced in advance and open to the public. Exceptions are made on advice of legal counsel.

There are standard guides for parliamentary procedure in conducting meetings. The two most frequently used are *Robert's Rules of Order*,

Minnie-Lou Lynch is a trustee and past president of the Allen Parish (Louisiana) Library Board of Control, and former president of the American Library Trustee Association.

which includes procedures for small boards of twelve or less, and *The Standard Code of Parliamentary Procedure* by Alice Sturgis, which is easily understood.

Preparing the Agenda

The librarian should prepare the agenda and supporting documents in close consultation with the board chairperson. Copies of the agenda should be sent out in advance to every board member so that none will attend the meeting unprepared.

In preparing the agenda, one chief aim should be kept always in mind: to make every board meeting meaningful. More absenteeism results from simple boredom than from any other cause. Routine business there always must be, but the community leaders who serve as members of the library board will come to feel repeated routine meetings a waste of their time, falling far short of their own purpose in undertaking trusteeship of the library. The library board that must resort to frantic last-minute calls to turn out a quorum is a library board in trouble, and the apathy of the "bored" members will be reflected by a stagnating library program.

There is plenty of latitude in the category of "new business" to offset this threat. Library boards are the planning officials of the library, and time should be allowed at every board meeting for consideration of the library's next progressive step. Creative thinking by the board may be sparked in any number of ways: by reports from trustees or special committees assigned to explore new trends, by informed professional advice and suggestions from the librarian, by presentations of staff members regarding various service programs offered by the library, by reports on regional and national conferences, and by visits to other libraries. Here is an ideal spot for board members to benefit from talks by professional consultants from the state library or elsewhere. Whatever broadens the horizons of the board and stimulates creative thinking for library progress should be provided for and included to some degree in the agenda for every board meeting.

The Order of Business

Consultation of the literature and of handbooks of many state trustee associations reveals the following order of business as approved by the majority of library boards:

Roll call

Reading of minutes of previous meeting

Correspondence and communications

Report of librarian

Financial report and approval of expenditures

Report of standing committees

Report of special committees

Unfinished business

New business

Adjournment

Routine business should be disposed of as quickly as possible to allow time for discussion of other matters. The board's long-range plans should always be kept as a "live" subject for such discussions, and never shelved or taken for granted. The board's continuing study of the standards and ways of achieving them should also be kept before the members.

Some library boards move the librarian's report out of the "routine business" category into the area of stimulating discussion by using this report as a basis for evaluating the work of the librarian and the progress being made on the library's overall program. Both board and librarian can gain much in this manner, as accomplishments, obstacles, and plans are reviewed.

The Role of the Chairperson

Leadership and tact are called for in almost equal degrees in the chairperson of a library board. A thorough knowledge of library programs and problems is needed for intelligent conduct of board meetings. Cordial cooperation with the librarian and with other board members smooths the way for efficient operation of library business.

Almost every group contains one voice which is heard more often and more loudly than the others. Sometimes this articulate voice denotes superior leadership and information; sometimes not. It is part of the chairperson's responsibility to discern this tendency and tactfully hold it in check, making sure that every board member has a chance to be heard. It is entirely possible that the most valuable contributions will come from some less vocal member. If all are democratically given a voice and a vote, the board will avoid the risk of being a mirror for the opinions of any one member.

Orientation of New Members

As soon as a new trustee is appointed, the chairperson and the librarian should give the new board member a helpful welcome by following the Trustee Orientation Program as developed by the American Library Trustee Association (see Appendix 1). This program may be used either at a full board meeting, or informally in the librarian's office, with the chairperson, the librarian, and the new trustee forming a question-and-answer trio. The more informal group is recommended for a relaxed and personal atmosphere, but at least one orientation should be given before the board for its inspirational effect.

The orientation program summarizes the meaning of trusteeship, grounds the new board member in information about the library, introduces the trustee to staff members and to the organization and administration of the library, and arms him or her with general information about the responsibilities of trusteeship at state and national, as well as local, levels. The librarian should supplement the program with materials drawn from the recommended reading list, for the new member's self-education.

At the new trustee's first board meeting, a wise chairperson will immediately give the new member an assignment, enabling the novice to identify with the library program and the board's function from the very outset of his or her service.

Standing and Special Committees

Some library boards, usually those of larger libraries, maintain standing committees of three or more board members who are assigned to follow various phases of the library's operation and program and report to the board with recommendations.

However, there is a decided trend to have the board work as a committee of the whole in general areas of library operation, programs, and expansion. This method involves each member in every phase of library development and avoids creating "specialists" artificially.

Special committees may be created from time to time to carry out limited projects on which the total board cannot spend its time. These committees may be empowered to seek advice from members of the community and to do research as background for a decision by the whole board.

Individual library boards will find useful ways in which to involve all members, preferably in the total library picture.

Controversies, Private and Public

Disagreements, differences of opinion, and personality clashes are bound to occur from time to time in any group. Library boards should be democratically administered, with every member having the right to express an opinion and vote accordingly. A sagacious chairperson will encourage discussion while not allowing matters to get out of hand, and persons qualified to serve on a library board should include among those qualifications an adult acceptance of the will of the majority.

Esprit de corps should be bigger than any individual feelings; consequently disagreements among board members should not emerge from the board room, to the public detriment of the library. Here is another place where the trustee's devotion to the welfare of the library should ensure the board standing shoulder to shoulder as a solid entity behind its policies and behind the librarian in carrying out those policies.

The field of library service is in the realm of ideas, and it is but natural that, from time to time, citizens or citizen groups who are adherents of ideas opposing the policies of the board will wish to be heard. This is entirely within their rights, and the board's written policies should provide for such contingencies.

Such a request for hearing should be made in writing, and the conditions of the hearing should be made clear in advance to the petitioners. After the hearing, the board should take such matters under advisement to allow time for its deliberations and action. Once the board has voted its decision, the trustees should again be governed by esprit de corps outside the board room. Loyalty to library welfare will not encourage either schisms on the board or feuds within the community.

Need for Board to Retain an Attorney

Library boards should hire and retain the services of a competent attorney. Every important step in building, property management, contracts, and the framing of favorable library legislation requires legal advice. Should controversial questions arise, particularly in the area of attempted censorship or limitation of the right of freedom to read, the board should be represented by legal counsel.

Sharing Opportunities

Opportunities for assuming responsibility such as being the president officer of the board or of subcommittees should be rotated among board members to avoid domination of the board by a privileged clique. Educational benefits, such as payment of expenses to trustee workshops and conferences, should also be shared democratically among the board members, so that every member has an opportunity to acquire the experience and knowledge of trusteeship to be gained.

Further Reading

Robert, Henry M. *The Scott, Foresman Robert's Rules of Order Newly Revised.* Glenview, Ill.: Scott, Foresman, 1990.

Sturgis, Alice. *The Standard Code of Parliamentary Procedure*, 3rd ed. New and revised. New York: McGraw-Hill, 1993

5 The Trustee as Policymaker

Virginia G. Young

ibrary policy has been compared to a road map, and policy, like a map, should be clearly drawn on paper. This written policy should set out the terms of the library's operation: the what, when, where, and how, frequently the who, and sometimes the why.

Policy determines the pulse of a community library service—availability of library service, terms of staff employment, the objectives of the library program, and the intellectual freedom which the community has a right to expect. These factors are the structural steel on which a library in its true meaning is raised. Although the development of policy is accomplished in consultation with the librarian and staff, the final determination of library policy and its adoption are the responsibility of the library board. Except for the employment of a librarian, no other duty is more important to the library and its welfare.

What Policy Should Cover

Every library board should determine and record its policies on:

1. General library objectives.
2. Hours open; hours of staff duty; holidays.
3. Vacation and sick leave for librarian and staff.
4. Salary schedule; personnel classification chart; retirement provisions.
5. Type and quality of books and other library materials to be added to the library collection.
6. Charges for lost books; fines on overdue books.

7. Services to specialized groups.
8. Special services: to nonresident borrowers, use of meeting rooms, etc.
9. Cooperation with other libraries.
10. Acceptance of gifts and memorials.
11. Methods of extending services: branch libraries, bookmobiles, participation in library system, etc.
12. Public relations and publicity.
13. Payment of expenses for trustees and staff to attend library conferences, workshops, and professional meetings.
14. Payment of state and national association dues for board members and for the library.
15. Local circumstances may dictate the development of additional policies.

Flexibility Where Needed

Policy should be clearly stated. It serves as a public relations tool. Policy should provide a firm foundation for the librarian's administration of the library and should support the relationship of the staff with the public. Policies should be made known to the public so that they are clearly understood. Except where details are essential, as in hours of operation, salary schedules, and the like, library policy should be expressed in broad terms, since it is a basis for procedure and need not include details of procedure. It goes without saying that policy must rest upon the legal basis of laws applicable to the operation of libraries.

Library board members should carefully consider each item of policy before it is adopted and recorded. Most often the librarian is a source of informed recommendation for new or changed policy, growing out of day-to-day administration of policy and constant contact with the public. Once adopted, a policy should have the support of the entire board, the librarian, and the staff, and it is the board's moral obligation to stand behind the librarian in carrying out policies. Boards are most frequently called upon to support policies in the field of public relations and of book selection. Heat-of-the-moment decisions can be avoided and crises are much less likely to occur if the relevant policy, which is written, can be cited.

Firmness of policy and its administration should not denote rigidity, and the library board should keep an open mind toward needed changes and revisions of policy. Frequently new needs supersede previous ones; often a community's whole picture can change in a short space of years. The library board should be prepared to move with the times, and to revise or change its policies accordingly. Provision for an annual review of policies should be made to keep them current.

Policy on Operation

Library boards should make every effort to have the library open as long as possible. Hours of operation should conform as closely as possible to community needs. The library standing closed and locked is a dead and expensive library so far as the community is concerned.

Hours of staff duty, salary schedules, leave, retirement provisions, and fringe benefits should be as generously framed and administered as the library's financial resources permit. A library board, like every other employer, will get exactly what it pays for, and cut-rate salaries offer no inducement to good librarians and staff members. Consultant service from the state library, reference to the library periodicals, and comparison with similar libraries are the best guides for a library board in determination of salary schedules and working conditions for the librarian and staff.

Book Selection Policies

Once a fairly routine item in library policy, book selection has come to be a vital area in today's world of controversial ideas and approaches. Library board members must make an honest appraisal of the question of intellectual freedom before framing their policies in this field. Once the policy is adopted, it should be adhered to fairly and impartially.

As administrator of the board's policies, the librarian is sometimes caught up in the crosscurrents of opposing ideas. Here again, devotion to the library and its welfare should weld the board into solid backing for the librarian and defense of intellectual freedom for the community.

The American Library Association (ALA) Committee on Intellectual Freedom serves as an advisory body to the Association, to the profession, and to trustees faced with the problem of censorship and interference with intellectual freedom in the library.

Library boards should also be familiar with the provisions of the "Library Bill of Rights," adopted by the Council of the American Library Association to meet new demands, and with the "Freedom to Read Statement" endorsed by the Council of ALA. These statements (see Appendixes 3 and 4) constitute strong backing from the American Library Association offering encouragement to the library board faced with controversy and litigation.

Whether such controversy arrives from the ill-informed, the malcontent, or from honest opposition of ideas, the library board must stand firm and unified behind the principle of intellectual freedom, and behind its librarian in carrying out that principle.

Special Services

Groups

Special services offered by libraries provide an excellent channel for public relations, and for building up warm and friendly support for the library within the community. Civic clubs, study clubs, Great Books groups, garden clubs, and business firms and associations have found the local library a rewarding host. In cooperation with the librarian, additions to the library collection covering the special interests of such groups are often made, and their gratitude is usually expressed in practical gifts and appreciative support for the library.

Most specialized groups are keenly interested in knowing what the library offers in their particular fields, in suggesting additions to the collection, and often in donations of books and related materials. The library board should be alert to the needs of these groups in making long-range plans for the library program. Too often, libraries operate on the basis of what is available to these groups, whereas every effort should be made to ascertain their needs and provide for them.

Use of the library meeting hall or boardroom by these groups is part of the library's community relationship. At times when the library needs support in an election, in the legislature, or before the governing body, services to these groups usually proved to have been bread cast upon the waters, and the members repay the library handsomely by backing the library's plans and programs.

The Friends of the Library is a unique group within the community, since it is organized for the purpose of serving the library. This group is discussed at more length in a separate chapter, but it must be included among any groups listed as "special." The library board and librarian who work cooperatively with the Friends of the Library will have cause for gratitude.

The Handicapped

Services to blind and otherwise handicapped individuals of the community should be a part of every library program to the fullest measure possible. It is important that consideration be given to services to the people within as well as outside the library building. These handicapped people are the citizens whose need of the library resources is perhaps greater than that of any others. Provision to meet their needs should be in every library budget to some degree.

The Library of Congress, Division for the Blind and Physically Handicapped, provides both books in Braille and Talking Books to various centrally located libraries designated as regional centers throughout the United States. These materials may be obtained from the regional centers. Librarians and trustees should be familiar with the center nearest them and should make every effort to provide and to publicize this service. Every library, no matter how small or poorly financed, can afford to take certain practical steps toward serving these patrons. Any library can manage to do some or all of the following:

1. Consult with the state library and the headquarters of the American Library Association as to free materials available.
2. Send the librarian or a designated staff member to workshops or conferences on the subject.
3. Build a collection of records and tapes for loan to the blind and the shut-in, but avoid duplicating materials that are available in the Library of Congress program.
4. Build a collection of visual aids for loan to the deaf. Consider the possibility of an in-house TTY (teletypewriter) machine for regular correspondence with deaf patrons.
5. Arrange pickup and delivery service of books, records, and materials to shut-ins.
6. Arrange at least one street-level entrance to the library to accommodate wheel chairs and crutches (see latest American Standards Institute accessibility standards for buildings).

Delivery service to shut-ins should include cooperation with local hospital programs. If the library site and location preclude a street-level entrance, the construction of a ramp (also appreciated by heart patients, the aging, and any temporarily handicapped individuals) is always desirable. The library board must consider these patrons and their interests, and provide for them. Federal law requires that physically handicapped people be given access to public buildings. Every effort should be made to eliminate architectural barriers. Government documents are available which may be helpful in this planning. Title I of the Library Services and Construction Act makes federal funds available to the states to provide library services to the physically handicapped, including the blind.

Nonresident Borrowers

Many libraries make a charge for services to nonresident borrowers, feeling this a proper discrimination between the borrower who is not a taxpayer and the regular patrons of the community. Other libraries will not lend directly to nonresidents, insisting that the request must come through the nonresident's own library. This is an indirect and time-consuming method frustrating to the would-be borrower.

The growing trend among libraries today, with increased extension of library support, is for reciprocal lending service to patrons, with the feeling that a responsible borrower who holds a card from his or her home library should be welcome as such in every other library. The idea of a statewide library card, giving the borrower privileges in every library in his or her home state, is gaining adherents and a universally accepted library card seems an even more desirable goal.

Individual libraries whose boards have accepted the worth of the idea are pioneering it in their own communities by extending their policies to allow full privileges to nonresident library card holders, and reciprocal agreements with other libraries. Many library systems already have one card for any library in the system and reciprocal borrowing privileges are also being set up between systems.

Charges and Fines Levied

Boards today are concerned with the possibility of charging for some costly services, such as extended online searching, video services, in some instances, and interlibrary loans.

Libraries properly charge for lost and damaged books. More and more libraries have found it necessary to utilize security systems, which are designed to protect against the theft of library materials. These systems are expensive, so a decision must be based on cost-effectiveness in relation to material. Moreover, a public relations program should be promoted explaining the use of the system in advance of its installation. This will help allay any apprehension on the part of the public. Some states have within their library laws a general provision making the keeping of library property a misdemeanor after suitable notification has been given. In that case, board policy is formed within such a framework.

Some libraries are instituting the practice of no charge for overdue books, and report very favorable results in returned books. It has been proven that there are no more books overdue under this system than in systems where fines are charged. Many patrons feel the charging of fines is punitive, and the elimination of this resentment and annoyance opens the way for books to be returned even if somewhat past their due date. Moreover, it has been found in many instances that the staff time consumed in handling fines, if used in service to the public, would be much more valuable than any income derived from fines collected. That most patrons would prefer to return the library books if they could do so without penalty is shown by the enthusiastic response to the annual or semiannual "Forgiveness Day" instituted by some libraries, when patrons are invited to return missing books, "no questions asked."

Policy statements in the area of lost and damaged books and fines levied are best stated in broad terms that will make possible the widest use of materials and the fewest abuses.

Memorials and Gifts

The practice of contributing memorial gifts to the library has added many fine volumes, record albums, prints, paintings, and art objects to library collections. Often the gift is sent with the indication of some special field of interest held by the person to be memorialized, and the book is chosen accordingly. Just as frequently, the librarian is given carte blanche to expend the money as the library needs indicate. These gifts confer lasting benefits and an enduring memorial.

On a larger scale, legacies have provided libraries with gifts ranging from new buildings to reading patios. Even a modest bequest can memorialize the donor to the library's benefit. It is one of the library trustee's responsibilities to present this suggestion to potential donors, estate attorneys, trust officers, and other possible benefactors.

Friends of the Library have provided a pattern for donors by consulting with the librarian and the board before embarking on any projected gift or improvement. A prospective donor or legator might be encouraged to similar wisdom and forethought.

Unfortunately, many donors consult only their own wishes, and the library finds itself the unwilling recipient of a legacy earmarked for one specific purpose, or crippled by other restrictions laid down by the testator. Frequently the legacy or gift is in the form of a collection built around some personal interest of the donor, but of little practical general use to the library. If the gift is made free and clear to the library, it may be sold and the proceeds used to acquire necessities, but frequently the gift is hedged with conditions and the title is not clear.

As the royal gift of a white elephant ruined the hapless recipient by upkeep of the princely present, so the gift which a library may not legally dispose of harnesses the library to its maintenance. Unless the library policy on acceptance of gifts clearly gives the librarian a free hand in their disposition, precious space and staff time will go to the unwelcome addition. The small library in need of funds is a particular sufferer in such cases, whereas the proceeds from the sale of a valuable rare book or art object or special collection could have been translated into the practical benefit of new floor covering, additional reference books, or the convenience of an extension telephone.

Accordingly, the board should work out a policy governing the acceptance of gifts which will enable board members and librarian to be tactfully firm as to the conditions permitted.

Extending Library Service

Every library needs to plan for expanding and extending its services both in scope and in population served. As part of the long-range planning, this should be frequently discussed at board meetings, with particular reference to the next step to be taken. Consideration should be given to extending service within local boundaries as well as participation in library networks and systems. The board's policies governing these channels of extending the library service should be worked out in consultation with the librarian who may call in specialists in the field from the state library, ALA headquarters, and other libraries.

More and more libraries are providing electronic access to information through Internet and community computing networks. These services are designed to see that total library resources are available to every individual. Library trustees can take a leadership role to see that the goal is accomplished.

Library cooperation has a long and honorable history, evolving first as contractual agreements between libraries of similar type for the purpose of sharing certain resources, including staff and materials. Today cooperation has formalized into network systems in which all types of libraries (public, school, academic, special) located in a geographic area share resources on a regional basis. Each regional network system, in turn, affiliates with other systems in the state to form a statewide network. Eventually, these statewide networks will evolve into a national network through the auspices of which information and materials can be made available to the smallest member library in any state regional network.

Two factors have dictated the development of networking: patron demand for information and materials unavailable on the local level and the prohibitive cost of supplying such information and materials on a local level. By sharing resources through participation in a network, the local library can assure its patrons accessibility to expanded resources through the most feasible and economical means available today.

The library board should investigate, as a policy priority, participation in—or formulation of—a network in the library's local area. To do so would be to underline the library's basic goal of service to people.

The Library's Public Relations

Public relations is but another name for the communication between the library and the people it serves. Channels for this communication are many, and like varying wavelengths, may be beamed to reach different groups who make up the general public. It is this communication that creates the community's awareness of the library and acceptance of its program.

So important is a good public relations program in defining the library's place in the community that ample provision should be made in the annual budget to carry on such a program. Furthermore, maintenance of good public relations for the library is part of the obligation of everyone connected with the institution, from the janitor to the chairperson of the board.

The most direct contact with and influence upon the public are, of course, carried on by the librarian and staff, and every good librarian instills this understanding in the staff members supervised. But board members, too, have a very particular and very pressing obligation toward the library's public relations, since trustees are tacitly accepted by the public as "image-makers" of the library.

Specifics of the obligations of trustees toward library public relations are discussed in another chapter, both for library boards and for individual members. From the standpoint of policymaking, an effective and comprehensive program of public relations should be outlined and constantly maintained.

Organization Dues and Meetings

Since it is good management practice for employers to assist employees in maintaining good professional standing, the policy of the library board should be as liberal as finances permit regarding payment of state and national association dues for the librarian. If possible, the board should arrange payment of these dues for other staff members also, as a proper part of in-service training. In making up the budget, provision should be made for funds to cover the expenses of the librarian and other members of the staff (perhaps in rotation) for attending state and national association meetings. These professional meetings are necessary to the growth in librarianship of both head librarian and staff members, and the board owes them every encouragement to participate.

The trustee's need for membership in state and national organizations, and the value of such memberships, are discussed in another chapter. Too often in the past it has been left to the individual board member to pay such association dues personally, which worked a hardship on a trustee whose circumstances were not affluent. The unfortunate result has been limitation of self-education in trusteeship by too many board members.

Every library board member should be a member of the state association, and of the American Library Trustee Association, the trustee division of the American Library Association. The board's policy in this matter should be to make provision for payment of these dues for the members if financially possible; if not, at least the chairperson should be enrolled as a member of both associations and his or her dues paid.

At least once during a term of office, every library board member should attend an annual conference of the American Library Association, participating particularly in the programs arranged by the American Library Trustee Association. Expenses for the trip should be included in the library budget, and the privilege should be rotated among board members from year to year, giving all a part in the educational benefits of the national meeting.

The entire board should attend the annual meetings and workshops of the state association. Policy of the board should provide for this participation as additional education in trusteeship and in the trends of the library movement.

The Importance of Policymaking

The foregoing sections sketch the broad framework of library policy, giving some idea of its all-inclusive importance to the operation of the library. Devised as it must be to meet immediate needs, policy also necessarily has a far-reaching effect, and this fact should always be kept in mind by the board members as policy is worked out and adopted in various areas.

Policies determined by the library board set the conditions of the library's day-to-day operation and its program through the years, and policymaking demands the best in thought and planning from every library trustee.

6 Trustee Relationships with Librarian and Staff

Virginia G. Young

uman relationships determine the inner climate of the library, and if those relationships are cordial and understanding, the climate will be as warm and pleasant as a June day. Chief among these relationships, because of its effect on the overall library administration, is that between the library board and the librarian. Policies drawn by the library board delineate the conditions of library operation; the librarian chosen by the board carries out these policies. It is for this reason that the board's duties of policymaking and employment of a librarian are always shown as of equal and leading importance in any list of trustee responsibilities.

Employment of a Librarian

Since every library board naturally wishes to employ the best talent available to direct the library, care and thought must be taken in filling the post. The first step should be a realistic appraisal of the situation: what particular qualifications are required in the librarian, and what the library can offer the librarian. Consultation with the state library is helpful here, perhaps assisting the board to adjust its requirements or to provide additional inducements to prospective candidates.

Before employing a librarian, the board should be thoroughly familiar with federal and state statutes concerning equal opportunity and affirmative action. It is also advisable to review the American Library Association policy statement[1] in the *ALA Policy Manual*, which is in-

1. *ALA Policy Manual*, 54.3.

cluded in the annual publication of the *ALA Handbook of Organization.* These matters should be covered in the written policy procedures of the library.

Salaries for professional librarians, including the director, should meet national averages for libraries of similar size, and most definitely should be on a par with other similar professional positions in the local community. *The ALA Survey of Librarian Salaries,*[2] which is published annually and summarized in *American Libraries,* can be most useful in this regard. Trustees should approve salary ranges that entice the best people available at every level of library employment.

Once the basis for employment has been settled upon, the board should consult approved sources of personnel information, such as the state library, professional publications, and accredited library schools. Background and references of applicants should be checked and personal data evaluated by the board before the interviews are arranged. Should the board invite a candidate for a personal interview, the board should pay all or part of the applicant's travel expenses.

The final decision requires careful weighing in the balance of personal and professional factors, always with the aim of employing the librarian who will best serve the library program.

In employing a librarian, the board has always one primary responsibility: to fill a worthwhile job with a worthy candidate. If this is done, the welfare and progress of the library are assured.

What the Librarian Should Expect of the Board

Once employed, the librarian can properly expect to count on the board's solid support in carrying out the policies of library operation. Decisions of the board and changes in policy are not always universally popular. It is the librarian, carrying out those policies in constant direct contact with the public, who is in the line of fire, drawing the criticism of displeased groups or individuals. The board should at all times give unqualified support in defense of the librarian's administration of its policies. This is done with the understanding that the director will administer these policies with tact and diplomacy and keep the board advised. In the controversial area of "freedom to read," which today produces so

2. Mary Jo Lynch, along with Margaret Myers and Jeniece Guy, *The ALA Survey of Librarian Salaries* (Chicago: ALA, Office of Research and Statistics; American Library Association, Office for Library Personnel Resources, 1994); Mary Jo Lynch, "Librarians Salaries: Moving Upward at a Higher Rate," *American Libraries* (Nov. 1994): 954

many incidents between library and public, the board should be prepared to stand firm behind its policy on intellectual freedom, and behind the librarian in carrying out this policy.

Book selection and purchase are invariably sensitive areas, both between librarian and board, and between library and public. The librarian has a right to expect the board to draw up policy covering this field, stating in broad general terms the type, quality, and standards governing books and other library materials to be added to the library collection. Individual volumes and items selected and purchased within the terms of such policy are the responsibility of the librarian, and a trained competent librarian expects to conduct book selection and purchase without interference. Any questions or criticisms arising should be discussed between librarian and board at a full board meeting. Any decision made, within the framework of the total library program, by the majority at such a meeting should be unanimously supported by board members regardless of personalities involved.

The librarian has a right to expect support from the board in administering the library operations. Of course, the director may call on any trustee's expertise when needed. As shown by the chart of comparable duties and responsibilities of board and librarian in Chapter 2, it is the librarian's responsibility to interview, recommend, and employ the staff of the library, and to supervise its work, even though in some cases, a board may be required to approve staff appointments.

A librarian therefore can properly be expected to confer with the board regarding these matters should it become necessary, but to carry out the supervisory and administrative work without interference by the board or any of its members. The above-mentioned chart plainly shows that the two lists of duties and responsibilities are in many ways parallel, but do not overlap, and probably more internal discord springs from overbusy trustees or boards interfering with the librarian's direction of the library and staff than from any other source.

The board is charged with the responsibility of approving job specifications and salary scale for library staff members. Once these are adopted by the board, the staff positions and their incumbents are supervised by the librarian, and communication between board and staff is properly carried on through the librarian. Should dissatisfaction arise among the personnel, and members of the board are directly approached to intervene, the matter should first be brought to the attention of the librarian. Later it may be necessary for the matter to come up for discussion before a full meeting of the board with the librarian. Any other action by overzealous board members will undermine the librarian's authority and probably produce the unhappy result of opposing factions and general disorganization within the library.

Protection of the librarian's professional standing and advancement is a clear obligation of the board. In addition to encouragement and financial support for membership in the state and national professional associations and attendance at meetings, the librarian should be able to count on time to read in order to stay conversant with trends in books and periodicals. It is taken for granted by the community that the librarian will assume a leading place in cultural affairs, but many librarians find themselves so bogged down in housekeeping aspects of library management that the professional standards of librarianship are nearly impossible to maintain. Protection of the librarian's time and opportunity for this important segment of professional advancement should be assured by the board.

Should another post offering professional advancement be tendered the librarian, the board should be entirely willing to cooperate. Often a librarian identifies so completely with a library and a community that such a person becomes a permanent resident by choice, but every librarian must be free to move on at any time toward improved professional and financial status.

What has been lightheartedly termed "the care and feeding of a librarian" is squarely up the library board. The librarian necessarily looks to the board to provide an environment of library operation in which creative librarianship can flourish.

What the Board Should Expect

Top-notch professional performance, personal integrity, and a forward-moving library program are sought by every board in appointing a librarian, and every librarian worthy of the name is prepared to meet these expectations.

There is another legitimate claim which the board should make upon the librarian: to be the board's "open door" into the professional library world. Sometimes a library board is not sufficiently alert to its need for education in developments in the library world to make this demand. Sometimes the librarian does not fully recognize this professional obligation to the board members, and consequently does not do enough to introduce trustees to the library's problems or keep the board properly informed. Yet such an expectation on the part of the board, fulfilled by the librarian, is an implicit part of any valid relationship between trustees and librarian.

The ways in which the librarian can meet this expectation are various. Every board meeting offers a number of opportunities for such illumination of the members' thinking. Suggestions as to new policy, and the reasoning behind recommendations for changed or amended policy, will inform the board members about the different aspects of the library operation. The period during which the librarian's report is discussed and evaluated at board meetings offers limitless opportunity for exchange of information between librarian and board. The time reserved at board meetings for creative thought and planning, and for discussion of long-range library programs, gives the librarian a chance to broaden the horizons of the library board by reports and suggestions on new and progressive trends in the library world.

The librarian's obligation in this respect also applies to relationships with individual board members who show an interest in learning about their trusteeship. Many highly effective library trustees are frank to give credit for their achievements to the inspiration of a dedicated librarian.

The Two Interpreters

No reciprocal relationship can be built between librarian and board unless at all times it is remembered that each is charged with the responsibility as interpreter to the other: the librarian and board as interpreter of the library world to the lay person, the board as interpreter of the community to the librarian. The two interpreter roles are of equal importance. Both viewpoints must be weighed in the balance before the library can take its proper place in the community.

Many a librarian, armed with shining new professional theory, has shattered a lance on the seeming obstinacy and conservatism of the library board. Yet if each recognized the obligation of the other to interpret, a workable understanding could easily be reached. A librarian should be expected to interpret professional trends to the board; the board should be expected to interpret the community picture to the librarian. Each should welcome the other side of the story as completing the full picture.

The board which persists in considering any innovation proposed by the librarian as a challenge to a duel in the sun is likely to end up standing in its own light. The librarian who persists in proposing an unwelcome innovation simply because it has worked elsewhere should strive for closer rapport with the community. Sometimes all that is needed to bring about a happy ending is a period of preparation and education for the community's final acceptance. This necessity for seeing both sides of the question should bring together the board and the librarian as partners rather than as duelists.

A thoughtful and respectful hearing of one another's point of view is frequently all that is required to bridge the gap and to weld the two interpretations into a common language.

Agreeing to Disagree

Natural differences of opinion arise in every human relationship, and those which occur between library board and librarian can usually be solved by a moderate and understanding approach on both sides. It sometimes happens, however, that differences of opinion go beyond disagreement into dissension, and the working relationship is so severely ruptured that its continuation is not possible.

If the difficulty cannot be resolved by private conference with the librarian, usually undertaken by the chairperson at the request of the board, decisive official action must be taken by a full meeting of the board. It is only just to all concerned that the cause of disagreement and resulting board action be clearly stated.

Sometimes it is felt that a librarian has demonstrated deficiencies in filling the post and that a more adequate replacement should be sought. Again, a private conference communicating the board's decision with courtesy and candor is recommended. Termination of an unsatisfactory connection need not embarrass the librarian's professional future elsewhere.

When dissatisfaction is felt by either side regarding policies, program, or administration of the library, it has been found that impartial consultant service is useful. Analysis of weaknesses and recommenda tions for strengthening the program can solve an unsettled situation in a constructive fashion. The state library is in a position to counsel and give assistance upon request.

It should be constantly kept in mind that the board's first responsibility is toward the public, to provide adequate and satisfactory library service, and this obligation takes precedence over personalities, prejudices, and partisanship.

The Board's Relationship with the Staff

The library board's relationship with staff members should be exactly that of a corporate board of directors with employees: one of cordial and friendly interest, entirely free from personal intervention between staff member and supervisor. Policy governing job specifications, salaries, and other terms of employment is the responsibility of the board; selection and supervision of personnel are part of the librarian's administrative duties.

It is entirely possible for board members to make provision for the welfare and job advancement opportunities of the library staff without entering into any too personal friendships or criticisms involving individual employees. Nepotism should also be shunned, and employment of a close relative of any board member should not be considered.

Staff associations are often valuable to promote in-service training and to give the staff members an impersonal channel through which to communicate requests, suggestions, and complaints to the board. Formation of such a staff association should receive every encouragement from board and librarian.

While employee organizations in the public sector, and particularly in libraries, have not been common, there is an increasing trend toward the formation of such organizations, and they should be recognized. In the matter of economic considerations, such organizations bargain collectively with the agency or body authorized to make financial commitment on behalf of the governmental unit. The board is involved in negotiating those terms and conditions of employment over which they have discretion and authority to act. For example, such areas usually include a grievance procedure with an impasse provision. Although there may seem to be certain elements of basic opposition of interests in the relationship between management and employees, it can be, in fact, a most cordial and productive relationship.

Relationships Sound the Keynote

The working relationships which prevail within the library determine the attitudes of librarian and staff, which in turn determine the quality of the service offered to the public. It is from these attitudes that the public forms its judgments of the library.

There is no field connected with trusteeship which more richly repays the board's thought and effort than the one of human relationships within the library walls. It is the ultimate responsibility of the library board to make sure that an atmosphere of mutual understanding and cordial cooperation exists. Only in this way can the board, the librarian, and the staff unite in a harmonious team effort toward their common goal of better library service.

7 The Trustee and Labor-Management Relations

Donald J. Sager

he most important element in creating and maintaining high-quality public library service is the staff. The best collection, facilities, and public service policies will be of limited value without a competent, motivated, and dedicated team of personnel. Salaries and benefits also constitute the largest portion of the library budget. Therefore, when the library staff is represented by a bargaining unit, it is especially important for the library trustee to know how to foster effective labor-management relations within the context of collective bargaining.

Since a majority of public libraries in the United States and in other nations are legally departments or units of municipal or country government, many trustees will find that they are not directly involved in the negotiations or implementation of labor bargaining agreements, even though they may be vested with full policy-making and fiscal responsibility for the library under state law. This is one of the gray areas of local governance where the library board delegates its authority to the city or county either because of home rule provisions in state law and local ordinances, or because the bargaining unit may encompass many or all units of the city or county, and it is more efficient to have one labor negotiator who specializes in labor law responsible for negotiation and administration. A comparable relationship may exist with a civil service or merit system involving the library personnel. The library board, once again, may have the legal responsibility for all aspects of the library, but it may

Donald J. Sager is publisher of Highsmith Press. He previously served as director of the Milwaukee, Chicago, Columbus, and Mobile public libraries.

defer to the city or county personnel board for recruitment, testing, selection, and other aspects of personnel administration.

Therefore, it is common for labor negotiations to be conducted by an official or a consultant appointed by and reporting to the city or county administration and council. That does not mean that the library and its board of trustees do not have a role in labor relations. The same responsibility exists even when a library does not have a formally recognized bargaining unit. Some libraries have informal staff associations that may seek to affect compensation policies and work rules, and the library board may need to define its role and policies in those circumstances.

Governance and management have historically been ambivalent toward labor unions and the collective bargaining process. Like some businesses and industries, some libraries have sought to avoid creation of a bargaining unit in the belief that it would reduce management and governance control and/or lead to inefficiencies in operations or service. Development of compensation plans, working conditions, and personnel practices and policies in those circumstances may have been influenced by what proposals would discourage creation of a bargaining unit. Some boards and library administrators have the belief that a decision by the library staff to form a bargaining unit is an indictment against their policies, and something to be avoided at all costs. On the other hand, some libraries believe that the establishment of a union to represent the staff will improve personnel policies and public service because it formally involves staff, through their representatives, in decision making, planning, and goal setting. Some administrators and library boards find that personnel administration is easier when a collective bargaining agreement defines rights and responsibilities.

Staff Association as Bargaining Unit

There can be any number of reasons why a staff wishes to form a bargaining unit. The community may have a history supporting collective bargaining, or local economic conditions may stimulate organization. Staff may also be seeking greater participation in policy making or development of the institution. While union membership has generally declined during the recent past, this is at least partially due to the restructuring and downsizing of many industries that historically had large labor membership. The growth of the service industries has led to gains, especially in those industries that employ a high percentage of women.

Whatever the feelings and policies of the library board toward bargaining units or staff associations, it is important to recognize that collective bargaining is protected by federal and state laws and regulations. No board or administrator may seek to prevent an election or the formation of a bargaining unit, and there are rules and guidelines that must be followed in the event a majority of the library staff or a majority in a defined work classification wishes to engage in collective bargaining. If a library board or administrator learns or is informed that an organizing effort is underway, professional help should be sought to ensure that no violations occur and to explain the available options. Many law firms have attorneys who specialize in labor law, and there are consulting firms that can also provide assistance.

National Labor Relations Board

The National Labor Relations Board (NLRB), a federal agency (1717 Pennsylvania Avenue, N.W., Washington, D.C. [202-632-4950]) is charged with the responsibility to administer laws that prohibit unfair labor practices by either management or unions in the United States, and they maintain fifty-two field offices throughout the nation to oversee elections associated with the establishment of a bargaining unit. A key element in the election is the definition of which classes of employees will be included, and who will represent them. At one time it was common practice to have different unions representing craft or trade employees, custodial, clerical, and professional staff. However, the growth of many service or governmental unions such as the American Federation of State, County, and Municipal Employees (AFSCME) has changed that pattern, and the board may find that the organizers may be seeking to include almost all classes of employees in the bargaining unit. The organizers will obviously wish to exclude those classes of employees who may be inclined to vote against creation of a bargaining unit, and for that reason middle management positions are often excluded. If a sufficient number of employees seek representation under provisions of the NLRB, then strict regulations must be followed. Both management and labor have the right to petition the NLRB if they believe some violation or irregularity occurred.

Negotiating Process

Many library boards are fortunate to have members who may be union officials or attorneys or consultants who have experience in labor-management relations. While their advice will certainly be valuable, it is important to ensure there is no conflict of interest, or the appearance of a conflict of interest. Even an attorney who does not specialize in labor law may be a partner in a firm that is active in this field representing either management or labor unions.

While most, if not all, library boards must adhere to strict open meetings laws and provisions, discussion on labor negotiations are often exempt. With proper notice, the board may be able to go into executive session to consider various actions. However, the board will usually have to reconvene in open session to take formal action. The library's legal adviser should be asked to clarify the open meetings act relative to labor issues. The board and management should also anticipate attendance by a bargaining unit representative at board meetings. Unfortunately, many board meetings are often only attended by management, and the media on occasion. The initial appearance of a representative of the bargaining unit may be of concern, despite the existence of open meetings policies and laws. Representation should be welcomed as evidence of the board's interest in maintaining good communications. If the representative is a library employee, it is generally good policy to grant pay or compensatory time off for the period of attendance. The board should not go to the extent of inviting comments or opinions on various agenda items as a regular practice, since this will cloud the roles of labor and management, besides slowing the flow of board business. The board president may wish to make an exception to this, depending on the nature of the agenda item, but if bargaining unit input is sought, it is best to establish some other mechanism, such as delegation to management or an appropriate board committee where the library administration can review its position.

In those instances where the board does have responsibility to negotiate directly with the bargaining unit, it is recommended that an experienced labor negotiator be retained. There are several reasons for this alternative. First, it is unlikely that the board or library management will be familiar with the technicalities of labor law. A trustee with this knowledge is likely to have a conflict of interest. Second, the board and management is at a disadvantage if it is directly involved in the negotiations. They typical bargaining unit is usually represented at the table by a negotiating committee that reports back to the unit officers or executive committee. Any terms they negotiate usually must be approved by the membership, invariably by an election.

This gives the bargaining unit negotiating committee the opportunity to tell management representatives that they do not have the power to make a final decision, but that they will convey management's offer for consideration. In negotiations of any sort it is well to have a "cutout" such as this, since it forces the party with direct decision-making power to make greater concessions in an effort to gain acceptance. If a labor negotiator represents the board and management, he or she can insulate them, and serve as a cutout in the negotiating process.

Designating the library director or a member of top management as chief negotiator is also unwise. This places that individual in a situation where he or she has a conflict of interest, especially where working conditions are under negotiation. The administrator would normally be adverse to changes that might erode management's authority, and might take the requested changes as a personal criticism. In fact, friction between the administrator and the bargaining unit that may arise during negotiations could carry forward into everyday communications and destroy rapport. There will be many library directors, as well as some trustees, who will be reluctant to work through a third-party labor negotiator because of their fear of what the negotiator may offer as concessions, but there is a clear procedure that will avoid that risk.

Key to the labor negotiation process are the terms (or "demands" as they are described in an adversarial situation) which are first advanced by the bargaining unit, and the offer or response extended by management. Labor's terms are usually carefully developed and prioritized, and its negotiating committee is given clear instructions as to the limits of their negotiating powers. Management's representative reviews labor's demands with the library administration, the board, or both, depending on how the board delegates negotiating responsibilities. Ideally, the labor negotiator should report to a committee consisting of representatives of the board, such as its personnel committee, and members of the management team, preferably the director and the deputy and personnel officer, if these positions exist. Following a review of labor's terms, management's representative is given careful instructions as to which terms are acceptable or unacceptable, as well as any concessions that would be required of labor as a condition of acceptance. Again, the limits of the negotiator's powers are determined, and he or she goes back to the bargaining table.

This process will repeat itself until agreement is reached, and the terms are formally accepted by the board and the rank and file. If an impasse occurs, there are several alternatives to a labor strike. Some states require binding arbitration. In some instances it might be prudent for the board and the bargaining unit to request the intervention of the chief elected official of the political jurisdiction, such as the mayor our county executive. This is particularly appropriate if the impasse might necessitate a compromise that would require greater tax support. A third alternative that negotiating parties should consider is voluntary arbitration.

The American Arbitration Association (AAA) is an independent, nonprofit organization (140 W. 51st Street, New York, N.Y. 10020 [212-484-4000]) dedicated to the attainment of all types of agreements, including labor-management contracts. The Association maintains panels of disinterested parties who have qualifications in a wide range of specialties, and who are familiar with the precedents that have been established through negotiations in similar settings, such as public libraries. A third party arbitrator might be able to take a fresh approach that will lead to a compromise acceptable to labor and management.

Labor Agreement and Working Conditions

There are usually two key documents guiding labor and management relations when the staff is organized as a bargaining unit. The first of these is the labor contract or memorandum of agreement. This will contain terms such as the number of positions in each classification, their salaries or wages, fringe benefits, and the proverbial "kitchen sink" of other issues the bargaining unit and management have agreed to, for the specified period of the agreement.

The second key document addresses the working conditions. These include the policies that generally affect all employees, such as the length of the work week, disciplinary procedures, policies governing discharge, promotion, and related matters. While these might be included in the bargaining agreement, they are usually separate because they affect both represented and nonrepresented employees.

If the library is treated as part of a larger bargaining unit such as the city or county, and a chief labor negotiator reports to the larger jurisdiction, the library board and administration should be involved in evaluating the terms or demands, and should participate in developing a response which would include any desired concessions. If this opportunity is not customarily provided, discussions should be initiated by the board with the chief elected officials of the jurisdiction. A lack of participation in the collective bargaining process will seriously weaken the role of the library board and administration in controlling the library's finances and public service.

Labor agreements or the working conditions will usually provide for a grievance procedure. This may be used by the bargaining unit when it is believed a violation in the contract occurred, when there was a disagreement between a supervisor and a member of the bargaining unit, or to ensure that due process occurs. Some agreements designate the library board as a source of appeal in the grievance process. If so, care should be taken to ensure that the issue is not brought before the board until management has had the opportunity to resolve the disagreement.

When the matter does come to the board, it should be realized that this may take the form of a legal action, depending on the nature of the grievance procedure. In the instance where discipline or discharge is the issue, the individual is often entitled to an attorney, and the rules of legal evidence and cross-examination apply. It would be prudent for the board to delegate grievance issues to its personnel committee, request the assistance of their legal counsel, retain a court reporter to record the proceedings, and ensure that the library administration thoroughly prepares its side of the case. Grievance hearings involving the board or a board committee are generally open, but the committee may go into executive session for discussion. Votes on decisions must usually be held in open session, and be affirmed by the full board.

Conclusion

A final point concerns the trustee's contacts with members of the bargaining unit and its officers. It is always important for any member of the library staff, represented or not, to have the opportunity to communicate with members of the board. Every employee is a member of the team, and suggestions that will improve service or control costs should be welcomed. However, when an employee offers complaints or criticisms involving management, work rules, or the labor contract, the trustee may always remember that there are at least two sides to every issue. Both suggestions and complaints should always be referred to management. A request for follow-up should be made if a response is merited. A trustee who does not permit management to first address complaints, concerns, or suggestions raised by the staff, will seriously erode the role and effectiveness of the library administrative team.

Further Reading

Collective Bargaining Negotiations and Contracts. 2 vols. Washington, D.C.: Bureau of National Affairs. Published annually, updated weekly. It describes strategies and how to effectively administer an agreement.

Commerce Clearing House. *Guidebook to Labor Relations.* 24th ed. Chicago: Commerce Clearing House, 1987. Summarizes federal labor relations law. Ready reference handbook for finding information.

Flexman, E. "Library Unionization and Its Ties to the Public Sector: History, Issues, and Trends." *Indiana Libraries* 10; no. 2 (1991): 27–44.

Holman, N. "Forces for Change in the Future of Collective Bargaining in Public Libraries." *Journal of Library Administration* 11; no. 1 (1989): 53–65.

Kenny, John J. *Primer of Labor Relations.* 23rd ed. Washington, D.C.: Bureau of National Affairs, 1986. Summarizes the law and major cases. Outlines legal procedures in forming a bargaining unit.

O'Reilly, Robert C., and Marjorie I. *Librarians and Labor Relations: Employment under Union Contracts.* Westport, Conn.: Greenwood, 1981.

Seide, Katherine, ed. *A Dictionary of Arbitration and Its Terms.* (Published for the Eastman Library of the American Arbitration Association). Dobbs Ferry, N.Y.: Oceana, 1970. This is an encyclopedia on arbitration and its practice.

Todd, Katherine. "Collective Bargaining and Professional Associations in the Library Field." *Library Quarterly* 55; no. 4 (1985): 284–99.

Vignone, Joseph A. *Collective Bargaining Procedures for Public Library Employees: An Inquiry into the Opinions and Attitudes of Public Librarians, Directors, and Board Members.* Metuchen, N.J.: Scarecrow, 1971. Reports a study on library labor relations. Contains a model framework for collective bargaining procedures.

Weatherford, John W. *Librarians' Agreements: Bargaining for a Heterogeneous Profession.* Metuchen, N.J.: Scarecrow, 1988. Contains contracts developed by the Boston Public Library, University of California, and the State University System of Florida.

The Trustee
and Planning

Virginia G. Young
Minnie-Lou Lynch

lanning, in this day of ever-increasing demands on the library coupled with a growing competition for the scarce tax dollar, has become a most important responsibility of trustees. One of the duties listed in Chapter 2 is "know the program and needs of the library in relation to the community; keep abreast of standards and library trends; plan and carry out the library program." Planning has always been the means of recognizing the present situation, of identifying needs, of determining objectives and assigning priorities, and of deciding the action to be taken to achieve the stated goals.

Planning is essentially preparation for change—the look before the leap. Library trustees must never be willing to simply drift from year to year. Practices from the past can be carried forward by sheer inertia. But today's trusteeship calls for creative thinking and positive action.

Someone has said that "it is often easier to act ourselves into a new way of thinking than it is to think ourselves into a new way of acting." Planning means to think ourselves into a new way of acting.

To move the library forward in an age of change necessitates careful planning today. There are some basic assumptions with which trustees will want to begin: (1) planning is essential; (2) the librarian and board are partners in planning; (3) the end objective of library planning is service to people; and (4) local planning should be related to the overall state plan where one exists.

The planning process in relation to the library requires answers to some basic questions: (1) Where are we? (2) Where do we want to go? (3) How do we get there?

Where Are We?

Important elements in answering the first question include examining the library in relation to the community, examining the library in relation to other libraries and informational components in the area, and examining the library in relation to its stated goals and objectives. The board will want to take a good look at the community and its needs. A community survey which will show population patterns and shifts, the general level of education, the kind of employment, the organizational structures present, and other relevant data is invaluable.

There are a number of ways to gather this information. Experts may be brought in. Local groups may be able to furnish parts of the information required. The state library may be able to provide advice and assistance. There is literature on how to survey the community to which the American Library Association (ALA) has provided a notable contribution. The ALA publications *Planning and Role Setting for Public Libraries* and *Output Measures for Public Libraries* are invaluable tools in the planning process.

It is essential to assess the resources and services of other libraries and other information agencies in order to determine to what extent they are or can be made accessible to all of the people. It is also valuable to measure the library in relation to the goals and objectives which the board has established.

With this evaluation, it is important to keep in mind the necessity of interpretation with reference to the actual community and not to some mythical situation. The data must be good and the interpretation honest.

If the board and librarian have performed well, they should now be able to see in a clear light the community and its needs and whether these needs are being met by present library services and resources.

Where Do We Want to Go?

Here one recognizes a basic difference between "where we are" and "where we want to go" in the matter of the attitude of the decision maker. "Where we are" could be arrived at by any person or team or persons who are skilled in the techniques of gathering information.

But "where we want to go" is something else. This will not only require correct background for evaluation judgment, but will require a commitment to good library service and to its importance in the total community climate. It is this commitment that is the basic responsibility of the trustee as a holder of the public trust.

The library trustee must see the library as the service organization that is basic to all community education and culture, as well as a source of recreation and refreshment.

It is here that planning is clearly related to the goals and objectives of the library. These, of course, should be clearly defined and written down. In order to do this, there must be a definite understanding of the overall philosophy of the library and the function that it serves. In other words, what are the goals of the public library? What is the library trying to do? Who are the people the library is trying to serve? What resources does the library need to achieve these ends? It should be recognized that goals are simply purposes to be achieved. To express them in terms of short- and long-range plans clarifies the decision maker's intent and assists in the determination of exactly what needs to be accomplished and in what order.

Another important point to remember is that questions asked and judgments made in planning cannot transpire in a vacuum. People who are library users and nonusers, as well as community interpreters, must be involved, i.e., community leaders, city planners, and various related agencies. The ideas and suggestions of these groups must be sought and evaluated.

Before setting down plans, attention should be given also to the overall statewide plan for library development and the place the local library may be expected to fill. State and national standards should be consulted (see Chapter 17).

Then the board will want to actually set down long-range and short-term plans, assign priorities, write down what will be involved to achieve the plans, and the steps to be taken in their accomplishment. It is here that the board will have to take a hard look at the budget and at the realistic possibilities for its increase.

Planning often is attempted without serious consideration of the budget, just as budgets sometimes are assembled with little relation to the planning process. Consideration must be given to establishing a basic planning budget, as well as recognizing the implications that planning recommendations have on the library budget.

Examples of plans set down are many and varied and many include such items as longer hours and strengthened staff, increased tax support, building program, addition of audiovisual materials, strengthened young adult program, additional services to children, service to hospitals, cooperation with all types of libraries in centralized procedures at state and regional levels, and total utilization of community library resources.

Planning is not a "single shot" activity. It is a continuing process and iterative in nature. It is well to keep in mind that this may include the possibility of entirely new ideas as well as ways to ensure the best utilization of resources and services now in existence.

Since the end objective of library services is to serve people, since people have been involved in the deliberations at every step, there is one final area in which people are of first importance. This is in the acceptance of the planning by the people, the citizens whom the board represents.

How Do We Get There?

The acceptance and support of the people for whom the board plans will make the achievement of the objectives possible. Essentially this involves communication. All the way through, trustees must communicate, communicate, communicate.

And communication is half-achieved if the community has been a part of the planning procedure. It was a wise man who said that "the greatest obstacle to effective communication is the illusion that it has been accomplished." Take nothing for granted when it comes to community understanding of what the library needs to make it a real center of education, information, and enrichment.

There are many ways to communicate, but there are two that are really essential. One is the political process at every level—local, state, and national. It means keeping in constant touch with government officials, giving service to them, and keeping them informed of the services of the library to the people to whom they are responsible, their constituency. Second, there must be a strong program of public relations. There should be, of course, the library's planned program of public relations. But equally important in public relations is the trustee telling the library story, utilizing every informal opportunity. The support that a well-informed Friends group can provide also is invaluable.

Summary

Library trustees and librarians are concerned with service to people through the institution of the library and their planning is to that end. Planning is a way of making sure that there is a strategy for library development always interpreted in terms of people. It is important to remember that library trustees stand or fall in their responsibility and public trust on what the individual user gets from the library. Trustees must recognize that the human element is paramount. The budget, building, or program are important only as they affect service to people.

By examining where we are, where we want to go, and how we propose to get there, trustees have a basic structure for the planning process.

Libraries are essentially a product of change, and change is vital to their development. Planning is simply controlled change. How well trustees and librarians plan today, how well they instigate and control change, will determine the effectiveness of the library tomorrow.

9 Trustee Education

Gene Martin
Alice Bennett Ihrig
Virginia G. Young

t is an American tradition to have lay citizen boards charged with responsibility for public institutions, including libraries. In order to perform their duties, library trustees must be *informed*—informed concerning the library, informed concerning community, informed concerning state and national influences.

As libraries move more and more toward cooperative ventures linking them to a wider range of resources, the more vital becomes the trustee's part in designing a viable service program to meet constituent needs. Basic—and continuing—education will be the instrument by which trustees can develop the necessary skills and abilities that will assist them in fulfilling the fundamental responsibilities of trusteeship.

Learning at the Local Level

Boards which hope to recruit excellence in board membership do well to offer information about a trustee role prior to elections or appointments. Appointing officials should be provided with criteria that can be utilized as a basis for making appointments; prospective board members running for election should be given information about the trustee role,

Gene Martin is former director, Daniel Boone Regional Library, Columbia, Missouri.

Alice Bennett Ihrig is former president, Illinois Library Association and the American Library Trustee Association preferably in a formal board session designed for that purpose and to which all candidates are invited.

The present members of the board have a responsibility, also, in seeking out qualified prospective nominees for trusteeship. The Friends of the Library, for example, is an organization that offers an excellent source of potential trustees. An informational program on library governance and procedure directed at the membership might well capture the interest of those already involved in service to the library.

The Preorientation

A library offering a short course in trusteeship for potential trustees should consider the following as minimum points for inclusion in such a program:

1. How the library is governed, including state laws and local ordinances; the responsibilities of the trustees, individually and collectively; the operational responsibilities of the administration; and the role of the public.
2. How the library is funded, including legal base for financing, the current budget, and the legislative support role expected of a trustee.
3. How the library operates from day to day, including services offered, use by the public, short- and long-range plans, and library needs.
4. How the local library is linked to other resources, including explanations of the interlibrary loan procedure, sharing of resources, system relationships, state library services and technological advances that do or will affect the local library service program.
5. The trustee's role, including the establishment of policy, attendance at board meetings, service on committees or task forces, involvement in regional, state, and national library developments.

The preorientation program serves as a means to create enthusiastic potential trustees with a good grasp of the possibilities of the position, to weed out persons with a passing interest, and to identify new talent to appointing officials.

The Orientation

The provision of learning experiences for the new appointed or elected trustee is the dual responsibility of the administrative librarian and the present members of the library board. Basic to the trustee's education will be the orientation session (see Appendix 1 for a sample orientation session).

This session should provide the necessary information to instill in the new trustee a sense of confidence and a desire to become involved in a responsible manner. While the orientation consists of sharing important documents and conveying facts, it can serve also as a friendly introduction to both the board and the staff.

It can convey pleasantly the admonition that trustees make policy but do not run library operations; the advice to remember that the board operates as a whole and that an individual trustee does not speak for the board except when authorized to do so; and the counsel to remember that trusteeship is exactly what it implies, the responsibilities of which are to be performed openly and for the benefit of the public.

The board can consciously offer new trustees some understanding of what the community needs and expects, how the library is involved beyond community boundaries, and how state and federal laws and services affect the library. However, the best education of the trustee will come through self-involvement.

Trustees should become visible in the community, serving as conduits, listeners, and spokespersons for citizen needs and desires. Of necessity, trustees should become more knowledgeable about the local community—its census figures, its economic and occupational levels, its ethnic and special interest groups, and—most important of all—the needs which bring people to the library for help and the barriers which keep people from using the library.

Many boards have found that board retreats of a day or day and a half have been useful in discussing and learning more about library needs, the library in relation to the community, and involvement in the planning process.

The Library Association as Trustee Educator

Good performance by trustees in the community is of the highest priority. This performance can be enhanced if the library board makes every effort possible for its members to take part in other educational opportunities available outside of the local area. Such opportunities are afforded by attendance at workshops and seminars sponsored by state library agencies, educational institutions, and regional, state, and national library association.

The American Library Trustee Association (ALTA) developed a model workshop in 1982, that could be replicated in every state and province. It is known as ALTA WILL (Workshop in Library Leadership). It has been widely used and has now been revised and updated.

Most state library associations include a trustee organization either as a division of the organization or as an independent unit. Such associations expect to sponsor meetings for trustees and to include trustees in their target audiences for other meetings. Trustees who understand the scope of library service, who will work to develop and support needed legislation, and who will join in promoting standards and other means for improving library service and upgrading the qualifications of library staff have an important and welcome role to play in association activities.

Trustees involved on the association level in program planning have assisted in managing, promoting, and following up on seminars and workshops that have dealt with censorship, public relations, personnel policies, development of new services, setting of goals, library systems, technology, and many other topics. All such seminars have been designed to enrich and to expand the knowledge of trustees in their role as a governing body.

Library Education and the Trustee

Increasingly, colleges and universities offering a master's degree in library science have involved the trustee in the curriculum. Many schools invite a trustee to give guest lectures on the relationship between the public librarian and the library board. Through such sessions, trustees have been able to expand the knowledge of future librarians with regard to trustee responsibilities. In turn, trustees have become more aware of the kind of educational experiences made available to the student, thus permitting a more effective exchange of views in the board-staff arena.

Trustee Education and the State Library Agency

The state library agency, utilizing federal and state monies, often funds trustee workshops as well as other institutes in which trustees are invited to participate. In addition to serving, also, as a source for general information and publications of interest to trustees, many state library agencies maintain a meaningful and effective consultant service.

If a board senses a lack in the staff, the services, or the materials collection of the local library, for example, a lack with which either the board or staff finds itself inadequate to deal, a request for consultant service from the state library agency might well be the first step in securing a workable solution. The role of the state library in such instances will not be to dictate, but to work with the board and staff in surveying existing conditions and in exploring possible proposals to remedy the situation.

The concerned trustee should remember that the local library does not operate in a vacuum. When information is needed or help sought, the board should think first of its own state library agency.

Trustee Education at the National Level

Trustees who have participated in national conferences of the American Library Association, of which the American Library Trustee Association is an active unit, speak to the value of meeting with a cross section of trustees and librarians from throughout the country. It is at the national level that the trustee often picks up ideas, identifies trends, sharpens skills, and increases his or her value to the local library. Subject matter covered at national conferences—and often at regional meetings—is of a higher level in that broad issues pertaining to the advancement of libraries nationally are addressed.

If possible, the local library should include in its budget one or more memberships in the American Library Trustee Association. *The Trustee Voice*, published quarterly by ALTA, and *American Libraries*, published monthly by ALA, are useful educational tools accompanying the membership. Trustees, as well, should be urged to find ways to attend the national meetings, thus keeping the local board in touch with the library world.

Reading to Learn

In addition to the publications mentioned in the preceding paragraph, the library should call the board's attention to articles of interest generated by the library press and the general media. Trustees should make it a habit to peruse substantive materials on future library problems and trends (population speculations, use of leisure time, predictions of economic trends, etc.) to keep abreast of state and national legislation, to seek out information on what services other libraries have found to be successful, etc.

It is the joint responsibility of the librarian and trustee to accumulate significant materials for inclusion in a trustee reading shelf. Some of the articles contained therein should be presented at meetings for board discussion.

Governor's Conference

Through the years, a number of states have held a governor's conference on libraries with the emphasis being placed upon securing attendance at such conferences by nonlibrary related persons. These conferences are designed to reach community leaders and representatives of diversified interest groups for the purpose of explaining the present standing of the state libraries. Suggestions and support for the improvement of services are sought from the delegates. Such conferences are a viable process for the education of trustees and the lay public.

White House Conferences on Library and Information Services

Both the first White House Conference held in 1979 and the second held in 1991 greatly influenced the development of library services nationwide. They particularly drew attention to the role of libraries and assisted greatly in increasing funding for libraries.

Do-It-Yourself Workshops

Owing to a number of factors, not the least of which are limited time on the part of the trustee and the sharp increase in travel costs, the popularity of the one-day area workshop within a state is increasing. Even so light a consumption of trustee time carries with it the obligation to plan carefully for specific and limited objectives.

A few key points in planning a workshop are:

1. Decide what the workshop should do and state an objective which can be used to test the planning and the results. Describe the desired audience.
2. Keep the workshop simple. Do not cram it with topics unless there is a way to jump logically from topic to topic.
3. Plan every detail from invitations or notices to clean-up.
4. Involve enough committee members to accomplish the objectives and handle the details. (Speedy registration and prompt lunch, for example, may be important factors in the success of the workshop.)
5. Present topics in the most suitable manner. Use a speaker or a film or a panel or audience participation as *conscious* choices designed to make the workshop more valuable.

6. Be sure that all information is accurate, needed, up-to-date, and interesting.
7. Provide suitable material to take home. An exhibit at the workshop of other resources may be helpful.
8. Provide an evaluation sheet that will let the planners know how well the workshop accomplished its purpose, what went right and what went wrong, what other issues will be of interest for future workshops.

The Benefits of Trustee Education

From whatever source or at whatever level, information and ideas imparted to trustees benefit the library. In the last analysis, an informed trustee is a confident trustee, better able to assume and to carry out the responsibilities of the position. Rather than reticence, there will be exuberance; rather than static withdrawal, there will be active participation, for informed trustees working together as an intelligent library board will always search for the right choices to benefit both the library and the community.

10 The Trustee and the Law

Robert R. McClarren
Richard E. Thompson

 t is generally agreed that positions of public trust are not for the timid!

The provision of public library service, accessible to all people, without discrimination, and supported from public resources has been a traditional element of public policy of every state of the United States. Every citizen, who, as a member of a public board, officially has been selected to implement the library service policy on behalf of all citizens, has a legal trust obligation.[1] That obligation requires the aggressive advancement as well as the aggressive protection of the public library service. The volume and strength of the law applicable to libraries leaves the trustee with no excuse for timidity.

The Legal Context of Library Trusteeship

The constitutionality, statutory, and administrative or regulatory laws of the state are the bases for the creation, direction, support, and continuance of public libraries.[2]

Robert R. McClarren is system director emeritus, North Suburban Library System, Wheeling, Illinois, and former state librarian of Indiana.

Richard E. Thompson is director Wilmette (Illinois) Public Library District and holds a law degree from the University of Chicago.

1. While most trustees for public library service are members of public library boards, so designated, in some cases members of other boards, such as school boards, county commissions, city councils, and state boards of education, have the responsibility for such service and thus are de facto public library trustees.

2. Constitutional law is that expressed in the Constitution of the United States or of the respective state; statutory law is that enacted by the Congress or state legislature, as the case may be, and signed into law; and administrative

While only a very few states refer in their constitutions to the state's obligation for the provision of public library service, every state has specific statutory provisions for the establishment and operation of public libraries as a governmental responsibility.[3]

As is traditional and customary in American government, the responsibility for implementing the laws relative to local public library development and establishment, organization, support, and operation usually is vested as a trust in a group of citizens, a board of trustees. For most public library activity, this board is a board whose sole focus is the library. A few public libraries do not have a board of library trustees as such. For those libraries, the board responsibilities are held solely by a board of trustees of general purpose government (e.g., a city council or county board) or by a board of trustees of special purpose (nonlibrary) government (e.g., a school board), for whom the public library responsibility is a specifically added and oftentimes a remote secondary responsibility. These latter trustees, nevertheless, are library trustees also, and, despite the priorities of their own responsibilities, should so view themselves and act accordingly.

In that majority of public library organizations which have a library board so designated, the range of the degree of independent responsibility is wide. A relatively few boards are wholly independent units of special government with full financial, personnel, program-related and other operations self-determined.[4] Most other boards have self-determi-

---

or regulatory is that promulgated in regulation, ordinance, resolution, rule, order, etc., by the legally empowered library board of other body or unit of federal, state, or local government under appropriate law to adopt such regulation, etc. All of these laws may be voided or modified by case law, i.e., law established as judicial decisions in court cases involving the specific laws. The laws referred to in this footnote have force in the order of precedence indicated by their order of listing (i.e., constitutional law is superior to statutory and administrative or regulatory law; statutory law is superior to administrative or regulatory law.)

3. Note of several other relevant areas of statutory law is in order: state statutes provide for nonprofit, charitable corporations. Many states also statutorily provide for the provision of services—including library services—on an interstate basis. Most states have laws for intrastate or regional systems of multiple public libraries; increasingly, these systems are multitype, with membership including public and one or more other type of library (e.g., school, special, or academic).

4. According to the U.S. Bureau of the Census, 1987. . . . *Census of Government* . . . , *Government Finances* . . . , *Finances of Special Districts* (the latest issued, February 1990), independent public libraries, as defined by the Bureau, exist in 16, or 32 percent, of the 50 states. (In the previous report, 1982, the numbers, respectively, were 13 and 26.) In 3 states, the majority of public libraries are independent. Of the public libraries in the United States in 1987, 839, or approximately 9½ percent were independent. (In 1982 the respective figures were 638 and 7 percent.)

nation in some areas (e.g., programs) and are subordinate to a board of general purpose government (e.g., city or county) in other areas (e.g., finance and personnel). A few boards may have some limited responsibilities but have little or no legal power, being primarily or wholly advisory to the managers of a unit of general government, to a board of general purpose government, or to a school or other special purpose (nonlibrary) board. A great variety exists from state to state, and even within a state there may be a variety in the limits of the authority and relationships of boards of trustees responsible for public library service. (Several states have as many as ten different forms of public libraries.) This circumstance should caution trustees in their reading about, discussing, or comparing public libraries other than their own to be certain that they are aware of the possible legal and other differences and to reflect that awareness in any conclusions which they may draw.

Library Trustees as Public Officials

By virtue of being a member of the board of trustees of a public library established under the library laws, the library trustee is a public official. As a public official, the trustee of a public library has a special and preeminent status and commensurate responsibilities. Legally, the trustee is responsible for:

1. Having a broad, current knowledge of basic legal concepts and principles and of the relevant local, state, and federal library and general laws (any major applicable judicial opinions) of significance in the library's administration and operation.
2. Understanding in detail the governance, organization, financing, and administration, under law, of the trustee's library.
3. Recognizing the administrative law powers, duties, and functions of the trustee's own board of trustees, and encouraging and supporting the adoption of such administrative laws as will facilitate the library operation.
4. Securing for the board on a regular, continuing basis, the services of a competent, responsive, and effective independent legal counsel, knowledgeable in library and governmental law.
5. Complying at all times with the letter of the law, or in the absence of a specific law, complying with the spirit of the law, and supporting the fullest compliance of the board and its members, of the head librarian and other staff members, and of the library's agents with all applicable laws.
6. Using the law to its fullest capacity to achieve the board's goals and objectives.

7. Knowing and being involved regularly in the legislative process in order to secure passage of legislation favorable to libraries, or to prevent such existing legislation from being unfavorably amended or repealed. (Not only is legislative activity by a trustee legal and appropriate, this activity is imperative if a trustee is to fulfill totally the obligation to support in every legal way possible the library's mission. If trustees and the other members of the library community don't look out for the library interests, who will?)

8. Knowing and using the rules of parliamentary procedure to expedite and to facilitate the conduct of meetings of the board of library trustees.

9. Promoting the development, expansion, and preservation of public library service. (In cases involving the power of public library trustees, courts have held that trustees not only have broad authority in their operation of the library, but implicitly, as a part of their trust, they also are responsible for undertaking such political and other actions which may further the development of the institution for which they are trustees.)

Legal Bases for Establishment of Libraries

The power of the board of a public library derives from library statutes or from ordinances or resolutions of nonlibrary units of local government.

A common provision of state library law is the establishment of a public library by the corporate authority of a local general-purpose government under its administrative powers (i.e., by ordinance or resolution). Under the laws of some states, a public library may be established by such an entity upon the petition of legal residents. A third basis is the passage by voters of a public library establishment referendum.

Provisions for the financing of public libraries in a state usually is found in the state's library law. Customarily, the authority to tax for library purposes rests with the corporate authority of the local general purpose government, although in a few states and for a few libraries, the taxing power lies with the library board. (In the rare instance where the funding provision is not in library law, the authority rests in the general powers of the local general-purpose government.)

Provisions for the public library's governance constitute the third basic element in library establishment law. Included in the specifications will be the library board or other form of governance, number and term(s) of the members of the board, and method of their selection, their powers and duties, and, perhaps, other special provisions such as an oath of office, honesty bonding, representational composition of the board, and terms of disqualification of a board member.

Legal Powers of Library Boards

Except for the few library boards which are honorific or otherwise generally powerless, and with the recognition that from state to state some powers in a general list may or may not apply, the legal powers of a board of library trustees ordinarily include:

1. Determination of the library's mission, and of the goals and objectives, and the programs and activities necessary to fulfill that mission.[5] Upon board approval of the mission (or its amendment, as the case may be), the library director should be responsible for developing and executing the program of response to and fulfillment of that mission, and the resulting goals and objectives.

2. Authority to make rules and regulations (administrative law) governing the operation and the management of the library. Examples of areas for which rules and regulations are made are days and hours open, the circulation of materials, the selection of materials, the use of meeting rooms, user eligibility, user registration, nonresident use, fines and fees, and the conduct of board meetings.

3. Control, management, and care of all real and personal property. The library board normally owns and has exclusive control and possession of personal property, such as books and other materi-

---

5. Somewhat surprisingly, the laws of the various states omit references to the philosophical, social, and broad general purpose(s) of the public library. At most, there may be statements that the law's purpose is the establishment of free public libraries and reading rooms, the provision of a physical facility for the library, and the purchase of books and other library materials. The attention is to the basic resources needed to meet an assumed mission, rather than to an identification of that mission. For the legalistic, the ambiguity resulting from the omission in the law of a statement of purpose may be perceived as a weakness and significant handicap. Others will appreciate that the omission gives each library great latitude in identifying and responding to the needs of its community and in determining what specifically is or is not appropriate in responding to that need. In any case, the library director, with the assistance of the appropriate library staff and of the trustees, should be responsible for identifying and formalizing the library's mission statement. With the board's adoption of that statement, the mission becomes the legal basis on which the library's activities rest.

als, bookstacks, furniture, and movable equipment. For an independent public library or special library district the board normally also owns the library's real property (the library site, and the building and other physical improvements), has the right to construct, purchase, improve, and repair its building, to dispose of its building and other real property through sale or other means, and to borrow money for these purposes. For other public libraries, the board may have powers similar to those of independent libraries, but more often the library board at best has a qualified control, subject to the ultimate control of the corporate authority of the "parent" local general-purpose government. Too, for those public libraries, the will of the corporate authority applies to the library's construction, purchase, and improvement. For most libraries, whether independent or subordinate to a unit of local general-purpose government, a referendum approving the financing of major real property projects (through the sale of bonds, etc.), and the general conditions applying to that financing may be necessary.

Most states have provision for the acquisition of property for public buildings, including libraries, by the exercise of the power of eminent domain. However, in only a few states do library boards have that power; normally the privilege of exercising this power on behalf of a public library rests with the corporate authority of the local general-purpose government.

4. Determination of the amount of funds needed, source(s) of the funds, and the amounts such may provide, and preparation of the budget based on need and realistic funding possibilities. Depending upon the respective state revenue-raising method, the basic and major financial support for public libraries normally either is (a) a dedicated tax for libraries upon property, primarily, if not exclusively, real property (usually expressed as a percentage or as a millage rate of the assessed value of the taxable property), or (b) a lump-sum appropriation from the general revenue, i.e., the aggregate of all the local general-purpose government's income from the various taxes and other sources. The first source, a property tax dedicated to libraries, is the most prevalent basis of library financial support. Sometimes the minimum and almost always the maximum tax rate which may be levied for library purposes is specified in law. (While the property tax remains the major source of library funding in all but a few states, this form of taxation increasingly is in disfavor. Unfortunately, no generally acceptable alternative for library funding has appeared, and the finding of an alternative source as the

legal basis for library funding increasingly is an imperative for trustees and others in positions of library leadership.)

For all but the relatively few independent libraries, the funding authority, whether the library funding is from the library taxes on property or from appropriations from general revenues, is a local government body other than the board of library trustees.

Under such circumstances a most important consideration is the type of relationship that exists between the library board and the corporate authorities. If through the years the trustees have been successful in presenting the library's position . . . in a persuasive manner, then the board should experience little or no difficulty in convincing the political power structure that a substantial tax levy or a generous appropriation is required. In interpreting the library to the corporate authorities and in obtaining adequate financing, the library board must employ political sagacity, diplomacy, firmness, and even the use of political pressure if necessary. There are many library boards that have established excellent working relationships with the . . . [financing] authorities and as a consequence they are virtually able to set the library tax rate to be levied or to determine the amount of an appropriation even though officially the levy or appropriation must be made by the corpo rate body.[6]

5. Disbursement of the library's funds in accordance with the approved budget and any other legal authorization.

In the discharge of this power, accountability is the fundamental responsibility of the library trustee and of the board, collectively, of which the trustee is a member. Every state has laws requiring the accountability of public officials and of public bodies, which include trustees and library boards. The letter of the law is an absolute, and requires accountability "to the penny" for all monies held in trust, all disbursements (in amount and in legality of expenditure), all assets, all liabilities, and all funds in safekeeping.

In addition, some states require honesty and fidelity bonding in an amount adequate to cover fiscal officers in the total indicated risk and require, also, an annual audit by a legally acceptable auditor. Whether or not the law specifically requires an honesty bond, the purchase of such a bond to cover all board members and employees who are—or conceivably will

6. Alex Ladenson, "The Trustee and the Law," in Virginia G. Young, ed., *The Library Trustee: A Practical Guidebook*, 3d ed. (New York: Bowker, 1978), 56.

be—involved in fiscal activities and responsibilities is advisable. As well, the conduct of an annual audit by a certified public accountant with a resulting management letter pointing out areas for improving the library's fiscal practices should be required.

As to the service responsibility, although fiscal responsibility is in order, the "saving of the taxpayer's money" at the expense of the fulfillment the library's service obligation is a violation of the trust.

A few words are appropriate regarding public library trustees and conflicts of interest. Differences in objectives of an individual and of a group with which the person is identified are common. Such differences or conflicts of interest are not by general definition illegal or necessarily inappropriate; indeed, differences of interest and acts arising from those differences are a basic condition in and for a dynamic democratic society. However, a public library trustee, as a public official, must always be free of the taint as well as the act of using the office for a personal benefit. Principles of good government and public practice, even when not spelled out in the laws of the respective states, require that the trustee not be a party to any action of the board, which action will or may personally benefit the trustee, members of the trustee's family, or trustee's business connections. In some states, abstaining from voting on a matter in which this condition of conflict of interest exists is not sufficient; in this case, the only solution is for the trustee to resign.

6. Conduct of the library personnel activities.

The degree to which this authority rests solely with the board of public library trustees and the degree to which the authority may be reserved to another governing authority varies from state to state and may vary among various types of public libraries within a state. For those libraries which are subordinate to the corporate authority of another unit of local government, that authority's personnel or civil service regulations may apply and the key power of a library's control of its personnel is seriously curtailed. In practice, where the library board generally has the authority for personnel, the library director is assigned the responsibility for the various day-to-day personnel activities as a part of the overall administrative duties. (However, the ultimate responsibility for the staffing and other personnel matters rests with the trustees. To that end—and in particular in a time of increased litigation involving personnel matters—the continuous monitoring of this area of operations is imperative.)

7. Power to contract for library or library-related services with other public or governmental libraries or other public bodies when a board of trustees determines that library service can best be provided by contracting for any or all services from another entity. (In some states, this contractual authority extends to contracts with not-for-profit and other private corporations for the provision of library services. For other than independent public libraries, this contractual power may be reserved to a superior unit of local government. In some cases, the authority for intergovernmental contracts is specific for libraries; in other cases, this power exists under a general governmental provision. The names for such contracts vary from state to state: common names include interlocal government agreements, interstate compacts, and joint exercise of powers agreements.)

Library Trustees and Nonlibrary Local, State, and Federal Laws

While the library trustee's primary focus is on the library laws of the respective state, the body of general local, state, and federal law applicable to governmental institutions such as public libraries is voluminous. This large body of law is not to be overlooked. (Examples of the subjects of these laws include building construction, commercial contracts, copyright, elections and public office, fair labor practices, discrimination, employee benefits, employee disability, Freedom of Information, access for the disabled, legal notice and publication, liability insurance, obscenity and pornography, postal rates, privacy, purchasing, safety, site and property maintenance, taxes and taxation, tax-free gifts and donations, telecommunication, unemployment, and zoning.)

Although a trustee's primary legal awareness and knowledge should focus on state law, the trustee should develop a broad awareness and knowledge of applicable local and federal law.

Library Trustees and Indemnification

In an era of increased litigation, public officials, including public library trustees, are at some risk, notwithstanding their good faith and their attempts to perform to the best of their ability and in the public interest. Trustees risk being sued for acts or alleged acts while acting officially on behalf of the library. Examples of acts conceivably subject to such suits include unfair labor practices, deprivation of personal rights, and negligence in the operation of the library. Although the instances of public library trustees being sued are limited, nevertheless the possibility is ever-present. Indemnification of individual trustees (as well as of members of the library staff) against judgments, fines, and other liabilities, include amounts paid in settlement and for reasonable expenses such as attorney's fees incurred as a result of a suit, should, to the extent possible under law, be a responsibility of the public library. Some states have tort immunity acts which grant authority to local public entities, including public libraries, to defend trustees and employees against a claim or action of this sort and to pay court costs, judgments, or settlements. Trustees and other members of the library community in states without tort immunity laws and where such laws are enactable should work for the passage of laws to provide indemnification to library trustees and staff members.

A board of public library trustees alternatively or additionally may purchase insurance, sometimes called an Officers and Directors Errors and Omissions Liability insurance, to provide indemnification should it be necessary. (Care should be taken that such a policy covers at least all of the most likely areas of possible risk.)

Summary

The law provides the basis for the creation, support, development, and preservation of the public library. As such, the law is at the heart of the institution.

Library trustees should have a knowledge of the library laws and the applicable general local, state, and federal laws, and operate in accord with those laws. Trustees should recognize their roles, responsibilities, powers, and opportunities as public officials, and work to improve the laws under which libraries operate.

> Law is not static or immutable . . . legislation does not originate in a vacuum. Law and legislation are deeply rooted in the social, economic, and political soil of society and reflect the changes that evolve in every facet of community life. For this reason, it is vital that trustees seek to improve and expand legislation on a continuing basis, so that libraries can function more effectively and make a greater contribution to the educational and cultural life of this nation.[7]

7. Ibid, 59.

11 The Trustee and Finances

Herbert H. Davis

igh on the list of responsibilities of a board of trustees is the task of assuring adequate funds for the operations of the library; and also the task of adopting a budget for the expenditure of those funds so as to fulfill the policies and programs which have been adopted. Money is the driving force that makes things happen. Without funding, the most appealing and worthwhile plans of action are dead in the water.

The Budget

The annual responsibility for the adoption of a budget is the time when all of the attention of the library board of trustees becomes focused on a single document which will affect every aspect of library service to the community in the coming year. As the summation of the best thinking of the library director and staff, the budget provides the most important single opportunity for the board to exercise its responsibilities.

Basically, the development of a budget is a matching process: available income versus proposed expenditures. A plan which calls for spending more money than can reasonably be expected to be received is unrealistic and bound to cause misunderstandings, and, in the worse case, an emergency curtailment of services toward the end of the budget year. Assigning priorities in the service program is the beginning point in

Herbert A. Davis is past president of the Baltimore County, Maryland, Libraries board and former president of the American Library Trustee Association.

the budget process. Only the trustee who has systematically analyzed and evaluated the service program can intelligently discriminate among the myriad of appealing opportunities and balance the ambition of the board and staff for implementation of every good idea against the inevitable shortage of funds to do everything.

Sources of Revenue

A board of trustees which limits its financial responsibility to the allocation and budgeting of available resources has failed to recognize the ultimate and most important task of the board, which is to investigate all income sources and to maximize their yield. Sources of income will vary from state to state, and between libraries within a state. Often these sources are dictated by law, and sometimes the board will find that income generated by the library's activities will revert to the governmental funding source, which is a severe limitation on the suggestions which follow.

In most cases the major support for public library services will come from legislated sources such as state statutes permitting the establishment of tax levies and bond issues on the local level. Such sources can be affected by the influence that trustees can—and should—wield with legislators at the state and national level, and with local representative bodies. Influence is most effective if exercised over time. The politically savvy trustee will build bridges at every opportunity, and not limit contacts with governmental sources of support to budget time alone. The trustee will find that there is intense competition for funds at every level of the budget process, but that a well-presented and intelligently reasoned presentation of the library's case will receive an attentive hearing.

Revenues generated by library operations are playing an increasing role in the overall funding of library services. This is a subject of much ongoing discussion in the library profession and among trustees. Charges for overdues, reserved books, copying services, and parking are generally accepted. More controversial are fees for computerized database access, video rental, meeting room charges, and book sales. Solicitation of contribution and grants is sometimes negated by a policy of the governmental funding source of subtracting such receipts from the annual appropriation. Although each library will have a context in which the following discussion should be viewed, in general these ideas will prove useful, if adopted by the board.

Fines

Although there is a divergence of opinion regarding the effectiveness of a fine policy, money collected from patrons for overdue materials can amount to a significant income source. At the Baltimore County Public Library (Maryland) (1993 circulation 10,989,985), the charge for keeping the book or other item is now called "extended loan fee." Only one notice is sent, after the item is three weeks overdue. No threats or "penalty language" is included, but the next time the patron visits a branch the charges will appear on the computer screen and will be collected before any additional items can be borrowed. Revenue from this source in 1993 was $1,242,164. This income provided funding for many additional copies of popular titles, allowing for the extended loan program to be implemented without inconvenience to other borrowers.

Caution should be exercised to make sure that the cost incurred in notifying patrons of overdue materials as well as the staff time devoted to this process and the actual collection of the money are in proportion to the revenue received. Some libraries have a no-fine policy, opting instead to have staff time devoted to public service. There is a feeling by many, as well, that a fine policy is a negative rather than a positive public relations tool. As to the inauguration of a fine (extended loan fee) policy, this is a philosophical tenet each board of trustees will have to settle.

Copying Machines

The income from a copying machine will usually pay for the machine and provide significant revenue as well. In most communities machines can be leased or purchased, and a service contract can be obtained from the vendor that will provide for everything but resupplying the paper cassettes. If the utilization warrants, two machines at each location is a good idea, because nothing is more frustrating to a patron who has traveled a long distance with the intention of making a copy than to find the machine out of order. Providing facilities for copying is a great convenience to the library user and often results in materials remaining in the library for others to use, and tends to reduce mutilation of reference materials.

FAX Reference Service

Many reference callers have access to a FAX machine, and prefer having the answer to their inquiry sent to them instead of recited over the telephone. In libraries with computerized borrower files, the cost of a FAX response can be charged to their library card and collected upon the patron's next visit. Often, from the reference librarian's point of view, FAX responses are timesavers, resulting in better service to a large number of callers.

Reserve Fees

It has been common practice to charge a fee for the privilege of "standing in line" for a book. However, the revenue generated rarely does more than cover the cost of operating a reserve system. Some libraries achieve a dramatic reduction in reserve requests by refusing to accept "reserves" for current best sellers. Of course, this plan is only practical when a sufficient number of copies of best sellers is purchased at the time of publication.

Books/Materials Sales

At noted above, in some jurisdictions the proceeds from the sale of library property reverts to the general fund of the governmental funding source. In this case the task of the board is to lobby for a change in policy or law, so that sales revenues can be retained by the library for the purchase of replacement materials.

Where the library can have a book sale and keep the money, it should be a regular practice for two reasons: first, the money collected can be used to buy current books and materials to replace those withdrawn, and, second, having sales (or a continuous sale, for that matter) is a big help in furthering a policy for continuously weeding the collection. The value of a library's holdings is in direct relationship to the usefulness to the user. A building full of an obsolete collection will be expensive to maintain, and will provide very little help to the patron. One library routinely buys up to 1,200 copies of current best sellers to meet the immediate demand upon publication, and puts the excess copies on sale (priced at library's cost) within two or three months, revolving the money to buy the next hot item. Although a one time appropriation was required to get this revolving fund started, funds for keeping it going are available from the sale of the extra copies which would not have been purchased ordinarily, and from the extended loan fees generated by these popular fiction and nonfiction books.

Fees for Rental

The discussion in library circles among professional librarians and trustees with regard to the appropriateness of charging fees for services provided by a public library is still going on. In some states, such charges are prohibited by law, and in most communities the tradition of "free" service is deeply rooted. Where the law prohibits charges, it was probably enacted before the invention of expensive services libraries will be providing, such as data base access through computer terminals in the library and video cassettes. In the absence of fees, it is difficult to justify the expense where the service meets the needs of such a relatively small number of users.

It is not uncommon for libraries to maintain a "pay duplicate" collection of video cassettes and/or books. In this way the library can purchase more copies of some titles than they would otherwise be able to afford.

Board members and library staff will be called upon to make some philosophical judgments with regard to this issue, and some practical solution sought.

Grants

Money from federal, state, and local governments; from foundations; from community groups and private sources is available to fund everything from experimentation with new programs to study existing patterns of behavior, to planning for new or expanded programs, to training staff and research of every sort. The point to remember is that in almost every case you have to ask for the money. Often, grantors will even offer assistance in preparing a request. A word of caution: programs initiated with grant money will have to be funded from general revenues when the grant money has run out, unless the program replaces another or generates income of its own for its continuance.

Contracts with Other Libraries

Short of combining systems, some libraries have linked togethor contractually with beneficial financial results for both parties. In one instance, a small three-branch system contracted with a larger, geographically adjacent system of twenty-three branches for certain specified services:

1. Computerized circulation control
2. Computerized materials selection and ordering
3. Interbranch delivery service
4. CD-ROM (compact disc-read only memory catalog services).

The small library pays $50,000 annually for those services, which would have cost between $100,000 and $120,000 annually had the services been developed in-house. The large system, on the other hand, provided the services at no discernable cost to the system. Consequently, each party found itself better off by $50,000.

More common, and often separately funded, are regional libraries which provide many services for local libraries within their assigned territory. As materials continue to escalate in cost, and the practicality of online interconnectivity is better understood, such alliances are likely to enable the local library to afford the quality of service the patron deserves without dramatic and unaffordable increases in budget. Often the initiative for such a linked service is best found at the local level. Otherwise, the difficult questions of control and autonomy are likely to prevent a cooperative arrangement which would benefit everyone.

Friends of the Library

The recognition and support of a Friends group is a task in which trustees should be directly involved. In a large system Friends for each branch can be initiated. The Friends, individually and collectively, can be the library board's most visible and valuable support. Often these organizations can fund a service or activity which would otherwise be beyond the budget. Also a well-organized volunteer group can have a dramatic effect upon the ability of a library to expand its outreach.

Publications

Some libraries have been successful with ventures into publishing books, maps, directories, and catalogs generally relating to the library's local setting. Although not likely to produce huge sums of additional revenue, there can be a small profit. Often such ventures are undertaken in conjunction with a Friends group or a commercial publisher/printer.

Expenditures

There is no point in planning to spend more money than will be available from tax income, appropriations, fees for service, and any other revenue sources. Once this dollar amount has been agreed upon by staff and board, the process of allocation can begin. Establishment of priorities is the prerogative of the board. The choices are difficult, since there is no such things as "enough money" to accomplish all of the desirable goals and to fulfill all of the opportunities for better library service.

The usual process involves providing funds for staff salaries and benefits, plus any COLA adjustments; predicting costs for utilities, fuel, maintenance of buildings, telephone and supplies; allowing for contractual services such as janitorial service and equipment maintenance; and other such "standing commitments."

Then follows the "discretionary" list: books, audiovisual materials, reference materials, including computer data bases and equipment of all sorts required for the library to fulfill its mission. Often, the budget is balanced by adjusting the "discretionary" items to fit the money left over after the so-called standing commitments have been provided for.

A much sounder basis for budgeting is a plan whereby every category of cost is scrutinized annually. Believing that a library is "books and materials" rather than a building, some library boards will allocate a percentage of the total funds available to books and materials first; then divide the remaining money among the other budget categories. In times of budget cuts, this program will result in staff reductions, branch closings, shorter hours, and "more natural" landscaping (cutting the grass less often).

The Materials Budget

The board should also be conscious of the rapidly rising cost of books and materials and be wary of complacency. The same dollar amount expended annually will usually buy fewer items. Library systems of all sizes have to cope with the same threat. Unless priorities are agreed upon in advance, the budget will balance itself on the basis on appropriating funds for all of those things which have been traditional categories of expense with the materials budget receiving what is left over. To prevent this from happening, the board should establish a priority for the materials needed in order to maintain the collection at a minimum level, and should allow nothing to prevent at least this much money being allocated to this category. The startling increase in the dollar amount required to achieve this important goal should not mask the necessity of at least keeping even with the previous year's purchases.

Obsolescence is another factor affecting the materials budget. Unless the collection is routinely purged of outdated, worn-out, or unused materials, the trustee might assume that the collection was adequate solely on the basis of the number of items held, rather than on the basis of its timely usefulness. Weeding the collection should be *routine*, and provision should be made for its impact upon the budget.

Equipment

In addition to budgeting for new equipment, funds for the replacement of obsolete or worn-out items must be included. It is important to check the budgeted total for replacement and new equipment against the total investment in such items. The equipment budget total should be at least 5 percent of such investment (twenty-year life expectancy), and, ideally, closer to 10 percent.

The Capital Budget

Whether the money to meet the capital needs of the library is to come from an appropriation from general funds (government), a bond issue, a building tax levy, or from a capital drive in the private sector, a five-year forward-looking capital expenditure budget should be updated every year. The impact upon the operating budget can then be antici- pated. Many library boards, having acquired a new facility, have discov- ered that the cost of operating it was so much higher than the old build- ing that it was impossible to fund the materials and staff required for good library service.

One way of insuring the success of an expansion program is to in- clude in any campaign for funds from the private sector a sum to function as an endowment to offset the increased cost of operating a new facility. Most universities, for example, now will refuse to accept money for the construction of a new building on the campus unless the contribution is accompanied by an adequate sum to provide an endowment to cover the cost of operating the facility once it has been constructed.

Insurance

Arrangements for covering the insurable risk exposures of library boards and libraries are as varied as the insurance industry itself. Li- brary systems functioning in metropolitan settings often are covered under the insurance umbrella of the municipality or the county which, in many instances, is self-insured for most potential losses. In this in- stance it is the board's responsibility to assure that the governmental body is fully aware of the value of the assets under the library board's control.

In other instances the library is entirely responsible for its own insurance coverages. In such situations the board should exercise its fiduciary responsibility by making certain that there is a thorough re- view of library insurance needs by a competent, independent insurance analyst at least once every three years. This analysis should cover types of coverage required, and appropriate limits. Not to be overlooked is the desirability of D & O (directors and officers) liability insurance coverage to protect members of the board in the event of a lawsuit related to his or her board activities.

Conclusion

It is not the function of the board of trustees or of its individual members to second-guess the library director at budget time. Rather, the board should look at the budget as a measure of the library's current position, anticipate the hard choices to be made in the relatively small part of the budget susceptible to manipulation, and direct its major thrust toward providing adequate resources so that the choices become less trouble- some. Lobbying the governmental funding source, soliciting special purpose contributions, or initiating and conducting a successful election campaign to increase the library's tax levy are clearly the trustee's bailiwick.

Public libraries have been described as the road to learning. If this is the case, then we need to find the link between libraries and highways. If one considers the staggering sums of money spent to build highways and roads in the United States, the funding of libraries is pitifully small. Trustees need to build a case for adequate funding of library service in this country on a scale comparable to that which has funded the development of the interstate highway system. Only then will we have a true highway to learning adequate to the task.

12 A Fundraising Primer for Public Library Trustees

Glen E. Holt
Thomas F. Schlafly

undraising is a financial necessity for most American public libraries. Libraries define this necessity differently. Some need to supplement meager budgets. Others seek to raise the quality of good basic services. Still others look for outside income to initiate innovative programs. Finally, there are those that seek funds for special projects, including capital developments like a building addition or an entirely new library.

As public libraries become more dependent on information technology, the imperative for fundraising is likely to become even more compelling. In simple terms, traveling the information superhighway is considerably more expensive than circulating best sellers. In many cases the price of improved electronic services will be higher than local tax payers are willing to pay. To keep up in the electronic age, many public libraries will have to find additional money beyond their funding base.

The Library's Fundraising Image

If libraries have not raised funds previously or they want to raise the level of giving to their institutions, they need to develop a fundraising culture inside their institutions and within their communities.

A fundraising culture can vary according to the needs and image

Glen E. Holt is executive director of the St. Louis Public Library.
Thomas F. Schlafly is president of the board of the St. Louis Public Library.

of an institution. Some institutions thrive because of their community prestige (e.g., universities, art museums, or orchestras). Others appeal to donors' sense of compassion (e.g., homeless shelters).

In most communities public libraries fall somewhere in between. As public agencies, they are often not regarded as exclusive or prestigious as the area art museum. At the same time library patrons are not viewed as being as needy as clients of a homeless shelter.

Because they are primarily funded through taxes, public libraries face another identity problem. Many potential donors resist contributing to agencies already receiving their tax dollars. In this view libraries are seen as a public utility like the fire, police, or water departments. Both the community perception and the library's sense of its own identity need to be kept in mind when building a fundraising culture.

Building a Fundraising Culture

Building a fundraising culture usually begins with institutional planning. A plan may be comprehensive, covering the future of the whole institution; or strategic, emphasizing the critical shifts necessary to move the institution forward.

An effective planning process involves board, administration, and staff. Good planning leads inevitably to the consideration of resources. In the process the entire library staff, board, and, quite often, influential members of the community begin to see the institution in a new light.

As part of institutional planning, the library needs to prepare a financial priorities statement. Partly narrative and partly statistical, this document presents a clear statement of current financial resources and the amount of new revenue needed to reach the visualized future articulated in the plan. Board members and donors often ask for an additional statement of what the library will do if new funds are not obtained.

Research

While preparing the plan and the priorities statement, knowledgeable board members, friends and/or staff need to undertake four kinds of research.

First, research on the institution itself. Areas for analysis might include defining operational style; marking out critical service constituencies, including those unserved; assessing current and potential supporters; and evaluating the library's future against area demographic trends and in comparison with similar institutions in other communities. In making this assessment, library leaders need to decide which service programs or projects merit private-sector support.

Potential donors should be included in the generation of this assessment. The greater the sense of ownership, the greater the probability that the support will occur initially—and will continue at a higher level. If a potential donor shows an interest in seeing the library undertake a particular project, the task of library leadership is to make it easy for that donor to have a project to fund. If the library does not follow through with the donor, the donor will have no trouble moving support to another institution.

Second, the library needs to gain a sense of the local community's fundraising style. In some communities, for example, it is easier to raise money for special programs; in others, it is easier to raise funds for buildings. Research helps determine the general pattern of community giving—the fundraising style.

Third, the library needs to identify donor prospects. That is accomplished by gathering local news about who is giving for what—from publications, electronic news outlets, and through conversations with potential donors and those who have experience in raising funds.

One way to begin this identification process is by looking at published lists of donors to other area cultural and educational institutions. The more an institution resembles the library, the greater is the likelihood of its potential support. It is also important not to focus merely on institutional similarity but also on programs that are like library programs. Supporters of similar programs at a dissimilar institution are good candidates for supporting a comparable program at the library, particularly if they have a role in helping design it.

Identification, Organization, and Training of Campaign Leadership

A fourth type of research is that undertaken to identify campaign leadership. In many communities library board members are likely to have more influence and contacts than the library director. In other communities the reverse is true. In some cases the library board members and administration will have to recruit well-known community leaders who have a record of giving and of soliciting gifts to lead the library campaign.

Many libraries have started philanthropic foundations to attract well-known community leaders who promise to give high-visibility leadership to the institution.

Private foundations have numerous advantages. Their funds are often not subject to the same legal restrictions as the public monies of libraries, e.g., limitations on type of investments. Moreover, serving on a foundation can give donors a sense of ownership in the library without the commitment of time and energy required by membership on the board of trustees.

Whether or not a foundation is created, the campaign leadership has to be ready to give the time and energy necessary to make the library development program a success. Campaign leadership is a demanding job, and it is critical to the success of any development program.

The training of campaign spokespersons is essential. Those who speak for the library, especially those who articulate its financial priorities, must speak with a clear, unified voice. Board members, high-level staff, and any campaign volunteers all need to learn the library fundraising story and how to tell it before approaches are made to donors.

Administrative Issues

Before beginning a campaign, trustees should give careful thought to establishing procedures for maintaining donor records. Also, library staff and trustees should develop an appropriate gift-processing system to ensure timely gift acknowledgements and pledge reminders and to meet donor and government tax requirements. For example, in compliance with Internal Revenue Service regulations pertaining to the Revenue Reconciliation Act of 1993, the organization may be required to notify donors at year-end not only of accumulative contributions but also of any premiums, goods, or services that were received in conjunction with their gifts; these goods or services may reduce the deductible amount. The gift-processing system should also accommodate record keeping for gifts of tangible personal property and other noncash items.

Well in advance of developing campaign communications, trustees will want to clearly identify what types of gifts will be accepted for the campaign and how they will be counted toward campaign goals. This is particularly important for planned or deferred gifts.

Types of gifts might include outright gifts of cash, cash pledges, personal property, real estate, in-kind service, equipment, and other assets, such as securities. For donors with assets that have been held long-term and that have appreciated in value, there may be significant tax advantages for the donor to contribute them to a qualifying charitable organization.

Special attention should be given to planned gifts because of their potential for being relatively large gifts. Planned gifts typically include bequests, life insurance policies, and life income gifts, such as charitable remainder trusts, charitable lead trusts, gift annuities, and pooled income funds.

Trustees may want to seek technical advice on gift policies and solicitation strategies for noncash gifts from a local attorney specializing in tax/estate planning or from a planned giving development specialist.

Donor Recognition

Another important part of fundraising preparations is to work out a donor recognition plan. Most donors want thoughtful recognition. That recognition can take many forms: the naming of a program, endowment fund, or building room for the person making the gift; organizing a recognition event with the donor inviting close friends or relatives to see the recognition given; or appropriate name recognition in sponsored programs and publications, to name only a few. Generally, the higher the level of donation, the more unique the recognition.

In this context it again is important to keep in mind the value of letting potential donors help shape what they are being asked to fund. Asking donors for advice and counsel—and then acting on it—is one of the most sincere forms of recognition a library can give.

Public Relations

A library needs to prepare for and support its development effort by a marketing campaign that positions the institution in the community. Favorable publicity is especially important if the institution is new to fundraising. Depending on the proposed nature of the campaign, library publicity themes might show how the institution provides services that meet community needs, operates in a businesslike way, and could play an even more important role in the community if more funding were provided.

From Fundraising to Philanthropy

Many institutions raise funds without ever really understanding philanthropy. Successful fundraising institutions always capture the spirit of philanthropy. That is, they respect individuals and work with them to find unique ways in which they can express their feelings through donation of their precious assets—their wisdom, their time, and their wealth.

People give for many different motives. Fundraising consultants Robert Hartsook and Suzanne Walters, at a fundraising seminar for libraries given a few years ago, summarized philanthropic motives this way:

1. Demonstrated spiritual love of humankind gained from spiritual teachings.
2. Philanthropic concern for humankind through gifts of time or resources or both.
3. Personal gratitude for life or services rendered.
4. Perpetuation of personal ideals, values, and goals.
5. Joining in success to assure organizational goals.
6. Fear—prevention of want; assurance of service.

Hartsook and Walters note that tax considerations are often crucial in gift giving, but even for these persons "the decision to give or not to give to any particular organization is based on non-tax considerations first, given the options to give to several thousand other philanthropies."[1]

The best fundraisers, whether for libraries or other institutions or charities, ignite these basic concerns in potential donors. If a library fundraising campaign does not deal with individual prospects on this level, then the institution may raise some money, but it will not motivate the philanthropic spirit in its donor constituents.

Cultivation

A library can convey this philanthropic spirit in the way it conducts donor cultivation and solicitation.

At is simplest, cultivation is getting to know individuals, families, or corporate representatives. At its best, it is a specialized form of courtship. Library representatives have two important responsibilities during cultivation: introducing the potential donor to the operations and needs of the institution, and getting to know the potential gift giver as well as possible. The latter usually involves careful questions and even more careful listening.

1. Robert Hartsook and Suzanne Walters, *Resource Development for Libraries* (Wichita, Kans., and Denver, Colo., typescript, 1992, 9).

Often the cultivation process can be hastened through introductions by a friend of the library who can be persuaded to take an interest in the campaign. But the listening process cannot be hastened. Potential donors almost always are willing to talk about themselves. In the process they provide important clues to their interests, motivations, and gift range.

Solicitation

At some point in the cultivation process, carefully planned and program solicitations are made to donors. No two solicitations are alike. Each solicitation is carefully planned to meet the needs of a potential donor. Solicitation is usually done in teams of two, with the role of each carefully scripted. Normally one person undertakes the presentation, with the second serving in a counterpoint and listening role. With two persons involved, all the facts and impressions of a presentation can be remembered, and nuances and details of emotionally charged conversations can be recalled and analyzed.

It is worth keeping in mind a truism of solicitation: the more personal it is, the more effective it is. A personal visit is more effective than a telephone call, which in turn is more effective than a letter.

Hartsook and Walters provide a "Checklist of Factors Solicitors Must Consider." They have prepared this list from the standpoint of the donor. It is an outstanding summary. Solicitors who have prepared answers for all of the questions for an individual donor are well prepared to ask for funds. Here are a majority of the points from Hartsook' and Walters' checklist:

1. Was the solicitation interview thoughtful, well stated, honest?
2. Were the volunteer/staff solicitors well prepared for determining my/our interests?
3. Did they give evidence that they really knew me/us sufficiently?
4. Did they get to the point in good time?
5. Did they really know the organization, the plan, the (fundraising) program?
6. Was the specific request well stated for a range of giving or merely a yes-or-no figure? Was it reasonable for me/us, given knowledge of my/our background?
7. Was the presentation persuasive or matter-of-fact? Were solicitors enthusiastic? Concerned for the urgency of (their institution's) success?
8. Is the organization really doing the jobs the solicitors stated? More so? Less so? Was their evidence convincing?

9. Am I/are we satisfied/grateful for the organization's services?
10. Do I/we really know the organization's leadership, management, staff, volunteers?
11. Is the organization well managed?
12. Is the plan for the future reasonable, impressive, persuasive?
13. Will our investment make a difference?
14. Should I/we provide a modest gift as a test of the organization's efficiency and see how the program progresses, or should I/we provide a real gift of confidence in the organization's plan, leadership, and volunteers?
15. Is this my/our best investment for our interests, concerns, ideals? Is this a way I/we should put back/provide for others as others have provided for us?
16. Who else is supporting the organization? What is their record? What is the record of governing board participation?
17. Did the presenters say what they were giving?
18. Why should I/we decide now?[2]

These questions and others like them form the pattern of expectations which potential donors bring to the solicitation interview. Library representatives will do well to prepare answers to even the most difficult of these questions before engaging in a solicitation.

The solicitation is not the end of the cultivation process. If the solicitation is successful, cultivation turns into a long-term relationship. It is not unusual for donors to give a second time—and at a higher level. Even if that is not expected, donors are precious to organizations, and they deserve the best possible treatment.

If the solicitation proves unsuccessful (if the research and cultivation have been done effectively, turndowns will not happen frequently), then cultivation may be continued in the hope of making another solicitation for a different objective.

Conclusion

As the title of this chapter suggests, the material presented here is only a primer to help library trustees begin thinking about how to organize their institution for fundraising.

If the library budget does not allow for a professional library development staff, more training is relatively easy to find. Area colleges and universities usually offer short courses on fundraising as part of their

2. Ibid., 7–8.

extension curricula. Almost every community has persons working as development officers for organizations like the Boy Scouts and Girl Scouts, National Cancer Society, or United Way. Most such individuals are quite willing to share their knowledge with those just starting out in the development field. Training and contact with area development officers can also be found in the programs organized by local chapters of the National Society of Fund Raising Executives (NSFRE).

At the outset of this chapter, its authors suggested that fundraising has become a necessity for most public libraries. Yet this necessity does not have to be unpleasant. The organization and carrying out of a development program is often the most rewarding and long-lasting part of library trusteeship. Good trustees are always ready to help find new sources of funding to help move their institutions forward toward a bright future.

Further Reading

Association of Research Libraries. *Library Development and Fundraising.* Washington, D.C.: Office of Management Services, 1993.
Burlingame, Dwight W., ed. *Library Development: A Future Imperative.* Binghamton, N.Y.: Haworth, 1990.

13 The Trustee and Library Buildings

Anders C. Dahlgren
Charles E. Reid

The public library provides a variety of programs and services that can hardly be matched by any other local institution or unit of government. The public library is a busy, dynamic hub in the community. The typical public library serves a quarter of the population regularly and a far greater proportion of the population occasionally on a budget that generally accounts for less than 2 percent of total local municipal funding. The library building provides a context within which all the library services and activities are organized.

Consider the myriad of diverse activities that occur at the library: patrons borrow and return books and other material; others browse through the latest magazines and books; still others come to study, alone or in groups; some make photocopies; others do research among the local history clipping files or utilize microfilm and microfiche collections; the staff answers reference questions and assists people in the use of the collection; they meet with sales representatives to order books; new books and materials are received, and they are cataloged and prepared for use; preschoolers attend storytimes that introduce them to the world of reading; their parents may attend programs that introduce them to microcomputers, or new cooking techniques, or a host of other topics, and so on.

Anders C. Dahlgren is a consultant for Public Library Construction and Planning, State of Wisconsin, Department of Public Instruction, Madison.

Charles E. Reid is former chairman of the U.S. National Commission on Library and Information Science and former president of the American Library Trustee Association.

The library building must support all of these activities and more. The trustees' attention more routinely may be directed toward issues like budget preparation, staff organization, or collection development, but the board must also keep in mind that the structure housing the library has a direct effect on what the library can or cannot accomplish.

When the limitations of the building itself stand in the way of delivering effective library service, the board is obligated to develop a facilities improvement program to correct the problems. The improvements may involve a major or minor remodeling, in addition, or the construction of a new building. The resulting capital project may be difficult and is challenging to undertake. It may be difficult because it involves an increased commitment of time and energy from the board, the staff, and others. It is challenging because it requires careful examination of the community's future needs.

A building project carefully planned will have an incomparable impact on the success of the library's services and programs for many years to come. Without careful planning today, the building will limit service options tomorrow. As Winston Churchill observed, "We shape our buildings; thereafter they shape us."

The Role of the Trustee

As a member of the library's policymaking body, a trustee bears a fundamental responsibility for initiating, organizing, and implementing a library building project. As the final authority for the project, the board will provide general oversight and direction, just as it provides direction in the establishment of policies directing the library's day-to-day operations. In broad terms, the board provides legal authority and fiscal authority as well as community representation for the project.

The library board is usually vested by law with the responsibility and authority to undertake a building project. This will vary somewhat from state to state, according to the specific provisions of the statutes. In some instances, the legal authority may rest with another governmental unit, in which case it is imperative that the library board and its attorney identify and work closely with the unit or office responsible. Typically, however, the library trustees are granted exclusive control over the construction and maintenance of library facilities.

Together with the authority to undertake a building project, the board is typically granted the fiscal authority to pursue the project. The board will establish a budget for the project. The board will evaluate financing options for the project. The board will recommend a financing option to the municipality or implement the preferred financing option directly if that is allowed. Once the project is under construction, the board will be responsible for reviewing and approving contractors' applications for payment.

The board also plays a crucial role as community liaison. As representatives of the public at large, trustees should hear the concerns of the general public and assimilate those concerns into the planning process. As representatives and advocates for the library, trustees should serve as advocates to press the library's case with the voters and any local boards or councils that may have a voice in the project's completion.

Each project develops in its own way according to its own schedule. Because each building project is unique, it may be artificial to outline the major steps in a building project. The exact process that works in one community may not work in another; there is no single, absolute model for a successful building project, only general guidelines. The steps outlined below may occur in a slightly different order for any particular project, and specific trustees' responsibilities may vary, but the board typically will:

1. Make the decision that a construction program is needed.
2. Select a qualified professional librarian if one isn't already employed to direct the service planning to be reflected in the building program.
3. Study the community, including broad demographic, economic, and other trends as they define library service needs.
4. Initiate a needs assessment based on the community study.
5. Direct the campaign to let the community know about the need for new or expanded facilities.
6. Approve a written building program statement describing present and future building needs.
7. Appoint a strong building committee from within the board membership, or if the board is small enough, name a committee of the whole.
8. Select and appoint a qualified library building consultant.
9. Select and appoint a qualified architect.
10. Select and appoint an attorney.
11. Select and appoint an interiors specialist.
12. Select and purchase a site with the advice and assistance of the planning team.
13. Approve preliminary plans, furniture, and equipment layouts.
14. Estimate the cost of operating the new building and seek assurance of adequate operating funds once it is completed.
15. Secure funds for the project if it is not endowed; activate the campaign, referendum, or whatever is needed financially.

16. Approve final plans and authorize the invitation for bids for the building.
17. Approve construction contracts.
18. Monitor project progress.
19. Approve furniture and equipment contracts.
20. Approve and pay invoices.
21. Arrange the dedication and open house, with announcements to the public.
22. Help acquaint the public with the new services and programs now possible and available.

As is always the case, it is crucial that the board prepare for planning and that sufficient lead time be allowed for each of these steps.

The Trustee and the Planning Team

One key to a successful project will be the selection of the library planning team. The trustees are responsible for bringing the team together in the early planning stages.

The participants in any successful building planning team are the library board, the librarian, the architect, and the building consultant. As described above, the library board bears the final responsibility and provides the overall vision for the project, and the board receives and acts upon recommendations regarding the project's direction. The librarian provides day-to-day administration of the project and acts as intermediary between the board and the architect. The architect brings general design experience to the project. And the consultant brings experience in assessing library service and space needs to the project.

The librarian serves as adviser to the board and coordinator between the board, the architect, and the consultant. The librarian is responsible for preparing an initial space needs assessment and building program statement (though the writing of these documents may actually be done by, or in cooperation with, the building consultant). From that point on, the librarian should be involved with all aspects of the project's development—from site selection through construction—to be able to advise the board more effectively. The librarian must involve the staff in the planning process. Staff review of plans will help evaluate how those plans will affect library operations. Staff involvement can also improve communications and reduce anxieties generated by the prospective move into a new facility.

The architect is hired to design a facility according to the goals outlined in a written building program statement approved by the library board. A building program statement is a summary of the library's service goals, its projected space needs, and its vision of how departments should interact to achieve those goals most effectively. Initially, the architect will prepare schematic designs. With board approval, these will be developed into detailed working drawings and specifications. The architect typically assists the board with soliciting and evaluating bids from contractors. Then, during construction, the architect will serve as the library's representative, monitoring progress and holding regular job coordination meetings with the contractor(s).

The building consultant combines library programming expertise with library building expertise. He or she is usually a librarian who is familiar with the assessment of library service needs and has had previous experience with library space planning. The consultant helps the trustees and staff assess their future service or program needs and calculate how those service needs affect space needs. The consultant can interpret the library's needs to an architect or engineer to help create a design that will be responsive to the library's projected service needs. In a delicate political environment, the consultant can also provide the impartiality needed to convince a municipal board of the need for the library's project.

Consultant assistance is usually recommended because in most cases librarians, trustees, and architects aren't routinely involved in the library facilities planning process and may not be aware of some of the unique planning requirements posed by a library building. A consultant's expertise can be valuable in avoiding ill-conceived design solutions to space needs. A smaller library may not be able to retain an independent building consultant, however, in which case planning assistance may be sought from the regional library system or the state library agency.

As the project continues, these four participants will be complemented by others. The city, for example, must be part of the process if the city has the ultimate financial authority for the project. If the project involves renovation of a historical structure, the State Historical Society will become involved. A friends group may provide additional support. The general contractor becomes a key player once the project is under construction. Still, the principal players will be the board, the librarian, the architect, and the library building consultant.

Assessing the Community's Needs

A building project must evolve from a thorough understanding of the community's library service needs. The board may initiate a study to assess the library's service and space needs, but the actual coordination of the study will likely be performed by the librarian, in conjunction with the building consultant. This assessment of service goals can become a statement of the board's vision for the future of the library, detailing how the library's service will evolve, considering the growth in the demand for service and the library's ability to meet that demand as well as newer technologies that can aid the library, the library patron, and the library staff.

Although projects are sometimes undertaken without due consideration, doing so invites short-sighted and haphazard planning. Even if it seems unlikely that an expanded building could be achieved soon, it is imperative that the board and staff have a sound knowledge of the community's library service needs and how those needs affect the library's space needs. Political winds can shift quickly and dramatically, or the library may be the beneficiary of an unexpected bequest, and if the board and the staff have not carefully considered the library's service and space needs they may be rushed into uninformed decisions.

A space needs assessment should be predicated on the services the library expects to offer to the community. These service needs find their expression in the roles the library plays in the community and in the library's goals and objectives. Before planners can begin to assess their space needs, they must first ask what type of library service does the community want and need now and in the future? The Public Library Association has developed tools to help local libraries evaluate their role(s) in the community and establish specific goals and objectives for local library service. *Planning and Role Setting for Public Libraries: A Manual of Options and Procedures* (Chicago: ALA, 1987) describes a planning methodology that can be used by libraries of all sizes. This methodology also includes descriptions of eight typical service roles to assist planners in creating a profile of services most appropriate to their community. Libraries completing this process will have a long-range plan—a road map, if you will—to outline how the library expects its services will develop.

State library agency or state library association standards can also be helpful in assessing community needs. The Public Library Association's *Public Library Data Service* annual statistical report provides data on libraries serving communities of similar size that can be used to establish benchmarks or targets for managing collection size and so on.

As the service needs are assessed, the planning team can start translating the service needs into space needs. In the past, public library space standards were based on a measure of floor space per capita. Such measures tend to be old (the last quantitative measure of public library floor space from the American Library Association appeared in *Interim Standards for Small Public Libraries*, published in 1962), and they don't account for differences in service programs among communities of equal size. Today, library space planners recommend that library space be programmed to meet the specific service needs of individual libraries.

Basically, to assess a library's long-term space need, it is necessary to know what the library must house to meet the community's future service needs. The board can set a series of targets that over a period of time (typically twenty years) the collection will grow to include a specified number of books and other library materials, and the library should provide a certain number of reader seats to meet the needs of the population twenty years hence, and so on. Targets like these are known as inputs because they quantify what a community puts into its library.

In turn, the inputs can be used to calculate a space need. For example, traditional library shelving installations can house an average of ten volumes per square foot, so a collection targeted to grow to 50,000 volumes would require approximately 5,000 square foot of floor space. Similar calculations can be made for other inputs or other types of floor space—reader seating space, staff work space, meeting room space, and so on. Further assistance regarding space needs assessment is readily available in the literature (see the bibliography for Holt's *The Wisconsin Library Building Project Handbook* and Dahlgren's "An Alternative to Library Building Standards").

Along with the service and space needs assessment, the planners should review the condition of the current building, noting its spatial and structural deficiencies, along with the aspects in which the building is particularly accomplished.

With an assessment of need in hand, the board and the other local planners can begin to evaluate options. Does the space needs assessment suggest that the library needs 10 percent more space? 50 percent? 100 percent? 200 percent? At what point in that range is an expanded building needed for the community? If an expansion is warranted, should it take the form of an addition or a new building? Is the present building in good enough condition to warrant the investment of an addition? Can any problems that exist with the present building be solved in the course of construction for the addition? If an addition is preferred, is there room on the present site to support the expanded building? Is there enough room on site for public and staff parking? Or must additional property be secured? If a new building is preferred, are there parcels on the market that are large enough to support the proposed structure? Or would the library have to exercise eminent domain to secure a proper site?

As part of the needs assessment process, operating costs should be considered as well. An expanded facility will require additional funding to operate, and the community will not be able to benefit from facilities improvements if the library has to reduce service hours because of operating budget constraints. The expanded facility will have a direct impact on utilities and maintenance costs, obviously, but other segments of the budget will be affected as well. Just as personnel represents the largest single share of a typical public library budget, so will increases in personnel costs likely represent the largest single share of the increased cost in the expanded building. Consider how the expanded building will allow the library to add new service points (a new children's service desk in a small-growing-to-medium-sized library or a fully staffed microcomputer lab in a larger library). Circulation and reference use will almost certainly increase as a result of renewed public interest resulting from the expanded facility; consider the impact of this increased use on staffing needs. An expanded building will often raise the community's expectations for service, which may also prompt a need to increase the library's materials budget to respond to the demand.

The Building Program Statement

Whenever a major capital project is undertaken, the board should direct the preparation of a written building program statement. Essentially, the building program statement is the planners' instructions to the architect, and as such the building program statement describes:

1. The library's space needs, including how the space should be subdivided or organized.
2. What is going to occur in each department or service subdivision, including at least a preliminary listing of the furniture and equipment that will be required to support those routines.
3. How those departments or subdivisions should interrelate for optimum efficiency (that is, what needs to be close to what).

The building program statement may include other information, such as a brief history of the library, a summary of the library goals and objectives, a description of the current building (sometimes known as the list of what to avoid!), or a preliminary projection of the construction budget and the operating budget in the expanded facility, but it must include at the very least the three elements listed above.

The program may be written by the librarian, or by the building consultant, or as a cooperative venture. Sometimes, particularly for projects in smaller communities, individual trustees or a committee of the board may become directly involved. When the statement is complete, the board should review and approve it. Copies should be shared with the library board's governing authority (if, for instance, the library operates as a city department), and it may be appropriate to have that authority endorse the building program.

It may begin as something as informal as some notes jotted down after visiting a neighboring library, but it should evolve into as thorough a description of the library's space need as possible. It will come to serve as a checklist of the library space needs. The checklist should be continually updated. Sample building program statements may be available from a regional library system or the state library agency (see the bibliography for Finney's "The Library Building Program: Key to Success" and Holt's *The Wisconsin Library Building Project Handbook*, which includes representative outlines for a building program statement).

The building program represents the planners' understanding of the library needs at a given point in time. It should be considered a working document, revised to reflect changing needs. If the project is delayed, new elements may be introduced into the planning mix that may affect the amount or type of space the library needs to provide for certain services. If the original budget is insufficient, plans may have to be modified or additional funding secured. These changes can be made in a more informed manner if the planning team has taken the time and effort to prepare a formal building program statement.

Financing the Project

As the project proceeds through the development of a building program statement, selection of a site and the development of a specific plan, budget estimates can become increasingly precise. It is one of the board's most important responsibilities to secure funding for the project.

Between 1988 and 1993, funding for public library construction nationwide had increased from $248 million to $428 million (see figure 13.1). Total spending in 1993 decreased from a high of $473 million the year before. It remains to be seen whether 1992 will come to represent a historic high, or a particular surge in an otherwise upward trend.

Most public library construction is funded at the local level. According to the December 1993 issue of *Library Journal*, 81.7 percent of public library construction funds for the preceding year came from local sources. During that year federal funds provided 1.86 percent of the total (LSCA Title II has been funded since 1983); state funds provided 8.68 percent (some states allocate money grants for public library construction), and the balance came from gifts. In recent years the propor-

Figure 13.1 Sources of Public Library Construction Spending

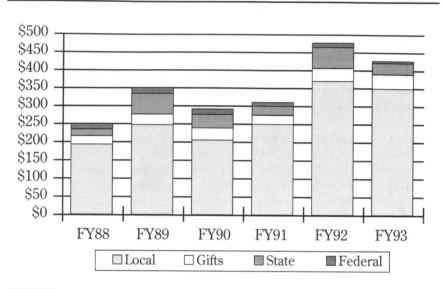

tion of local funding has increased slightly, while the share of federal funding has decreased.

Financing options open to the board will usually be dictated by state statute. These may include the sale of bonds, a direct appropriation from the municipality, a mortgage, private or foundation fundraising, endowments, leasing, any combination of these, or any other alternatives that may be allowed by state or local statute. (Note that some of the preceding options may be disallowed in some states or situations.)

If the board chooses to sell bonds and a referendum is required, it should be the board's responsibility to coordinate the information campaign to promote the library's need. This can be a great opportunity to involve a friends group directly and dramatically in supporting the library's goals. It may provide a chance to establish a friends group that can continue to support the library in years to come. Even if a referendum is not needed, it is important that the public be made aware of the library's needs and that they support the project. Positive public relations are essential.

Implementing the Project

After construction is underway, the board will be generally responsible for monitoring construction, reviewing contractors' applications for payment, and approving invoices. On a day-to-day basis the architect and the librarian will assist with these administrative duties.

During construction board members should be prepared to review changes, and all members of the building team should keep the board informed of possible causes for change. A change order is a formal request to deviate from or add to the working drawings prepared by the architect. A change may be initiated by the contractor, the architect, or the library for a number of reasons (the discovery of unforeseen subsurface conditions, the need to substitute a lower-cost material to stay within the budget, or the inability to secure a specified material because it is no longer manufactured, to name just a few). Because the need for a change can arise suddenly, and because maintaining the construction timetable can rely on a prompt resolution of the change, the librarian and the board must develop a mechanism for prompt review of changes.

The board should consider appointing a building committee from among its members. This committee should be small—three to five members—and draw from the board those members who may have particular planning, budgetary, or construction experience. The building committee can be expected to monitor the project more closely than the remaining library board members, and they can be expected to make reports to the full board at their regular meetings. When state statute allows, the committee should also be granted the authority to act upon change orders when immediate action is needed to keep the project on schedule. Then when the board next meets in regular session, they can ratify the change. Remember that the authority to delegate this responsibility to a building committee may vary from state to state.

Eventually, construction will reach a stage known as *substantial completion*. At this time the structure is complete and ready for occupancy, except for a few minor construction details. The contractor will so advise the architect, and a walk-through of the building will be scheduled. The architect and the contractor, along with the librarian and representatives of the library board, will go through the building room by room to identify work that remains to be completed.

From this inspection the architect should develop a *punch list*, which documents all the work that the contractor has yet to complete. Pending completion of the work, the library will withhold a portion of the money due to the contractor—usually 5 to 10 percent. This is known as the *retainage*. When the contractor accepts that list, the library can accept the building and move in. In the weeks or months to come, the contractor will complete the items on the punch list, and any problems with the mechanical and other systems should be smoothed out. When the punch list is completed, the contractor is due the last of the retainage.

The Trustee as Advocate

Throughout the planning of a new or expanded facility, the library board should actively represent the library's needs to the community and vice versa, just as its members do in the normal course of activities. Trustees should be highly visible in the promotion of the project to local residents and should be responsive to the concerns and suggestions of those residents.

Trustees should be prepared for some of the ways a building project is out of the ordinary. A building project will involve the board with long-range planning to a higher degree than usual. It will involve the trustee with larger budgets than are usually encountered in the daily operation of the library. Because a library building program is a major project in the development of any community it will draw more attention, and it may draw more controversy, than is customary for the library. For this reason, trustees should be prepared to advocate the library's cause assertively.

The Final Product

With careful planning and support from the other members of the team, the library board can meet its obligations to provide an adequate, responsive facility for the library. By taking a long view of the community's needs, the board can ensure that its plan to meet those needs will offer the community the most building for its construction dollar.

The finished building will provide sufficient space for the library collections to grow to meet community needs. It will provide a variety of user seating to meet the differing needs of its users, from preschoolers to senior citizens. It will provide comfortable and efficient surroundings for the staff. It will be conveniently located to provide access to the greatest number of residents. In most instances the building will include meeting rooms for library programs and other community activities. The building should be expanded. It should be adaptable so that future planners can respond to the changing service requirements of their time. And the building will offer a compelling invitation to enter and read and explore the collections and services housed therein.

Further Reading

Cohen, Aaron, and Elaine Cohen. *Designing and Space Planning for Library: A Behavioral Guide.* N.Y.: Bowker, 1979.

Dahlgren, Anders C. "An Alternative to Library Building Standards." *Illinois Libraries* 67 (Nov., 1985): 772–77.

Dahlgren, Anders C. *Planning the Small Public Library Building*. Chicago: ALA, 1985.

Finney, Lance C. "The Library Building Program: Key to Success." *Public Libraries* 23 (Fall 1984): 79–82.

Holt, Raymond M. *The Wisconsin Library Building Project Handbook*. 2d rev. ed. by Anders C. Dahlgren. Madison, Wisc.: Department of Public Instruction, 1990.

Library Journal. "Architectural Issue." December, annually.

Lueder, Diane, and Sally Webb. *Administrator's Guide to Library Building Maintenance*. Chicago: ALA, 1992.

Lushington, Nolan, and Willis N. Mills, Jr. *Libraries Designed for Users: A Planning Handbook*. Hamden, Conn.: Library Professional Publications, 1980.

Lushington, Nolan and James M. Kusack. *The Design and Evaluation of Public Library Buildings*. Hamden, Conn.: Library Professional Publications, 1991.

McClure, Charles R., Amy Owen, Douglas L. Zweizig, Mary Jo Lynch, and Nancy A. Van House. *Planning and Role Setting for Public Libraries: A Manual of Options and Procedures*. Chicago: ALA, 1987.

Martin, Ron G., ed. *Libraries for the Future: Planning Buildings that Work*. (Papers from the LAMA Library Buildings Preconference, June 27–28, 1991) Chicago: ALA, 1992.

Myller, Rolf. *The Design of the Small Public Library*. New York: Bowker, 1966.

Rohlf, Robert H. "Library Design: What Not to Do." *American Libraries* 17 (Feb., 1986): 100–104.

Rohlf, Robert H. "The Selection of an Architect." *Public Libraries* 21 (Spring 1982): 5–8.

Smith, Lester K. *Planning Library Buildings: From Decision to Design*. (Papers from a LAMA BES Preconference at the 1984 ALA Annual Conference, Dallas, TX) Chicago: ALA, 1986.

14 The Trustee as Advocate

Carol C. Henderson
Joan Ress Reeves

dvocate—active support—is one of the most challenging and exciting responsibilities of trusteeship. Advocacy represents the trustee's relationship with the community and embodies the strong support every trustee owes the library.

There are many aspects of library advocacy: (1) *legislative*, on the local, state, and federal levels; (2) *personal, social*, and *public relations*; (3) *financial* and *fundraising*; and (4) *attendance* at library functions, rallies, wherever you are needed.

Before you begin your advocacy efforts, there are some general principles that apply to any kind of advocacy.

The first is the first principle of marketing: Make sure you have a top-quality product. That is one of your responsibilities as a trustee.

Second, be knowledgeable. As a responsible trustee, it is important to have as much information as possible about your library and how it relates to the community.

Third, use your library. That way, you will get to see what really goes on there. Who is using the library? Do you see children doing their homework? Do you see elderly people reading newspapers and magazines? Do you see people using computer terminals to search electronic databases? All this is fodder for the fourth principle: tell stories. Ancedotal material is always more interesting and revealing to your

Carol C. Henderson is executive director of the American Library Association Washington Office.

Joan Ress Reeves is chair of the Library Board of Rhode Island and past chair of the White House Conference on Library and Information Services Taskforce (WHCLIST).

listener or reader than a recitation of facts. It is the equivalent of "A picture is worth a thousand words."

And the last principle is networking. While you must be knowledgeable, it is often not *what* you know, it is *whom* you know that counts. Trustees have connections beyond the library world. Those connections can help garner support for the library and bring in new supporters and new leadership.

The Legislative Imperative

Legislative advocacy is called lobbying, and it is all right to do so. Democracy depends on it. A state legislator from Pennsylvania once said, "Goodness is its own reward—in heaven. On earth, you have to lobby."

Never be shy about lobbying; you are doing it, not for yourself, but for the library to which you are dedicated.

You can make a difference; in most cases in a democracy it takes just one vote to carry an issue. As a trustee, you have great credibility. No one is a better lobbyist than a layperson who has no financial interest in the organization, who is there because you believe in the institution and its needs. As a trustee, you know the power people in government, or you know people who know them, so cultivate those contacts.

Giving Testimony

An important way to help your library legislatively is to give testimony before your city or town council, committees of your state legislature, and congressional committees. It is easier than you think. You need to know what you are talking about, but don't worry if you don't know all the facts and figures. If you are questioned, and you don't know an answer, say you will find out and let the questioner know later. Especially in oral testimony, don't bore the legislators with dry facts and statistics. Leave the documentation to the librarians, who are more likely to have the numbers at their fingertips. But if statistics are important to your testimony, use the dramatic ones, and include other relevant material in your written testimony or in an attachment.

Talk from your unique perspective, about your children, your parents, your elderly friends, and your own experiences with and feelings about libraries. Tell library stories that have human interest. After all, the legislators are probably not librarians either. They will relate to your "down-home" stories. Use "hooks"—attention getters—for your specific audience. For instance, refer to people or places in the constituency of the members to whom you are talking. Remember the "What's in it for me?" principle: the best way to persuade people is to show them how your library can help them.

Speak or write simply, not pedantically. Use lots of pronouns. Keep your words and sentences—all your oral testimony—short. Make eye contact with the people you are addressing. Smile. Use natural gestures.

At the state level, be sure to be in touch with your state library agency head, your state library association(s), statewide Friends and advocacy groups, and others before you testify. Nothing will kill a bill faster than testimony that exposes conflict within the library community.

Similarly, at the city and town level, prepare your testimony in conjunction with your library director, board president, and the rest of the board.

Some further tips about giving testimony—you are often called to testify on short notice. Be prepared to rush to the capitol for a hearing, to wait endlessly to be called—and then to be told either that the hearing on your issue will be postponed or it is cancelled. Don't be discouraged. While you are waiting around, you may get a chance to get to know the legislators, to network with them or with other lobbyists. It is a good idea to get to be known around the state house and identified with libraries. Persistence pays off.

When you give congressional testimony, you are usually asked to submit written testimony in advance, often in multiple copies. This may be any length—but, again, keep it interesting. Your oral testimony is usually confined to five minutes. This is terrifying. But it does force you to concentrate on the essentials. You need to cut, cut, cut. Be sure to feature the material that is dramatic, that makes your point strongly, that will keep the members awake and interested.

Visiting Representatives

Personal visits are the best way to persuade anyone to do anything. Make an appointment with your legislator in advance. Remember, your vote put the legislator into office, and, as a taxpayer, you are paying her/his salary. Your legislator should want to hear from you. Keep your meeting short and simple. If you can, give the legislator some brief written materials clearly illustrating your issue. Tell stories about what libraries mean to people. After the meeting, write to thank the legislator, and reiterate your point.

On the national level, you may or may not get through directly to your congressperson. He or she should be willing to see you at least once a year—for instance, on Library Legislative Day in Washington in April during National Library Week.

Generally though, your point of contact will be the member's legislative aide. The legislative aide is usually knowledgeable about library legislation, and provides the congressperson with the information he or she needs to make decisions. One of the sources of that information, especially about what is going on at home, is you. It is invaluable to develop a good relationship with your congressional legislative aides. Once you have built up a relationship of trust, you should be able to count on at least a fair hearing, if not a positive response, for your requests.

Phone Calls and Letters

Letter writing is another crucial advocacy tool. The very best letters are personally composed and heartfelt. A handwritten letter is fine; form letters are far less effective. Your letters don't have to be masterpieces of literature. They do have to be short and simple and stick to one issue. Make your point at the beginning (including bill number, title, and subject). Tell a story illustrating your point, and tell the legislator why he or she should vote for the bill. Thank the legislator for past and continuing support. You can never thank a legislator too often.

While you still have pen—or word processor—in hand, consider another way you can use letters for advocacy. Letters to the editor are not exactly legislative lobbying, but they are effective. When articles in the newspaper mention library issues, use that as an opportunity to thank the newspaper if the mention is favorable, or to comment if it is not. Be sure to talk about good things your library does. Or if libraries ought to be mentioned in an article but are not, write about that. When an important situation is breaking, such as a bond issue, think about writing an Op-Ed (the page opposite staff and syndicated editorials used for public expression) piece—and use every bit of influence you have to get it published. It is a good idea to check with the library director first.

Call your legislator on the telephone to make your feelings known, especially when a bill is coming up too soon to send a letter. If it is a federal bill, you can call the member either at her or his office in your home state, or at the Washington office, or call the legislative aide. Follow up with a letter or a fax so there is a record of your request.

Legislators welcome phone calls; after all, their job is to respond to their constituency. Not enough people do call. A local legislator told us that if she gets eight or ten calls on an issue, she considers it a mandate!

Other Forms of Advocacy

Another aspect of advocacy is what we call personal, social, or public relations advocacy. You are an ambassador for the library, both publicly and privately. You represent the library to the community; you can be a conduit of information between them about their needs. Talk about your library whenever you are among friends, at dinner parties, in various groups. Be a joiner: join library and other organizations to let people know that you support your library, and why. That is networking.

Financial and fundraising support is another form of advocacy. In public libraries, basic operating support should come from the local community and to a lesser extent from the state, with a small percentage from the federal government. More and more, public libraries are turning to the private sector for support—as long as it supplements, but does not supplant, the publicly supported budget.

A financial commitment to your library clearly expresses your own support. After all, if trustees don't support their institution, who will? That doesn't mean that you have to give huge sums beyond your means. It does mean that you should give appropriately, according to your own circumstances, when private funds are needed. Full trustee participation in a fund drive is almost as important as the dollars raised, because other funders look to see that the board is 100 percent behind the drive. And every trustee can be an advocate for the library by helping in fundraising efforts, whether by making phone calls, culling lists, writing letters, or planning the drive.

Finally, there is "being there." Your presence at library functions, rallies for support, wherever you are needed is another important expression of your advocacy for the library. By being there, you not only swell the crowd, but you let people know that you care about what the library is doing. And, again, if you are not willing to show up, why should anyone else?

Clearly, library trustees should make advocacy a top priority. As Deborah Miller eloquently stated:

> When we advocate better public library services, we advocate bettering the quality of life for today's citizens and America's future. It seems like an overwhelming task, but trustees have been doing just that for many years and continue to create success stories through library trustee advocacy.[1]

1. *Trustee Facts File,* "Advocacy and the Library Trustee," Illinois Library Association, 1986.

15 The Trustee and the State Library Agency

William G. Asp

ibrary trustees today plan and govern library services in an environment of accelerating change. Changing communities, changing technology, changing federal and state laws, and changing financial needs are just some of the challenges. State library agencies are a source of information and help for library trustees.

In every state there is an agency in state government responsible for development and improvement of public library services throughout the state. While organizational placement will vary from state to state, and while not all state library agencies offer exactly the same services, all do support the efforts of library trustees in governing public library services.

The state library agency provides valuable information and services for public library trustees. Staff at the state library agency can provide authoritative information on the state's laws governing libraries, on the state plan for development and improvement of public library services and library cooperation, and on grant programs which benefit public libraries. The state library also often provides education for trustees, through workshops and trustee handbooks. Staff can provide consultant assistance on any aspect of public library service.

State Library Laws

State laws govern public library services, and the state library agency is the best source of information on current state laws affecting libraries.

William G. Asp is director of the Minnesota Office of Library Development and Services.

Typically, state laws set out how a public library is organized—what action is required by a city or county government, for example, to establish public library service and whether that action can be taken by a city council or a board of county commissioners or whether it must be the result of a public referendum. State law, too, may set the size of the public library board, how and by whom board members are appointed, the length of terms, and whether the board member is subject to any limitation of term. The powers and duties of public library boards are generally established in state law as well, including the board's authorities and responsibilities for budget and finance.

In addition to specific library laws, public library boards need to know about general state laws relating to operations of governmental units because these laws may also apply to public library boards. Open meeting laws, for example, often require that the meeting of any agency of government, including a public library board, must be held at a time that is posted or otherwise made known to the public, and open to public attendance. If any part of a meeting may be closed or declared an executive session, the law will define exactly how that may be done. State law may also govern procurement of major equipment items, requiring bids for purchases over a dollar amount that is established in state statute. State law may also cover other financial actions of library boards, such as establishing requirements for audits.

The state library staff is knowledgeable about state library laws and other state laws affecting libraries. While the typical state library agency consultant is not an attorney, the staff knows of any attorney general's opinion relating to the specific statutes, as well as opinions written by county or city or other attorneys relating to library law.

The state library staff takes a leadership role in amending or modifying state library laws. When a state's library laws have become out-of-date and need to be recodified or when they need to be amended, it often is state library agency staff which takes the lead in working with the library community to develop and propose amendments to the legislative process.

State Plans for Statewide Library Development

No library can be independent; all libraries are increasingly interdependent. The day when any one library could fulfill all of the information needs of people in its community is long gone, if that day ever existed. State library agencies develop and implement state plans for development and improvement of library and information services statewide. The library trustee needs to be knowledgeable of these plans, so that local library planning and policymaking takes place within the context of public library services statewide.

The federal Library Services and Construction Act (LSCA) has required state library agencies to develop long-range programs for the use of federal library funds in each state. The long-range program identifies the needs for library services in the state at present and for the next three years, and shows how federal funds could be used to address those needs. The program addresses each of the priorities established in LSCA for the three titles administered by the state library agency: Title I—Public Library Services; Title II—Construction and Technology Enhancement of Public Libraries; and Title III—Interlibrary Cooperation and Resource Sharing.

Besides the federal long-range program, some state library agencies also develop state long-range plans that show how statewide library development programs and funds will be used to meet needs. These plans might address a wide range of topics, such as provision for multi-county library systems and networks, needs for personnel in libraries, continuing education for staff, specific needs for specific groups of users such as children or seniors, and specialized services for targeted populations who may be underusing libraries now. These plans will identify steps to be taken at the state level and encouraged at the local level, to meet the needs.

With technology becoming ever more important in delivery of library services, many states have developed plans for automation in all of the state's libraries. These plans may include standards libraries should follow in order to ensure compatibility among automated systems. The plans may show how automated library systems will be interconnected, how the state will foster participation of libraries in electronic networking and help libraries gain access to the coming "national information superhighway."

State Standards for Library Development

To guide local library planning, many state library agencies have developed and adopted standards or goals for public library service. Standards tend to be established when attainment determines the library's eligibility for state aid grants. Goals, in contrast, are established as targets—levels of service which a library would strive to achieve.

For many years goals or standards for libraries tended to be measures of input. Typical input standards included books per capita, audiovisual materials per capita, staff per capita, and the number of hours open to serve a population of a given size. In the late 1970s research began in measuring library effectiveness. Some states now have standards or goals that are measures of output, showing levels of service that the library is delivering. Examples of output measures are the number of registered borrowers as a percentage of the population to be served, frequency of use by registered borrowers, circulation per capita, and "fill rate" of requested items from the library's on-site collections.

In the 1990s governments at all levels are increasingly moving toward performance management. The goal is to establish measures to allow customers and funders of government services to know exactly what services are being delivered, at what cost, and with what impact on the receiver of the services. Output measures will have to be transformed into statements of performance outcomes, where there is ultimately an effort to measure the impact of library services on the user.

A starting point to help librarians and trustees develop output measures and performance outcomes is the state and the national data on public libraries made available under the Federal State Cooperative System (FSCS). FSCS is a partnership involving the National Center for Education Statistics (NCES), the National Commission on Libraries and Information Science, and the state library agencies. Standard statistical data on public libraries is submitted by each state to NCES. NCES aggregates the statistics from the states and also analyzes and summarizes the data. With the NCES reports, it is now possible to compare statistics on libraries in all of the states. This data can be very helpful in planning and in justifying requests for funding for the library.

The State Library Agency and Library Funding

Most state library agencies administer grant programs, from federal and state funds, to foster improvement of public library services and facilities. In a few states, statewide library services are operated by the state library agency in lieu of grants.

The federal Library Services and Construction Act (LSCA) originated in 1956 as the Library Services Act with a focus on establishing and strengthening library services to rural Americans. In successive revisions, the act was amended and broadened, responding to changing needs for library services by people in urban and suburban area as well as rural. Groups especially in need or targeted services, such as persons who are blind or disabled, were also made a priority. Funds were added for construction of library buildings and for renovation and additions to library buildings. Programs for sharing of library resources and networking among all types of libraries, as well as preservation of library materials, have been added. These funds are administered by the state library, an agency under the state long range program and annual plans. State library agency staff can provide trustees with information on these grant programs.

Several titles of LSCA are administered directly by the U.S. Department of Education rather than coming through the state library agency. The state library agency staff can provide information and assistance in applying for these funds. Examples are funds for library literacy programs for acquisition of materials in languages other than English.

State appropriations for public library services also are administered by the state library agency. Most often these state funds are for library operations. In a number of states they are granted to regional library systems rather than being awarded to local libraries. Some states also have state funds to assist in public library construction and renovation. State library agency staff can provide information on any state grants available.

The state library staff is frequently asked to provide information on sources of funds for public library services. Staff tries to monitor potential sources of funding from government as well as private sources. Staff can provide information and assistance in applying for project funds from foundations, and in setting up a local Friends of the Library group or a local library foundation or endowment fund.

Trustee Education

State library agencies and state library trustee associations often work together to create educational materials and workshops for library trustees. Trustee handbooks have been developed in many states, and these books become valuable reference sources for the trustee in carrying out ongoing responsibilities. State level and regional level workshops offer opportunities for trustees to work with colleagues from other libraries, exploring common interests and problems in trusteeship, learning about the newest developments in library and information services, and learning new skills. The American Library Trustee Association (ALTA) has been particularly active in developing model workshops for library trustees. ALTA publishes an array of books, pamphlets and other materials to assist the library trustees.

Consultant Assistance

Every state library agency has consultant staff ready to assist library trustees. State library agency consultants are prepared to respond to virtually any question about library organization, governance, or finance. They can assist trustees and librarians in developing long-range plans and in surveying their communities. They can assist in planning new library buildings. As a rule of thumb, when in doubt ask the staff at the state library agency! They will do their best to respond to your need.

When a public library board needs to hire a new library director, the state library agency consultant can be especially helpful. Hiring a director is something that most boards do very infrequently. It can be difficult to know where to begin. Based on experience working with other libraries, the state library agency staff can help a library board design a search process, prepare an up-to-date position description, prepare advertisements, assist with recruitment of potential applicants, assist in developing a process for evaluating applicants and in planning the interview for the finalists. Staff also will have up-to-date information on applicable federal and state legal requirements, including assistance in ensuring that the search and evaluation process is fair and nondiscriminatory.

Conclusion

While the range of responsibilities of the library trustee, and the amount of information needed by the trustee to carry out decision making in governing public library services may seem daunting, there are sources for advice and assistance. Chief among these sources is the state library agency, which has been assigned in state government the responsibilities of assisting in the strengthening and improvement of library services statewide. Library trustees play a major role in the strengthening and improvement of library services, and members of the state library agency staff are ready to help.

16 Federal Support for Libraries: A Guide for Trustees

Ray M. Fry

 n the early eighties the U.S. Department of Education's National Commission on Excellence in Education issued a devastating report, *A Nation at Risk*, on the quality of elementary and secondary education in America. The report enumerated several recommendations to lift our educational system out of mediocrity and to promote the creation of a "learning society."

In response to this clarion call for action, a national library effort was initiated to outline the role libraries could play in supporting the recommendations of *A Nation at Risk*. Out of that effort came *Alliance for Excellence: Librarians Respond to "A Nation at Risk."* In the foreword to this report, then U.S. Secretary of Education T. H. Bell, wrote:

> The challenge before us is of such magnitude, . . . that school and family will be a match for it only when they forge a grand alliance with a third institution—the library.

In 1989, at the historic educational summit at the University of Virginia, President George Bush and the fifty state governors agreed on six national education goals to remedy one of the major deficiencies of our schools as they were identified in *A Nation at Risk*. These six goals, along with two others added by Congress are shown in Table 16.1. Library leaders responded once more to a national challenge through the "America 2000—Library Partnership," announced by then

Ray M. Fry is director of the Office of Library Programs, Office of Educational Research and Improvement, U.S. Department of Education.

Figure 16.1 The National Education Goals

The National Education Goals, as set out in the Goals 2000: Educate America Act, articulate the desires and needs of Americans for improvement in education over the next several years. IN 1989, America's governors and the President met and developed the original six goals, and the U.S. Congress added two new goals. The goals have been recognized by every major group of parents, educators, and businesses.

The goals state that by the year 2000:

1. All children in America will start school ready to learn.

2. The high school graduation rate will increase to at least 90 percent.

3. All students will leave grades 4, 8, and 12 having demonstrated competency over challenging subject matter, including English, mathematics, science, foreign languages, civics and government, economics, arts, history, and geography, and every school in America will ensure that all students learn to use their minds well, so they may be prepared for responsible citizenship, further learning, and productive employment in our Nation's modern economy.

4. The Nation's teaching force will have access to programs for the continued improvement of their professional skills and the opportunity to acquire the knowledge and skills needed to instruct and prepare all American students for the next century.

5. United States students will be first in the world in mathematics and science achievement.

6. Every adult American will be literate and will possess the knowledge and skills necessary to compete in a global economy and exercise the rights and responsibilities of citizenship.

7. Every school in the United States will be free of drugs, violence, and the unauthorized presence of firearms and alcohol and will offer a disciplined environment conducive to learning.

8. Every school will promote partnerships that will increase parental involvement and participation in promoting the social, emotional, and academic growth of children.

U.S. Secretary of Education Lamar Alexander at the George Mason Regional Library in Fairfax, Virginia.

To support this effort, the U.S. Department of Education redirected some of the discretionary library grant programs. Part of the redirection involved funding for fellowships to train graduate students in library science in children's and young adult services, as well as funding for institutes to train library personnel in services related to the National Education Goals and the new information technology. To promote parental involvement in education, the Office of Library Programs, part of the U.S. Department of Education's Office of Educational Research and Improvement (OERI), mailed out copies of the "Helping Your Child" series to all public libraries to offer as a community resource. OERI developed these booklets to assist parents in helping children of all ages learn and succeed in school. In addition, Head Start undertook a partnership program with public libraries to strengthen services for at-risk children.

The redirection of the discretionary grant programs continues today. In addition, the Office of Library Programs is encouraging the states to use more of their Library Services and Construction Act (LSCA) funds on goals-related projects. And it appears the states are responding. According to the annual LSCA reports, states are supporting a variety of program directed toward the Goals. Programs include improving public access to the information highway, adult literacy for new immigrants, homework centers, summer reading initiatives, and outreach to Head Start and day-care centers.

Further support for library involvement with the National Education Goals came with the 1991 White House Conference on Library and Information Services. The Conference passed numerous recommendations related to the National Education Goals and the national information highway. For example, it recommended the Omnibus Children and Youth Literacy Initiative to invigorate library and information services for student learning and literacy; literacy initiatives to aid the disadvantaged; the designation of libraries as educational agencies; recognition of libraries as partners in lifelong learning; and the sharing of information via "network superhighways." These and other Conference recommendations are being considered as the reauthorization of the Library Services and Construction Act moves forward.

The importance of libraries to education was demonstrated in a 1993 survey, *The Roles of the Public Library in Society: The Results of a National Survey: Final Report*, by George D'Elia of the University of Minnesota in collaboration with the Gallup Organization. All of the groups surveyed, especially blacks and Hispanics, regard public libraries as a very important source of support for their community's educational aspirations. Also, the lower the education and income level of the public, the higher they rate the educational importance of their public library.

D'Elia's study on the roles of the public library in society was funded by a grant made under the Library Research and Demonstration Program (Title II-B of the Higher Education Act) administered by the Office of Library Programs. That office used the study as the basis for a free brochure, *Public Libraries Service Communities: Education is Job #1*. Since the spring of 1994 it has distributed nearly 90,000 copies of this brochure to public libraries, Friends of Libraries, trustees, and others interested in library policy. In addition, the Office of Library Programs has requested proposals for a major study, "Assessment of School/Library Contributions to Supporting the National Education Goals." Work under this contract began in late 1994.

In the spring of 1994, the "Goals 2000: Educate America Act," the most critical and comprehensive educational bill since the Elementary and Secondary Education Act of 1965, was passed by a strong bipartisan vote in Congress and signed into law by President Clinton. Its purpose is:

> To improve learning and teaching by providing a national framework for education reform; to promote the research, consensus building and systemic changes needed to ensure equitable educational opportunities and higher levels of educational achievement for all students; *to provide a framework for reauthorization of all Federal education programs*; to promote the development and adoption of a voluntary national system of skill standards and certifications. . . .

The law adds two National Education Goals (the eight goals are listed on page 114). More importantly, it promotes a full complement of community institutions, including the public library, to address local education needs. This positions the public library as a full participant and key player in education initiatives.

To take advantage of federal programs for these policy-driven opportunities, trustees must have a good understanding of federal funding sources—programs and agencies.

Major Library Programs in the U.S. Department of Education

Figure 16.2 at the end of this chapter presents the major library programs administered by federal agencies. Most of the programs benefiting public libraries are located in the U.S. Department of Education's Office of Library Programs. These programs are of two types: (1) formula grant programs in which state library agencies apply to the Department for funds which they then administer, and (2) discretionary grant programs in which libraries and other eligible entities apply directly to the Department of Education for funding. The major portion of this funding is in formula grant programs administered by the states under the Library Services and Construction Act.

Regardless of the status of the reauthorization of the Library and Construction Act or similar legislation, it is important for trustees to know how these programs can affect their libraries. Trustees can thus be effective in helping to achieve such legislation.

Library Programs in Other Federal Agencies

Although most of the federal programs benefiting libraries, especially public libraries, are administered by the U.S. Department of Education, there are programs in other federal agencies of interest to public libraries. Chief among them are programs in the National Endowment for the Humanities (NEH). NEH programs (for which libraries are eligible applicants) promote the preservation of educational materials relating to the humanities, encourage public understanding of the humanities, support humanities projects for out-of-school audiences, and support humanities research designed to deepen our understanding of science and technology and their role in our culture.

In recent years several new sources of federal funding for libraries have become available. Most important, the National Telecommunications and Information Administration in the Department of Commerce launched a competitive grant program in Fiscal Year 1994 which was created to advance the goals of the Administration's National Information Infrastructure initiative.

There are other federal agencies that undertake initiatives to promote libraries though they may not fund libraries directly. As part of the "America 2000—Library Partnership" initiative, Head Start, a part of the U.S. Department of Health and Human Services, in collaboration with the Center for the Book at the Library of Congress and the Association for Library Services to Children, launched a model program to demonstrate how Head Start agencies and public libraries can work together in literacy programs at the local level.

For a comprehensive guide to federal programs for libraries, consult the *Catalog of Federal Domestic Assistance.* For a listing of all U.S. Department of Education programs, consult the *Guide to U.S. Department of Education Programs.* A selected guide to library grants and services programs is offered in *Federal Grants and Services for Librar-*

ies—A Guide to Selected Programs, which is published by the American Library Association. (References for these publications are listed at the end of this chapter.)

Other Federal Sponsorship

In addition to the support given libraries by grant and special programs in the federal agencies, the Library of Congress, the three National Libraries—the National Library of Medicine, the National Agricultural Library, and the new National Education Library—and the National Commission on Libraries and Information Science all exert strong national leadership in library development through their services, resources, and programming.

The Library of Congress is the world's largest library with a collection of 105 million items. Because of its copyright deposit responsibilities, the Library receives about one million new items each year. About half of these items are added to the permanent research collection. Although its first requirements are to serve the members of Congress, the Library also provides many services to the nation's libraries.

These services include books for the blind and physically handicapped and the creation of catalog records. The more than twenty-six million catalog records in the Library's database are available to twenty million computer users, including libraries, through the Internet. Recently the Library has launched several new programs to make its incomparable collections more widely available to the public. These programs include a cable television program about the Library, an expanded exhibition program available to libraries throughout the country, and the creation of a multimedia digital archive to disseminate the collections electronically.

Two of the "national" libraries—the National Library of Medicine and the National Agricultural Library—have served their clienteles with distinction for decades. The National Library of Education, created by Congress in 1994, is expected to do the same. Its mission is to serve as the nation's chief education library information resource and service, providing access to information that will improve teaching and learning. The national libraries support networks and databases that represent their interests. The information available through these resources is used by libraries worldwide.

The National Commission on Libraries and Information Science, since its beginning in 1968, has held two critically important White House Conferences on Libraries and advises both the President and the Congress on matters relating to national library and information services, policies, and plans. The White House Conferences on Libraries have been instrumental in promoting policy development at the state and local levels as well as at the national level.

What Trustees Need to Know and Do

As discussed in the preceding sections, there are many grant programs, services, and resources in the federal government that can benefit libraries. Figure 16.2 at the end of this chapter summarizes the federal programs. Every trustee, in order to fulfill his or her policymaking role more effectively, must become familiar with all of these efforts. More specifically trustees should:

1. Understand the relationship among the local, state, and federal governments—their functions and responsibilities.
2. Become knowledgeable about major federal library grant programs, services, resources, and activities that support and enhance local libraries.
3. Be active at the policy level in local efforts to obtain funds, services, and resources that are available from the federal government either through the state library agency or directly from the federal government.

Summary

The environment at all levels of government is conducive to a greatly needed major overhaul of our educational system. Working with public schools and school libraries, academic libraries, literacy service providers, day-care centers, and others, libraries have a great deal to offer as partners in education reform. With the passage of the "Goals 2000: Educate America Act," we have an umbrella under which all federal education legislation will be developed. Trustees everywhere will need to be more aware of federal programs and how they can support state and local efforts.

Every library must become a dynamic learning center supporting a nation of students. A "grand alliance" of home and school and library must be forged for the attainment of the eight National Education Goals and the realization of a true "learning society" in our democracy.*

*Jeannie Coe, Christina Dunn, Kathryn Perkinson and Shirley Steele, members of the Library Programs staff, assisted in the preparation of this chapter.

Further Reading

1. *Alliance for Excellence: Librarians Respond to a Nation at Risk*. U.S. Department of Education, OERI, Center for Libraries and Education Improvement, 1984.† (ED243885)‡
2. *The 1994 Catalog of Federal Domestic Assistance*. Washington, D.C. Government Printing Office, 1994.†
3. "Goals 2000: Educate America Act," Public Law 103–227, March 31, 1994, GPO, Washington, D.C.†
4. Office of Library Programs Fact Sheets, free from the office of Library Programs, OERI, 555 New Jersey Avenue, NW, Washington, D.C. 20208-5571
5. The Guide to U.S. Department of Education Programs, free from the Office of Public Affairs, U.S. Department of Education, Washington, D.C. 20202.
6. *A Nation at Risk: The Imperative for Educational Reform*, by the National Commission on Excellence in Education, Washington, D.C., 1993.† (EF226006)‡
7. *The Roles of the Public Library in Society—The Results of a National Survey: Final Report*, by George D'Elia, Information and Decision Sciences Department, Carlson School of Management, University of Minnesota, in collaboration with the University of Minnesota center for Survey Research and the Gallup Organization. A printed copy may be purchased ($25 plus $4.50 shipping) from Urban Libraries Council, 1800 Ridge Avenue, Suite 208, Evanston, Ill. 60201.
8. *Public Libraries Serving Communities: Education Is Job #1* (based on report in 7 above), free from the Office of Library Programs OERI, 555 New Jersey Avenue, NW, Washington, D.C. 20208-5571.

†Copies of these documents are available through federal depository libraries or may be purchased from: Superintendent of Documents, U.S. Government Printing Office, Washington, DC 20402 (Order Desk: 202–512–1800).
‡ERIC Documents: 1-800-Let-ERIC.

**Figure 16.2 Selected Federal Programs of
Interest to Library Trustees**

Types of Assistance	Legislative Authority	Administering Federal Agency
1. Extends and improves public library services and strengthens services to special groups.	Library Services and Construction Act, Title I	Library Programs/OERI US Department of Education 555 New Jersey Ave, NW Washington, DC 20208-5571
2. Public library construction.	Library Services and Construction Act, Title II	Library Programs/OERI US Department of Education 555 New Jersey Ave, NW Washington, DC 20208-5571
3. Establishes and maintains cooperative activities among libraries.	Library Services and Construction Act, Title III	Library Programs/OERI US Department of Education 555 New Jersey Ave, NW Washington, DC 20208-5571
4. Assists eligible Indian Tribes and Hawaiian Native organizations to develop and improve public library services.	Library Services and Construction Act, Title IV	Library Programs/OERI US Department of Education 555 New Jersey Ave, NW Washington, DC 20208-5571
5. Assists state and local public libraries in support of adult literacy programs.	Library Services and Construction Act, Title VI	Library Programs/OERI US Department of Education 555 New Jersey Ave, NW Washington, DC 20208-5571
6. Supports innovative programs which improve access to and the quality of postsecondary education.	Higher Education Act of 1965, Title X	Funds for the Improvement of Postsecondary Education US Department of Education Washington, DC 20202
7. Library research and demonstration.	Higher Education Act, Title II-B	Library Programs/OERI US Department of Education 555 New Jersey Ave, NW Washington, DC 20208-5571

(Continued)

Figure 16.2 *Continued*

Types of Assistance	Legislative Authority	Administering Federal Agency
8. Library training, fellowships, and institutes.	Higher Education Act, Title II-B	Library Programs/OERI US Department of Education 555 New Jersey Ave, NW Washington, DC 20208-5571
9. Provides funding and leadership for research in development of digital libraries.	National Sciences Foundation Act of 1950, as amended	National Science Foundation Computer and Information Science and Engineering 4201 Wilson Blvd Arlington, VA 22230
10. Telecommunications and Information Infrastructure Assistance Program; advances the goals of the National Information Infrastructure (NII)	Department of Commerce Appropriations Act of 1993	US Department of Commerce National Telecommunications and Information Administration Washington, DC 20230
11. General revenue sharing for library services and construction.	State and Local Fiscal Assistance Act	US Department of Treasury Washington, DC 20220 Contact: Local Mayor's Office
12. Public library construction.	Housing and Community Development Act, Title I	Department of Housing and Urban Development Washington, DC 20202
13. Surplus books.		Library of Congress Washington, DC 20540 Contact: Representative or Senator
14. Books for the blind and physically handicapped.		Library of Congress Washington, DC 20540
15. Trains professional personnel and strengthens library and health information services.	Public Health Services Act, Title III, Part A, Title IV, Part D	Extramural Programs National Library of Medicine Bethesda, MD 20894

Types of Assistance	Legislative Authority	Administering Federal Agency
16. Encourages and improves the use of telecommunications, computer networks, and related advanced technologies to provide educational and medical benefits to people living in rural areas.	Food, Agriculture, Conservation and Tract Act of 1990, Title XIII	US Department of Agriculture Washington, DC 20250-1500
17. Provides support for projects of national significance designed to improve the quality of teaching and instruction and increases the access to such instruction.	Elementary and Secondary Education Act of 1965, Title II, Part A D.D. Eisenhower Mathematics and Science Education Act of 1988	Office of Reform Assistance and Dissemination/OERI US Department of Education 555 New Jersey Ave, NW Washington, DC 20208
18. Captioned films and instructional media for the educational, cultural, and vocational enrichment of the deaf.	Education of the Handicapped Act, Title VI	US Department of Education Office of Special Education and Rehabilitative Services Washington, DC 20202
19. Supports interchange of information and promotes public understanding and appreciation of the arts and humanities.	National Foundation on the Arts and Humanities Act of 1965	Division of Public Programs National Endowment for the Humanities Washington, DC 20506
20. Promotes the humanities through centers of formal education in libraries, museums, and cultural institutions.	National Foundation on the Arts and Humanities Act of 1965	Division of Public Programs National Endowment for the Humanities Washington, DC 20506
21. Development, access, and use of collections for research in the humanities.	National Foundation on the Arts and Humanities Act of 1965	Division of Preservation and Access National Endowment for the Humanities Washington, DC 20506

(Continued)

Figure 16.2 *Continued*

Types of Assistance	Legislative Authority	Administering Federal Agency
22. Provides support for college and university teachers and others employed by schools, museums, libraries, etc.	National Foundation on the Arts and Humanities Act of 1965	Division of Education Programs National Endowment for the Humanities Washington, DC 20506
23. Assists institutions of higher education in their efforts to improve the teaching of the humanities and faculty development and library acquisitions.	National Foundation on the Arts and Humanities Act of 1965	Division of Education Programs National Endowment for the Humanities Washington, DC 20506
24. Encourages public understanding of the humanities and stimulates interest in and use of academic and public libraries humanities resources.	National Foundation on the Arts and Humanities Act of 1965	Division of Public Programs National Endowment for the Humanities Washington, DC 20506
25. Supports interrelated research in well-defined subject areas through block fellowship grants at independent centers for advanced study, American research centers overseas, and independent research libraries.	National Foundation on the Arts and Humanities Act of 1965	Division of Education Programs National Endowment for the Humanities Washington, DC 20506
26. Funds projects which create research tools and reference material important to scholarly research.	National Foundation on the Arts and Humanities Act of 1965	Division of Research Programs National Endowment for the Humanities Washington, DC 20506

Types of Assistance	Legislative Authority	Administering Federal Agency
27. Supports educational and cultural institutions and organizations in order to increase their financial stability and sustain or improve the quality of humanities programs, services, or resources.	National Foundation on the Arts and Humanities Act of 1965	National Endowment for the Humanities Washington, DC 20506
28. Provides educational materials on Gallery's collections and exhibitions.	20 U.S.C. 71–75	National Gallery of Art Washington, DC 20565
29. Donates or lends obsolete combat material to veterans, soldiers' monument associations, state museums and incorporated municipalities.	10 U.S.C. 2572; 7308; 7445	Department of Defense Washington, DC 20301
30. Training and employment opportunities for the unemployed, underemployed, and disadvantaged.	Job Training Partnership Act of 1982	Employee Training Administration US Department of Labor Washington, DC 20213
31. Surplus personal property available to educational agencies including public libraries.	Federal Property and Administrative Services Act	General Service Administration Washington, DC 20405

NOTE: More information is available from the *Catalog of Federal Domestic Assistance.*
This table was prepared by John Blake, National Library of Education.

17 Standards for Public Libraries

Karen Krueger

s your library doing a good job? Does it serve your community well? What can it do better?

These are questions most public library trustees want answered. Not long ago trustees could have used national standards to answer these questions. However, these national standards have been replaced by the Public Library Development Program, a set of tools which assist libraries in planning, measurement, and evaluation. Many states, however, have state standards which trustees can use to help them improve library service. How do state standards mesh with the national program? If national standards were eliminated, are state standards valid? Will every library benefit from standards?

This chapter will describe the purposes of standards, the need for standards, the status of national and state standards in this country, and the steps a trustee can take to make the best use of the standards-related tools that are available.

What are Standards?

Although there is a dictionary definition of standards which could be cited, in public library practice the term *standards* has many meanings. Upon examination of forty-six documents called state standards, Amy Owen found that some were standards, others were guidelines, and still

Karen Krueger is director of the Janesville Public Library, Janesville, Wisconsin.

others were state aid requirements. She makes the distinction among the three as follows: Standards are developed by an entity with authority, and compliance or noncompliance has a specific impact, i.e., certification or recognition. Guidelines are developed with less formal authority, and compliance is voluntary; compliance is usually dependent on staff's professional pride and dedication. State aid requirements are usually found in statutes, administrative rules, or formal regulations, and are usually relatively simple and politically expedient.

For purposes of this chapter, standards are defined as any tools which are called standards by their creators and which attempt to prescribe specific activities and performance measures for libraries.

Purpose of Standards

Standards generally have had three purposes:

1. *Assessment*: To help library staff, board, and the community know whether their library is doing a good job.
2. *Encouragement*: To motivate libraries to improve services.
3. *Accountability*: To set a level of performance which is required by state government or other body, and upon which state aid or other funding is granted.

Need for Standards

Public library standards are generally minimum standards. Some libraries far surpass these minimums; others meet them comfortably; still others do not come close to meeting them. For certain libraries they can be very helpful. There may be a point in a library's development at which standards are needed to get the library headed in the right direction and functioning at a minimum service level. Such libraries may have low to modest financial support, a small or inexperienced staff, or may be a newly formed library.

There are probably many libraries in the United States which would not meet minimum standards set by their states. According to the 1991 report of the U.S. Department of Education's *Public Libraries in the United States*, 1,211 public libraries spent less than $10,000 in total operating expenditures the previous fiscal year, and 2,679 spent more than $10,000 but less than $50,000. In this same report, 1,786 libraries reported being open less than twenty hours a week. The differences on a state-by-state basis are large, from states with no libraries open less than ten hours a week to a state in which 38 percent of its libraries are open less than ten hours a week.

The above example demonstrates why it is possible and important for states to develop their own standards or guidelines to meet the needs of the libraries in those states at their present level of development. National standards could not possibly be pertinent to a large group of libraries with such ranges in performance levels.

National Standards

The last national public library standards were published in 1966. They were easy to use, and clearly identified some service and management areas that needed improvement. Despite this utility, they had serious flaws. National standards

- Were not based on actual measures of library performance, but were based on professional judgment.
- Were used both as minimum levels of service and as levels of excellence.
- Focused on the institution and not on the user or the community.
- Set levels for what a community should invest in its library (inputs), but did not tell the community what it should receive from its library (outputs).
- Did not allow local conditions to be taken into account.

Perhaps the most damaging flaw was the last one listed above: the assumption that libraries were alike and should strive to reach the same vision of "good" library.

In reality there is no *one* vision of a good library; there can't be. Libraries exist to serve the people in their communities. Those communities could be:

- A rural midwest village of 2,000 people, primarily agriculture-based.
- A rapidly growing city in Silicon Valley.
- A run-down, high-crime, ethnically diverse neighborhood in a large urban city.

Once the decision was made not to revise the traditional standards, the Public Library Association developed a number of tools to take their place, the latest being three publications produced between 1987 and 1989, which are referred to as the Public Library Development Program (PLDP): *Planning and Role Setting for Public Libraries*, *Output Measures for Public Libraries*, and *Public Library Data Service*.

The PLDP assumes that library staff, trustees, and representatives from the community can evaluate the library's service program and decide what needs to be improved rather than looking to an outside body to abuse them. Chapter 8 in this book, "The Trustee and Planning," describes the PLDP in more detail.

State Standards

Even though the public library community by and large embraced the new concept of community-based planning rather than national standards, there were needs defined at state levels which demanded more concrete directive guidelines for public library performance. Amy Owen's article on state standards published in 1992 is a wealth of information on the state of state standards.

Each state—whether it is the state library agency, the state library association, or other authority developing the standards—has specific goals it wants to accomplish through its standards: to demonstrate accountability, to encourage the improvement of library service, to distribute money, to establish minimum levels of service guaranteed to all state residents, etc.

State standards often include some quantitative measures of performance, input and/or output. While the old national standards included almost solely input measures, state standards often include both. The numbers, instead of being based on professional opinion, tend to be based on actual statewide experience. The norms in a particular state give libraries various levels of performance to strive toward. For example, state standards might specify that a library serving a population of 2,000 to 3,999 should be open thirty-four hours a week, which is the fiftieth percentile for all libraries of that size in the state. The same standards might specify that a library serving a population of 50,000 and over should circulate twelve items per capita to be considered an A library, ten and one-half items for a B library, and nine items for a C library. Such figures are usually based on actual statewide performance.

Although the weaknesses attributed to national standards apply to many state standards, with careful consideration, the state standards can avoid many of the pitfalls inherent in standards set nationally. Most states have clout, for instance, and can enforce some minimum level of service if they want to do so. With data collected statewide, quantitative standards can be based on realistic, achievable targets. However, state standards are inevitably minimums to achieve, not targets of excellence. While there may be a basic set of standards, such as the hours libraries are open, which must be met by every library, it is impossible to describe a uniform excellent library, given the differences in communities and their different needs and values.

Trustee-to-Do List

Find out if your state has standards.

Find out if they are mandatory or voluntary.

Find out if funding is tied to meeting the standards, or if there are other impacts.

If there are standards, ask if your library has measured itself against them and if there is a report or checklist showing the results.

Read the standards (and the report if one exists).

Determine the purpose of the state standards.

If state standards are voluntary, discuss with the library director and board if the standards will be useful in your situation.

Evaluate your library against them if you believe they will be helpful.

Compare your library to like libraries using data from your state and/ or the *Public Library Data Service* (PLDS) published by the Public Library Association.

If appropriate, share the results of your standards and PLDS review with the public, city council, press, etc.

Once your library is evaluated against the minimum standards, determine if you are ready to set your own standards of performance, i.e., goals and objectives.

Review the *Planning and Role Setting for Public Libraries* and *Output Measures for Public Libraries* manuals.

Follow the steps outlined in the planning manual, starting at a low or modest level of effort. (You may want to include as objectives some of the minimum standards you didn't meet.) The finished plan is your blueprint for achieving excellent library service for your community.

Conclusion

Trustees, library directors, and staff need to give careful consideration to any methods, including standards, which claim to result in better library service. Take the best from all approaches—use what is helpful to you. Who can best define "good service"? Who knows your community, its needs, and values? Who knows the resources of the library, and what is possible and what the priorities are? You are the experts. You may not feel that you are the library experts, but you are community experts, and that is what's most important in determining if you have a good library.

Further Reading

Owen, Amy. "Current Issues and Patterns in State Standards for Public Library Service." *Public Libraries* (July/Aug., 1992): 213–20.

McClure, Charles M., and others. *Planning and Role Setting for Public Libraries: A Manual of Options and Procedures.* Chicago: ALA, 1987.

Van House, Nancy and others. *Output Measures for Public Libraries: A Manual of Standardized Procedures*, 2d ed. Chicago: ALA, 1987.

Public Library Association. *Public Library Data Service: Statistical Report.* Chicago: ALA, 1988–   .

National Center for Education Statistics. *Public Libraries in the United States*: 1991. Washington, D.C.: U.S. Department of Education, 1993.

18 The U.S. National Commission on Libraries and Information Science: Purpose and Functions

Peter R. Young

T he U.S. National Commission on Libraries and Information Science (NCLIS) occupies a unique role in the world of libraries and information services. The Commission is involved with policy issues that relate to the informational needs of the American people. The National Commission functions as a national citizens' advisory group concerned about library and information services policy in much the same way that a board of library trustees is concerned about library and information services for a community. For the Commission, this concern is expressed in the following passage from a 1975 NCLIS publication:

> The National Commission views authors, publishers, and librarians as the principal participants in the production and dissemination of the intellectual and technical knowledge which powers our national development and nurtures our educational system. They are component parts of a national knowledge resource that must be strengthened, integrated, and sustained for all the people of the United States to use as needed in the course of their personal and economic pursuits.[1]

The Commission's focus includes different types of libraries as well as the full range of information service providers in the public, private, and government sectors, at the international, national, state, and local community levels. At the same time, because the Commission is an

Peter R. Young is executive director of the U.S. National Commission on Libraries and Information Science.
    1. U.S. National Commission on Libraries and Information Services, *Toward a National Program for Library and Information Services: Goals for Action.* (Washington, D.C., 1975). ix.

agency in the federal sector, a significant portion of NCLIS' attention is given to the role and influence of the federal government on libraries and information organizations.

NCLIS' Mission

In essence, the National Commission's mission and functional responsibilities were set by the 1970 federal law that established NCLIS (U.S. Public Law 91–345).[2] The primary rationale for establishing the National Commission was to develop overall plans and to coordinate activities at the federal, state, and local levels. The Commission is charged to consider all the adequacy of U.S. library and informational resources in meeting the information needs of the American people. NCLIS is a unique government agency with broad advisory responsibilities that relate to the ability of the nation's educational resources to address these informational needs.

Originating from the recommendation of a 1968 Advisory Commission, the National Commission took form as a federal agency responsible for planning national library and information services with a concentration on the development of plans and on advising appropriate governments and agencies, including the President and Congress, on the implementation of national policy. The Commission's membership includes professional librarians or information specialists, with the remainder composed of persons having special competence or interest in the needs of society for libraries and information services. Throughout the Commission's twenty-five years of activity, library trustees have constituted a large percentage of the appointees. Their wealth of experience, breadth of knowledge, and commitment to the principles of American public libraries have contributed significantly to the work of NCLIS.

The national importance of library and information science issues is reflected in the nature of the appointment process for the fourteen members comprising the National Commission: each Commission member is appointed by the President for a five-year term, by and with the advice and consent of the U.S. Senate. The Librarian of Congress also serves as a member of NCLIS. The President designates a chair from among the members.

2. Public Law 91–345 91st Congress, S. 1519, July 20, 1970, as amended by Public Law 93–29, Section 802, May 3, 1973, and Public Law 102–95, 95th Congress, S. 1593, Aug. 14, 1991.

Responsibility and Principles

The National Commission was established in response to a call for a permanent, continuing, independent federal agency charged with responsibility for conducting studies, surveys and analyses of the library and information needs of the nation, for appraising the adequacies and deficiencies of current library and information resources and services, evaluating the effectiveness of current library and information science programs, developing overall plans for meeting national library and informational needs, and for coordinating activities at the federal, state, and local levels. The National Commission should take into consideration all of the library and information resources of the nation to meet those needs.

Clear lines of responsibility were specified in the NCLIS authorizing legislation for advising federal, state, local, and private agencies regarding library and information sciences. By the inclusion of private commercial sector information concerns in the statutory authority of the National Commission, along with various other federal, state and local agencies, the Commission has wide discretion and responsibility to address a variety of information policy and services issues and topics affecting virtually every aspect of national library and information service activity. A key area of program focus for the Commission results from issues that arise in the boundaries between the various public and private sectors. These issues have gradually assumed more critical importance as the importance of networking has grown in the field of library and information services concerns over the last two decades.

In the late 1980s the Commission was charged by law[3] with planning and conducting the second White House Conference on Library and Information Services (WHCLIS). This Conference followed the first WHCLIS in 1979. The purpose of the 1991 WHCLIS was to develop recommendations for the further improvement of the library and information services of the nation and their use by the public.

Throughout the Commission's history, a number of principles have guided the selection of topics receiving the attention of the membership. These principles include: concern for equal access to library and information services; concern for coordination of activities at the federal, state, and local levels; concern for the impact of information technologies on libraries; concern about library and information services for special segments of the population including Native Americans, the elderly, minorities, children and youth, and rural residents; concern for

3. Public Law 100–382, Aug. 8, 1988, White House Conference on Library and Information Services.

providing effective mechanisms for dissemination of public information; concern for adequate U.S. representation in international library, information, and archival activities; concern for the economics of library and information services support; concern for assuring timely, reliable, and comprehensive statistics regarding American library activities; concern for clarifying the information policy issues arising from the interaction between the public and private sectors; concern for improving the education and training of library and information professionals; concern for the currency and responsiveness of the legal and regulatory processes affecting library and information services activities; and concern for coordinating the library and information–related programs and activities within the different governmental sectors.

NCLIS Actions

The listing attached to this chapter provides a list of selected examples of the major accomplishments of the NCLIS since 1969 that reflect these general principles. Many of these items reflect topics of interest to library trustees at the local level and, indeed, much of the Commission's policy work finds implementation at the local level.

The Commission's recent activity since the 1991 WHCLIS is directed toward implementing the priority recommendations from this second White House Conference. Thus, the Commission has programmed in the areas of library and information services for children and youth, as well as in the areas of libraries and the networked information infrastructure. Roughly speaking, these programs have focused on school library media center and public library programs for children and young adults, and on libraries of all types employing high-performance computing and communication networks, such as the National Research and Education Network (NREN), the Internet, and the National Information Infrastructure (NII).

The following activities reflect actions taken or initiated by the National Commission resulting from the Omnibus Children and Youth Literacy Initiative, which received strong support at the 1991 White House Conference on Library and Information Services:

July 5–9, 1991	WHCLIS, Washington D.C.: Passage of Omnibus Childrens and Youth Libraries Initiative.
Oct. 1991	NCLIS meeting with WHCLIS Advisory Committee, Annapolis, Md.: Synthesis of ninety-five WHCLIS Recommendations and preparation of synthesis of priority recommendations.

Nov. 1991	WHCLIS summary report transmitted to the President.
Mar. 10, 1992	NCLIS Open Forum on WHCLIS recommendations hears from twenty-seven organizational representatives.
Sept. 1992	NCLIS announces America 2000: Library partnership with the Department of Education, Center for the Book, National Library Institute, and NEH.
Nov. 1992	NCLIS Meeting in Washington, D.C. results in formation of coordinated program involving three NCLIS Committees (Education and Special Populations, Legislative and Library Statistics, and America 2000: Library Partnership).
Dec. 17, 1992	NCLIS/COSLA meeting to review plans for the Omnibus Children and Youth Literacy Initiative.
Jan. 18, 1993	NCLIS/ALA (ALSC, AASL, YASD, WHCLIS Community) meeting to review plans for Omnibus Children and Youth Literacy Initiative implementation.
Mar. 1993	NCLIS members visit Library Partnership representatives.
Apr. 26–27, 1993	NCLIS/COSLA/ALA invitational meeting on children and youth services initiatives to share information, strategies, and plans; to identify common goals, priorities, and positions; to suggest possible actions, programs, and activities; and to plan for coordinated activities.
May 4–5, 1993	NCLIS Forum on Children and Youth Services at the Boston Public Library—twenty-three representatives offered comments, suggestions, and views.
Aug.–Dec. 1993	NCLIS and ALA (ORS) plan School Library Statistics Project—collection of school library data from twelve states.
Sept. 2, 1993	Second NCLIS Forum on Children and Youth Services in Sacramento, California.
Dec. 2–3, 1993	Third NCLIS Forum on Children and Youth Services in Des Moines, Iowa.
Apr. 1994	NCLIS publishes *Public School Library Media Centers in 12 States: Report of the NCLIS/ALA Survey*.

Apr. 1994	NCLIS writes to selected members of Congress in support of proposal in the Elementary and Secondary Education Act reauthorization for school library funding.

The following activities reflect actions or programs of the National Commission resulting from the 1991 White House Conference on Library and Information Services that relate to information technology, networking, and the national information infrastructure:

July 9–13, 1991	WHCLIS delegates pass recommendations related to networking and the National Research and Education Network (NREN).
Oct. 1991	NCLIS meeting with WHCLIS Advisory Committee, Annapolis, Md.: Synthesis of ninety-five WHCLIS recommendations and preparation of synthesis of priority recommendations, including information networks.
Nov. 1991	1991 WHCLIS Summary Report transmitted to the President.
Mar. 10, 1992	NCLIS open forum on WHCLIS Recommendations hears from twenty-seven organizational representatives.
June 1992	NCLIS meeting in conjunction with OCLU Users Council hears presentation from the Coalition on Networked Information (CNI).
July 20–21, 1992	NCLIS open forum on library and information services roles in NREN hears from twenty-four organizations.
Nov. 13, 1992	NCLIS submits report on library and information services role in NREN to Office of Science and Technology Policy (OSTP).
Nov. 1992	NCLIS meeting in Washington, D.C., includes presentation by representatives from the Community Learning and Information Network (CLIN).
Dec. 1992	OSTP report on NREN to Congress includes reference to NCLIS report.
Jan. 1993	NCLIS meeting in Denver includes a presentation by representative from the National Governors Association concerning coordination of state and national information networks.
July 1993	NCLIS announces Dr. Chuck McClure as Dis-

	tinguished Researcher to study roles of libraries and information services in networking.
Aug. 6, 1993	NCLIS meeting in Philadelphia includes presentations for LibertyNet and the Ben Franklin Information Center representatives.
Aug. 1993	NCLIS involved in the Digital Resources Education and Training Working Group organized by OSTP to develop strategies for Federal information network dissemination.
Sept. 1993	NCLIS approves proposal to perform a national sample survey of current public Internet use and applications to provide a basis for recommending future NCLIS and federal program activities.
Mar. 1994	NCLIS chairperson report to the Public Library Association National Conference on results of a survey of the public library and the Internet.
Apr. 1994	NCLIS chairperson testifies at the Senate hearing on libraries and the information superhighway.
June 1994	NCLIS publishes *Public Libraries and the Internet: Study Results, Policy Issues, and Recommendations.*

As this chapter has outlined, programs of the National Commission provide an independent national perspective on issues and concerns of importance to the general library and information services community. Specifically this chapter explores those instance of current Commission program concentration arising from the Commission's statutory mission and arising from the Commission's historic program concerns. Given the rich mixture of topics, issues, concerns, and policies that the Commission has addressed, future NCLIS programs that will occupy the Commission's agenda in the future are likely to be: the reauthorization of the Library Services and Construction Act, the role of the federal government regarding library roles in the NII, and a selected number of other programs.

In addition, it is reasonably certain, based on historic and recent concerns, that future Commission program directions will relate directly and specifically to future programs of national libraries, as well as those state, regional, and local community libraries throughout the nation. It is also safe to bet that the focus and concentration of the National Commission will encompass those issues and concerns that are of vital interest to library trustees.

Selected Major Commission Achievements (1969–93)

1969   The National Advisory Commission on Libraries recommends legislation be enacted "to establish a National Library Policy and a permanent National Commission on Libraries and Information Science."

1970   Signing by President Nixon of P.O. 91–345 to establish the U.S. National Commission on Libraries and Information Science.

1971   Conduct of the first meeting of the Commission on September 20–21, 1971.

1972   Beginning exploration by an NCLIS committee on the application of new technology to library and information services.

1973   Hearing to develop a national program for library and information services.

1974   Study of continuing education needs of library personnel and recommendation from NCLIS to form Continuing Library Education Network and Exchange.

1975   Work with the Congress, the Register of Copyrights, and others to resolve copyright issues and revise legislation.

1976   Issuance of National Inventory of Library Needs and of a report on the role of the Library of Congress in a national network.

1977   NCLIS task forces' examination of three issues; the role of school libraries in a national network; computer network protocols; and standardization efforts for library services.

1978   Cosponsorship of consulting skills institutes for state library agency personnel.

1979   Conduct of the first White House Conference on Library and Information Services (WHCLIS).

1980   Work with Congress to amend existing library and information science legislation, based on WHCLIS resolutions, and on oversight hearings on the Library Services and Construction Act (LSCA).

1981   Publication of report of NCLIS Task Force on "Public/Private Sector Relations."

1982   Issuance of proceedings of hearings and development of the report from NCLIS Task Force on "Library and Information Services to Cultural Minorities."

1983   Beginning of work with State Department on alternative mechanisms to UNESCO to further international programs in library/information/archival areas.

1984   Publication of a report of NCLIS Blue Ribbon Panel on the information policy implications of archiving satellite data.

1985   Coordination of a joint congressional hearing on the changing information needs of rural America.

1986   Agreement with ACTION to promote improvement and better use of library and information services to the elderly through voluntary activities.

1987   Adoption of Glenerin Declaration, trilateral (United States, United Kingdom, and Canada) statement on the role of information in the economy.

At the request of the U.S. State Department, NCLIS undertakes monitoring and coordinating of proposals for International Conventions and Scientific Organizations Contributions (ICSOC) grants.

1988   NCLIS enters into interagency agreement with National Center for Education Statistics to establish the Federal-State Cooperative System for Public Library Data (FSCS).

Kickoff of cosponsored National Library Card Campaign.

1989   Cosponsorship of symposium, "Information Literacy and Education for the 21st Century."

1990   Twentieth Anniversary of the U.S. National Commission on Libraries and Information Science (NCLIS); development and adoption of the Principles of Public Information.

1991   Conduct of the second White House Conference on Library and Information Services (WHCLIS).

Passage of technical amendments of NCLIS' enabling legislation.

1992   Publication of 600-page report, *INFORMATION 2000, Library and Information Services for the 21st Century, Final Report of the 1991 White House Conference on Library and Services.*

Sponsorship of an open forum on recommendations of the White House Conference on Library and Information Services and released publication thereof.

Report of the Office of Science and Technology Policy on Library and Information Services' roles in the National Research and Education Network.

1993   Publication of the two-volume report titled *Improving Library and Information Services for Native American Peoples,* "Pathways to Excellence."

Sponsoring three regional forums on "Library Services for Children and Youth, Redefining the Federal Role for Libraries"; and publication of the forum proceedings.

Quick-response sample survey of school library media centers and public libraries in the Internet to identify potential Federal policies on the public library role in developing a national networked information infrastructure.

19 Participation in Library Systems

Frederick J. Raithel
Gina J. Millsap

ccess to materials and information is the primary objective of all public library service. Trustees and librarians together must adopt a broad range of innovative strategies to successfully accomplish an adequate level of access for all individuals in the community.

As the world economy moves quickly toward in information-based economy, information has become a commodity which can be bought and sold. The implication of this economic condition is that information may not always be available to everyone. While information has never been "free" (even libraries must pay for the books and materials they offer), libraries have served as the one institution which has provided community access without charge to these materials and information. *Universal access* for every member of the local community has been the defining characteristic of the modern American public library.

For small libraries, in particular, the cost of providing library services may be prohibitive. An adequate-size collection of materials, access to modern communications delivery systems, and properly trained personnel may be out of reach to many smaller libraries, especially in

Frederick J. Raithel is head of circulation, Daniel Boone Regional Library, Columbia, Missouri. He also serves as adjunct faculty at the University of Missouri-Columbia School of Library and Information Science.

Gina J. Millsap is head of computer services, Daniel Boone Regional Library, Columbia, Missouri. She also serves as coordinator of technical/user support for the Columbia Online Information Network (COIN).

rural areas. Participation in library systems may help the small library to achieve a level of service previously unattainable.

For the immediate future, participation in library systems provides greater access to the wealth of published materials and shared library services only the system can offer. For the future, residents of a community can gain access at the local level to the vast national and international communications networks of which libraries are increasingly becoming a part.

It is a basic responsibility of the trustee to become knowledgeable about the system concept and to work toward the establishment of such a system locally.

Organization and Administration of Systems

Cooperation has always been essential to the delivery of effective library service. The sharing of cataloging data began by the Library of Congress early in this century and served as an early attempt at cooperation. Presently, the sheer volume of published materials each year precludes any one library from providing access to all the materials. Consequently, cooperation and resource sharing have become an important goal of viable public library service.

There are essentially four types of library systems: consolidated, library district, cooperative, and network. The structure of the system and of the governing board will vary as statutory law varies from state to state.

A *consolidated system* authorizes the board of trustees to take office and operate under the statutory regulations which established the system. The board of trustees sets policy, secures funds, and carries out other legal responsibilities for the system. Frequently, a consolidated system comprises a large urban library system and its branches. The system may cover several counties. Two or more library jurisdictions may also legally merge, perhaps even across county lines.

A *library district* permits two or more county districts to form an administrative unit governed by one board of trustees through the decision of their respective boards. Usually, the trustees of the individual districts forming the district serve on the newly created board.

A *cooperative system* allows a group of libraries and/or library districts through joint action to provide specific services or materials for member libraries. The autonomy of each library or library district is maintained in this model. Each board governs its own library or library district. The shared materials and services are planned and coordinated by an advisory board for all of the network members.

A *network system*, sometimes called a *consortium*, serves all types of libraries (public, school, academic, special) through a formal agreement or contract. This advanced form of cooperative system provides services and materials which are planned and coordinated by an advisory board for the benefit of all network members.

In the early days the objective of library systems was to develop local geographic units of service which could then connect into a statewide network. State and multistate networks could cooperate until a national network for library services was established. Through this process the rich and varied resources of libraries everywhere could be shared nationally. The primary purpose for geographic networking in this new age of computers and communications is the attractiveness of a local or regional delivery system for documents. When more and more information and library services can be delivered electronically, it may well be that increasingly larger units of library services in the future will be based on communications systems rather the geographic proximity.

Communications

An effective means of communicating the service needs of one library to another is very important in systems and networks. A modern, efficient communication system has been identified frequently as integral to the development of successful cooperative ventures.

A major service of most systems and networks is the exchange of materials requested by the library users or interlibrary loan. Obviously, no single library can purchase all the materials which are published each year. When library users request materials that the individual library does not own, interlibrary loan provides a mechanism for the librarian to go beyond the boundaries of the in-house collection of materials and borrow the items elsewhere. In this way the library user can gain access to the varied and extensive library resources of a much larger unit of organization.

In order for libraries to exchange this information on their users' needs in a timely manner, most system members will need basic telecommunications equipment. With widespread use of small computers, even smaller libraries can benefit from the power of automation to transmit data on interlibrary loan as well as data on cataloging, book orders, and requests for reference searches and journal article photocopies.

The continuing sweeping acceptance and availability of computers in all types and sizes of libraries open up new opportunities for resource sharing. Remote telephone access to a central computer facility or in-house access to a computer optical disc that stores holdings information of member libraries can streamline the process of sharing materials. One can search the machine-readable information for an author, title, or subject entry, and, if a circulation checkout system is integrated into the cataloging database, one can even determine the availability of an item.

This increasing use of computers in systems and networks refocuses our attention on the catalog card record. The communication and sharing of cataloging data among many institutions prompted the emergence of a national standard for the computer storage of cataloging information. This national communications standard for the sharing of computer cataloging data became known as MARC (machine-readable cataloging). MARC is simply a standardized record format for storing cataloging data in various computer systems. As more libraries began to share their computerized holdings information with one another, the need for standards in the way we store the catalog record became imperative.

Finally, a regular delivery system provides the final link in the resource-sharing process which places the materials in the hands of the library user. The system or network might operate its own vehicular delivery system or make use of an existing service such as the U.S. Postal Service.

Systems and networks encourage the sharing of human as well as technological resources. Libraries are essentially communications systems for the transfer of culture and civilization. The communication of information needs among libraries is of paramount importance if they are to achieve their goal of improved library services for the users.

Key Components of Effective Library Systems

The most basic ingredient of any cooperative enterprise is the development of a shared mission or philosophical vision with a set of goals and objectives to which all parties have agreed. A mission establishes the goals for the venture and justifies the commitment to the accomplishment of those objectives. The mission focuses the organizational energy and allocates resources to the achievement of the vision.

Trustees of library systems must have a thorough understanding of and commitment to the library system's mission to assist in the development of systemwide policies that will further that mission. This commitment and understanding is critical to any decision-making process since an individual member of the system may have a different style of management, policies, or procedures that govern certain activities of services.

Consider, for example, a library system which has a policy of no fines for overdue materials: if a member library of that system wishes to implement fines, how with that affect the system as a whole? Will the member libraries be able to share materials and extend the same type of reciprocal borrowing privileges as they have previously? How will staff effectively implement two conflicting policies, and how will patrons respond to having to deal with two different policies when their library materials are overdue?

Ultimately, cooperating libraries must share and compromise in the process of implementing systemwide policies. Individual members may have to modify internal policies and procedures in order for the cooperative efforts to be successful. Trustees must balance the needs of the individual members with the needs of the system, paying particular attention to equity in the sharing of resources and the delivery of services.

Another key ingredient in successful library systems is the investment in a well-educated, trained, and compensated staff. In looking at critical resources of successful systems, professional, expert staff remains at the top of the list. A library can invest in the latest materials and technology, but without the staff expertise to implement and deliver those services to the patron, that investment is wasted.

Funding remains a major component of ongoing, viable library service. Adequate funding for library systems in the future requires the identification of specific, measurable benefits that can be derived from such a cooperative arrangement. It is essential that members of systems bring an adequate funding base to the system and that the system implement sound financial management practices that maximize the use of shared financial resources.

And adequate funding will supply other important pieces of the successful library system, including adequate numbers and types of materials to meet the information needs of the communities served and an attractive, inviting service environment, equipped with attractive, durable furniture and modern equipment. However, without a strong fiscal foundation, services may be curtailed or eliminated and the use of modern technologies may be sacrificed until the service program is no longer viable.

Finally, in much the same way that businesses strive for "market dominance" or market positioning in the minds of their customers, public libraries must preserve their political visibility in the minds of the individuals in their communities that make use of their many services. For cooperative systems which frequently include different political districts, types of libraries, and many facilities, this can be a real challenge. Key to this endeavor is the development of a strong public relations program. Libraries use a variety of activities to deliver information about the library's services and programs from publication of booklets to programming for National Library Week and other events. All media are utilized to reach patrons and potential patrons, including printed materials, newspaper articles, radio and television interviews, and most recently, computer bulletin boards and networks.

Library Systems and Networks in the Next Century: Building Coalitions for Service in the Community

Traditionally libraries have developed systems comprised of themselves, or, in other words, other libraries. Today libraries are building partnerships with municipal and county governments, school districts, higher education, businesses, and other nonlibrary organizations. Cooperative projects include everything from collaborative grant proposals to sharing resources. Those resources range from books and other materials located in a physical facility to computer networks and databases. The same vision that informs the development of a traditional library system drives these partnerships: the goal of providing equal access to information for their constituencies.

In the future the definition of library system may broaden to include organizations other than libraries. The same benefits that libraries enjoy through the formation of traditional library systems can also be realized through cooperation with other community organizations. One exciting example of this trend is the involvement of libraries in "freenets" or community information networks. These are computer information networks operating at the grassroots level to provide electronic access to both local information as well as access to the Internet, the "information superhighway." In many communities public libraries have become partners in, or have become founding members of, organizations to implement these community needs.

Library systems, whatever organizations they include, must share vision, goals, and resources. In that sharing the individual library or other organization is strengthened and is better equipped to provide the best service to its users.

20 Technology in the Modern Public Library

Jean Thibodeaux Kreamer

echnology presents public library trustees with a dilemma. It is an understatement to say that technology is changing rapidly; rather it is changing at an exponential rate.

Being a member of the policymaking body of a public library system, how can the individual trustee and/or board of control knowledgeably preside over the professional decisions involving enormously costly technology needs when most trustees are not technology gurus? A major responsibility of the trustee, however, is to do exactly that.

Generally and practically, trustees will find themselves increasingly asking questions about technology. While it is not necessary to become an expert in the exoterica of technology, it is necessary for the trustee to use common sense in approaching the technology needs of any library.

In a recent interview with Sona Domburian, who holds both the master's of library science and the master's of science in computer science degrees and who presently serves as assistant director of the Lafayette Public Library System, she stated, "The largest issue for any library is to balance its technology budget against its overall needs." For the uninitiated, both librarians and trustees, Domburian postulates that often uncertainty reigns supreme. In the quest to ask the right questions, those both practical and commonsensical, the best plan of

Jean Thibodeaux Kreamer is director of media and printing services in the Division of Computing and Information Services at the University of Southwestern Louisiana, Lafayette, Louisiana. She is a past president and a ten-year member of the Lafayette Public Library Board of Control.

attack is multifold and ought to include two major steps: information/education and future expansion.

Information and Education

The obvious first step is to formulate a plan for technology. This should be a joint effort between the library staff and the board. The plan ought to be a realistic one extending five years into the future.

A second series of steps falls under the umbrella of visits to other libraries for the purpose of viewing various technologies under consideration. These excursions should include both trustees and library staff. A summary report of these visits should be prepared for presentation to the full board.

A third informational step is to attend demonstrations of technology as often as appropriate. It is particularly important for members of the board to be included in planning for these demonstrations, again exercising their responsibility as planners and policymakers for the library. Such demonstrations can be arranged in-house as well as being viewed at state and national library conferences.

With a solid base of library literature serving as the fourth leg of this informational phase, sound technology decisions can be made. This information is timely and is published on a regular basis.

Future Expansion

When we approach the altar of technology for the first time, one's reaction is almost universally the same: dismay. The sheer complexity of technology and the high costs associated with it are breathtaking. It makes no difference whether one began as a trustee during the days of the library as a monolith housing the ubiquitous book, or whether one has become a trustee in this golden era of automation and the changing nature of libraries. An absolute truism associated with technology and its heart-stopping price tags is that all of this can be deadly for the trustee unless technology is viewed through the veil of the future.

Cycles seem to be emerging in technology circles. Approximately every six to ten years hardware changes appear to be occurring. When considering purchases of technology, from the lowly fax machine to the systemwide computer automation package, one might ask concrete questions with this six-to-ten-year cycle in mind. Brief examples of the type of querying trustees might consider are presented here.

Can this equipment be expanded to accommodate projected growth needs for this time span?

What sorts of contractual and/or written guarantees will a vendor give for expansion of products projected over a finite period of time?

How will upgrades of products be made? Are discounts given on upgrades? Are they part of the purchase package for a set period of time?

With what is this technology compatible? With what will it work? Other computers, networks, people?

It's one thing to buy the box that is the computer, but what software is used by that computer? How accessible is it and is it easy to use?

Software drives computers; look at it first, always.

Two clear and logical approaches to currentness for the trustee in library technology follows:

1. Keep an eye on the literature of libraries and technology.
   a. *Library Journal*, "Managing Technology Column."
   b. *Library Systems*, Library Technology Reports.
   c. *ProQuest Periodical Abstracts*.
2. Regularly request updates on library technology by the library staff or consultants.

A very effective method of updating the board of control is to regularly schedule reports of recent technological advances suitable for libraries. These might occur on a quarterly basis. The updates may be presented by knowledgeable library staff or by consultants with expertise in library technology. This is a relatively painless way to inform the board of innovations, trends, and activity in libraries. The relationship of libraries to technology is often very subtle; it is one which frequently is demand- or patron-driven. There have been few times, if any at all, when libraries have had adequate funds available to test new technologies in an orderly or ongoing basis. Libraries have increasingly found themselves in the position of responding on a consumer/patron/demand-driven situation rather than being in the fiscally luxurious position of being able to cyclically pilot test emerging technologies or materials.

Two examples are illustrative of this phenomenon:

1. Some years ago, when paperback books were in their popular ascendancy, many libraries were reluctant to add them to collec-

tions. Reasons centered around the ephemeral nature of the paperback itself. Public demand began to overshadow that concern, thus forcing libraries to add the lowly paperback to its bound collections. Likewise, public demand also drove the publishing market to make available greatly expanded title lists cancelling any overriding resistance to condemn paperbacks as unworthy.

2. A similar circumstance of demand for technology driving library acquisitions and services is exemplified with the emergence of video. Great opposition to video as an integrated and respected part of collections has existed in the recent past. Counter to this resistance is the overwhelming popularity of video as evidenced by the vast majority of American homes in happy possession of video recorders. Video has dramatically been the driving force of the library technology market. In a random sample survey of all types of libraries in the United States conducted over a three-year period, respondents have been circulating video collections for an average of five years. And space needs for growing video collections has shown significant increases.[1]

Trustees, of necessity, will have to debate what technologies to make available to the public. Translated into other terms, trustees are being boldly faced with the real problem of having to decide in which technologies to invest or not to invest. The underscoring issue is that often these library provisions for purchases may be the only access the public may have.

In providing access to technology, especially for those patrons who are unable to afford personal ownership or access, libraries and their boards are finding themselves as change agents in everything from the ubiquitous Internet to the marvels of multimedia.

Another side of this dilemma is the concept of libraries creating the demand for technology. With the high cost of technology, a strong case can be made for the tax-supported library being the only entity able to offer sophisticated and emerging formats and services. With stretched budgets and lightning changes in the technologies for libraries, this issue is not one to simply go away with time.

The trustee, as a policymaker charged with budget approvals, will increasingly be placed in the position of also needing the gift of prescience. Shall the library respond to the pounding demands borne on technology's shoulders? To what extent shall the library serve as the technology change agent? Will a library simply relax and follow the

1. Jean T. Kreamer, editor, *Video Annual III* (Santa Barbara, Calif.: ABC-Clio, 1993).

lead of technology, wherever that may go? Compelling to the mission of the public library is the charged choice which points to the library's responsibility to provide information and services to all patrons. Technology has shifted that choice dramatically.

A sparkling example of the breadth of the technology horizon is the Internet, which celebrated its twenty-fifth year in 1994. The origin of today's Internet was ARPANET, so-named for its founding entity the Department of Defense's Advanced Research Project Agency.[2] The goal of the project twenty-five years ago was to build a computer network enabling researchers around the country to allow users to share ideas. The problem then to be solved was that computers could not generally communicate with each other. The underlying driving force of the Internet was and still is to share computer resources. Today's Internet has electronically linked the globe into an information highway unlike any other before.

Availing patrons of the wonders of the Internet a short while ago would have been possible, but only in academic settings. The Internet reality has changed library services and the science of information creation, acquisitions, and retrieval. The Internet platform has made information available to huge chunks of the population instantaneously.

For the trustee, the issue is once again a demand driving the market. In the recent past, trustees might have calmly mused if a board should consider for the future technology like the Internet. The issue today is how soon can we have it (if we don't already) or how quickly can we expand our existing support? With a collective voice, the trustee may well ask what of tomorrow? With no clear answer in sight, one might be mildly comforted by recognizing that tomorrow is today. No longer are newer, faster technologies being developed annually, they are being developed daily.

Conclusion

In summary, trustees will find that presiding over libraries with their needs might be increasingly difficult. Balancing the library budget to accommodate growing technology needs and the overall needs of the library is becoming an entirely new issue for boards. Keeping abreast of innovations and practical applications of technology can be touchy for trustees; the reliance on top-notch library staff is a necessity. With

2. The Birth of the Internet," *Newsweek*, Aug. 8, 1994, 56–58.

technology, libraries are faced with a subtle new challenge: Shall the library become the technology change agent of the future, or shall the library find it is following the lead of the technology Pied Piper? And finally, libraries are finding that they are the only access point for emerging and expensive technologies in communities where patrons are unable to afford access on a personal basis.

The excitement and the promise of technology are unprecedented in the history of libraries. The problems presented to trustees in approaching and managing this excitement and promise are small when weighed against the possibilities. The future is no longer remote. With technology, it is only a moment away.

Further Reading

Corbin, John B. *Managing the Library Automation Project.* Phoenix, Ariz.: Oryx, 1985.

Wozny, Jay. *Checklists for Public Library Managers.* Metuchen, N.J.: Scarecrow, 1989.

Library Systems Newsletter. Library Technology Reports, American Library Association.

"Managing Technology Column." *Library Journal.*

21 The Trustee and Public Relations

Peggy Barber
Gloria T. Glaser

assivity is not a virtue; it is a position public libraries can no longer afford. Funding for all nonprofit institutions is tighter and harder to get. Demographic changes have put new burdens on library services. Twenty-three million people live in homes where a language other than English is spoken. Illiteracy even among native-born Americans has emerged as a major social and economic problem. A conservative shift has fueled the enthusiasm of censors. New technology offers great—but expensive—potential for libraries. If they are to survive, public libraries must relate effectively with the communities they serve.

Is your library mainstream or marginal? Are you involved in helping your community solve problems and improve the quality of life for all people?

The public library is a middle-aged institution too often taken for granted, even by the people who work there. Even the smallest public library can get set in its bureaucratic ways, become passive, and self-serving. We know that, if prompted, the American people use and appreciate libraries. The board of trustees is responsible for the prompting.

In the 1960s the dramatic turnaround of the New York Public Library provided a fine example of how an active and determined board can bring about social and financial success. It's still a good model.

Peggy Barber is associate executive director for Communications, American Library Association.

Gloria T. Glaser is a former president of the American Library Trustee Association.

According to Arthur Lubow in *Vanity Fair* (May 1986), "For a long time the library sprawled as sleepily as the two stone lions that guard its entrance. It was dim and dusty and nobody paid any attention to it." The board of trustees made the difference. They worked hard for the support of the mayor, appointed a dynamic director, set a style, and managed to get the city of New York involved in its library. To quote a fundraiser for another Manhattan institution:

> Now that it has come out of the shadows, the library is the perfect New York institution. It has a liberal aura, because it provides real services to the people of New York. The library casts a welcome glow of professionalism and intellect.

The New York experience suggests that the world is ready to love and support libraries, if we are ready to come out of the shadows. A planned program of public relations can help transform a passive public library into a perfect institution.

What Is Public Relations?

Simply defined, public relations is a planned and sustained effort to establish mutual understanding between an organization and its public. The practice of public relations involves research of the attitudes and opinions of the many publics served by an organization, developing policy that demonstrates responsiveness, communicating information about the organization, and constantly evaluating the effectiveness of all programs.

It is ironic that public relations (PR) has its own image problems. The term is often confused with publicity, which is one of its tools. Some see it as a smiling attitude of "Have a nice day." Others suspect PR is puffery and media stunts. Yet in spite of these misconceptions, PR has become a powerful and indispensable tool of management. PR practitioners insist that they do not create images; a good reputation must be earned.

Public relations was invented in the early twentieth century, when big business was forced to abandon its public-be-damned attitude. By the end of World War I, it was clear that words could be skillfully used to mold public opinion, and that public understanding was necessary for the survival of institutions. Although public relations was not defined in standard dictionaries until 1946, it has since become part of our everyday vocabulary. Few business or government organizations are without public relations departments.

Public libraries have made use of philosophy and techniques of public relations vigorously, but inconsistently. As early as 1910, John Cotton Dana horrified some of his more staid colleagues by using a billboard to advertise the library. He identified local interests and developed accordingly the libraries he directed in Denver, Colorado; Springfield, Massachusetts; and Newark, New Jersey. He believed in telling the community what the library had and did.

Yet as recently as the mid-1970s, librarians were still arguing the legitimacy of public relations and worrying about their dignity. A January 1974 *Library Journal* editorial protested the "Selling of the Public Library." The editor objected to aggressive PR messages, holding that people need and will use the public library just as they use hospitals, schools, and other essential services:

> This commercial pap, when applied to an institution like the public library, may be effective to a degree, if we want to pack 'em in, but beyond its lack of dignity, it overlooks the basic justification for all public services—that people need them. No other essential public service finds it necessary to peddle its wares as if they were new appliances for a consumer public that is tired of washing dishes, preparing food from scratch, or having hair with split ends.

My, how things have changed since 1974! Hospitals now "niche" market their specialized services to target audiences. Even attorneys advertise. Public funds are scarce and competition is fierce.

When public relations has slowly grown to be an accepted tool of library management, many library administrators are becoming still more interested in marketing. As defined by Philip Kotler, the guru of marketing for nonprofit organizations, marketing is "that function of the organization that can keep constant touch with the organization's consumers, read their needs, develop products that meet these needs and build a program of communications to express the organization's purposes." Theoretically, in turning to the consumer for information about the products and services to be developed, marketing goes beyond public relations. Selling focuses on the needs of the seller; marketing on the needs of the buyer.

All of this background about public relations and marketing has been included here to convince every trustee reading this book that you no longer need to waffle and debate the merits of applying either of these business concepts to the public library. As you well know, a business produces goods and services, and its bottom line is profit. A nonprofit organization such as the public library provides services, and its bottom line is *quality of life*, a concept considerably more difficult to measure than profit. It is dangerous for a library to assume that the importance of its cause will generate public support. Again, passivity is dangerous.

How to Organize a Public Relations Program

There are four basic steps in public relations: research, planning, communication, and evaluation. The responsibility for managing an effective PR program belongs to the library director, but it is vitally important for the board to know what's involved and to set the standards.

Research

Research involves identifying the library's publics and assessing their attitudes toward the library. These publics include the staff, board, Friends, users, and nonusers. Research should begin inside the library to determine how the staff and trustees view the library, how well they understand its goals and policies, and what they see as its strengths and weaknesses. It's also important to take an objective look at the physical appearance of the library, including access, signage, lighting, maintenance, and ambiance. All the print materials produced by the library should be reviewed. Do they reflect well on the library? What is the library's style? Does it have a style? Is it elegant, businesslike, friendly, cozy, elite, efficient? What should it be?

Even if you think you know your community, it is necessary to gather all available demographic information: age, income, ethnic background, occupation, religion, interests, community groups, and all other formal or informal data that are available. It's not necessary to hire the Gallup organization, but original research can also be undertaken, from mail questionnaires to telephone surveys, to informal meetings with community groups. The goal is constant sensitivity to public opinion. The research phase can be characterized as a *communications audit*—a public relations term for a full and careful study of all the ways the library communicates with its current and potential target audience.

Planning

Planning should make the PR process an integral part of the total library program. There should be a written PR policy and a plan with short- and long-term goals, a clear idea of the specific publics to be reached, a timetable and reporting schedule, a staffing plan, and a budget. Be willing to spend some money on public relations, but don't rush into publicity. You must have a plan.

If you watch the media and commercial advertising, you can't miss the fact that there is no longer a "general public." With the growth of cable channels and niche marketing, everyone with a message must have a plan and target audience. Yes, public libraries have the potential to serve everyone, but we must have a strategy to generate the support from these who "have" that will keep the doors open for those who "don't have."

Communication

Communication is the part of the public relations program that calls for the outreach, programming, and publicity suggested by your research and planning. The library should build and maintain a media list of publications and broadcast channels, including daily and weekly newspapers, radio, television and cable stations, community group newsletters, school newspapers, church bulletins, and any other media that may reach your target audience. Personal contact with people on the press list is especially important. Libraries are eligible for free public service advertising time and space from the media, but must compete with many good causes.

Beyond mass media, there are other publicity tools used successfully by libraries, including newsletters (internal and external), annual reports, posters, booklists, exhibitions and displays, special programs, film series, speakers bureaus, and more. Library journals are full of success stories and ideas to be borrowed.

The library director or designated public relations specialist should have the tools and techniques of PR firmly in hand, from how to write a press release to understanding the difference between news and feature material. Comparable to etiquette and the confidence to choose the right fork, PR skills provide an understanding to package everyday library happenings in a way that can capture public attention.

And before the board decides to make major investments in producing publicity materials, the members should know about and take advantage of national campaigns. There are more than fifteen thousand public libraries (McDonald's has only about ten thousand fast-food stores). Can you imagine what we could do if we all got together on a public service advertising campaign?

Every year the American Library Association produces print, radio, and television materials and a campaign book with ideas about how to use them. These materials are placed with the national media and marketed to libraries. This cooperative program provides professionally produced materials at a fraction of their actual cost.

Since 1990 the American Library Association has been leading even more aggressive national campaigns to rally support for libraries through grass roots advocacy efforts. Participating in these national campaigns has become a proven way to increase local, state, and national funding for libraries.

ALA also provides programs at every Annual Conference about marketing public relations, lobbying, and even media training—how-to-do interviews and make public presentations and a full schedule of promotional opportunities.

ALA sponsors National Library Week every year in April, a wonderful opportunity for local and national events to celebrate libraries. For more information on ALA materials and programs, contact the Public Information Office, American Library Association, 50 East Huron Street, Chicago, IL 60611. The toll free number is 1-800-545-2433.

Evaluation

Evaluation, the final step of the PR process, attempts to find out whether the communications program has met its stated objectives. Evaluation of a PR campaign might include clips of newspaper coverage, use of evaluation forms at programs, or surveys in the library to determine how users found out about various services. It is always difficult to prove a direct cause-and-effect relationship between a communications program and increased library usage, but an attempt should be made to measure the impact of the PR investment. Moreover, the library should constantly have its thumb on the pulse of the public opinion.

Evaluation brings the process full circle, or back to research. Consistent efforts to find out what people want will help your library become and stay essential—mainstream, not marginal.

What Is the Trustee's Role in Public Relations?

In addition to making sure that the library has a planned and effective PR program with a budget and written goals, trustees must be activists. Brooke Astor gave up her other board commitments to give her full energy to the New York Public Library. She gets instant recognition and identification with the New York Public Library.

Use your clout. If you've been appointed or elected to a library board, you have power and you know lots of people who have the potential for instant recognition and identification with the library. People should think LIBRARY whenever they see you. You should be an articulate spokesperson and have one or two quotes in mind—brief and well-turned phrases that express your thoughts and concerns about the library.

You should support the public relations program of the library, and have regularly scheduled reports on the board agenda. If your budget cannot support a PR staff member or your library staff is too small and overburdened to take on these duties, explore community resources. Is a local advertising agency willing to do work as a public service? What about cooperation from the nearby college or university?

Trustees must also be willing to take a chance. The biggest risk in launching any kind of outreach, marketing, or public relations program is that you'll promise more than the already overworked library staff can deliver. On the other hand, can you afford to wait passively for people to discover that your public library is the perfect institution and deserves their support?

Resources

Training Programs

An ALA preconference, "Speaking Up and Speaking Out," is held annually in June before the Annual Conference, in the conference city.

A National Library Week workshop is offered each year at the ALA Midwinter Meeting.

ALA's Public Information Office holds a PR Assembly during the midwinter and annual conference, usually on Sunday morning at 9:30 a.m.

Publications

American Library Association. *ALA Media Training Guide* is packed with tips and briefing materials. Sections include "How to Get Speaking Opportunities," "Speaking Successfully" and "Quotable Quotes." The publication also includes sample speeches, press materials, and fact sheets on topics of special concern. Order from the *ALA Graphics Catalog*.

American Library Association. *Library Advocacy Now! Action Pack.* Order from the *ALA Graphics Catalog*.

Lubow, Arthur. "The Studio 54 of Culture." *Vanity Fair*, May 1986, 110–14, 133.

Reed, Sally Gardner. *Save Your Library: A Guide to Getting, Using and Keeping the Power You Need.* Jefferson, N.C.: McFarland and Co., 1992.

Roberts, Anne F. *Public Relations for Librarians.* Englewood, Colo.: Libraries Unlimited, 1989.

Walters, Suzanne. *Marketing: A How-to-Do-It manual for Librarians.* New York: Neal-Schuman Publishers, 1992.

Videos

Controlling the Confrontation, 1989. Renowned media coach Arch Lustberg presents techniques for diffusing confrontations and delivering convincing messages. Includes discussion guide (44 minutes). Cost: $99. Order from the ALA Video/Library Video Network, 1-800-441-TAPE.

Library Stories, 1993. Produced by the New York Library Association, this inspirational video presents a vignettes of real-life library users telling how the library made a difference in their lives (14 minutes). Cost: $15 (plus $2 shipping). Order from NYLA Publications, 252 Hudson Ave., Albany, NY 12210-1802.

Promotional Materials

Posters, T-shirts, pens, and other promotional items with messages such as "Libraries Are Worth It!" and "Libraries Change Lives" can be ordered from the ALA Graphics Catalog. For a free catalog, call 1-800-545-2433, ext. 5046.

22 The Trustee and Intellectual Freedom

Judith F. Krug
Anne E. Penway

he fundamental mission of the public library is to make ideas and information that represent the full spectrum of human thought and experience available and accessible to all who want or need them. In the United States, publicly supported libraries function within a body of law interpreting and applying the First Amendment right to free speech—which includes the corollary right to receive expression. This right is recognized as essential to the survival of a free society. We expect our citizens to be self governors. To do so responsibly, they must have access to information from various points of view so that they can make informed decisions. A free society recognizes the value of imagination, the arts, and intellectual debate—offering to all the basic human right of freedom of thought, conscience, and expression.

The American Library Association and the Freedom to Read Foundation support the rights of libraries to collect and make available any work that may legally be acquired, and the rights of library users to have access to those materials. But it is the library trustee to whom falls the primary responsibility to ensure the protection of these fundamental rights—through well-crafted policy and clear communication with the community served. More than anything else, it is the trustee's commitment to intellectual freedom, reflected in the policies established and

Judith F. Krug is director of the American Library Association Office for Intellectual Freedom.

Anne E. Penway is assistant director of the American Library Association Office for Intellectual Freedom.

the support provided for implementation of those policies, that allows intellectual freedom to flourish in libraries. Protecting intellectual freedom is the trustee's highest duty and, in publicly supported institutions, a legal duty as well. The Constitution and Bill of Rights impose special responsibilities on trustees, including the responsibility to ensure that the collection is unbiased and free of viewpoint-based discrimination, and that rules governing access to the collection are applied fairly and without discrimination regarding types of users.

The Board's Responsibility: Book Selection and Reconsideration Policy

Foremost among the policies trustees must establish is the one governing materials selection. Incorporating the basic principles set forth in the *Library Bill of Rights* and the *Freedom to Read Statement* (see Appendixes 3 and 4), the policy will be based on the goals and objectives of the library. It should clearly delineate that the basic goal of the library is service to all members of the community and that the intent of the library is to circulate all legally protected materials which patrons need or want, regardless of viewpoint, even though officials or private persons may disapprove.

In setting policy, trustees must recognize that communities are made up of people of varied backgrounds, interests, religions, ethnic groups, and educational levels. The policy statement should take cognizance of these differences.

In any community the residents are going to hold conflicting and/or unformed opinions. The policy statement should make provision for the acquisition of materials reflecting those conflicting opinions and for the presentation of a diversity of points of view so that the reading public will have a chance to reach its own conclusions, even if those conclusions are not the ones held by the librarians or by the trustees. Internal censorship, whether it arises from the biases of the librarian or from the fear of public outcry, is as dangerous to intellectual freedom as external censorship by well-meaning citizens.

Problem areas—materials dealing with sex, for example—will become in some communities a main target for censorship. The selection policy must address such areas. For instance, the policy might contain a statement that says the library will include in its collection a broad range of materials on controversial issues of current concern. Here again, the policy should adhere to the principles of intellectual freedom. Neither the taste of the librarian nor that of the trustee should determine the basis for selection.

In conjunction with the selection policy, a second statement should be developed and adopted which delineates the proper procedure for handling complaints about specific materials within the collection. Such a procedure would obviate the harm that could result from an off-the-cuff defense of the materials or a heated argument with the complainant.

Although the policy for book selection will be formulated by the library staff in consultation with the trustees, the board of trustees must adopt it as basic operating policy. Furthermore, the daily work of selection is an administrative function and, as such, is one of the duties and responsibilities of the librarian and the professional staff, operating within the guidelines established by the selection policy. But remember that any book or library materials so selected will be held to be selected by the board.

The Board Must Support the Librarian

Once the trustees have chosen a librarian and approved the book selection policy to be followed, the board must be prepared to follow through and accept responsibility, along with the librarian, for the contents of the collection. The board must make it clear, both to the librarian and to the public, that books selected by the librarian are considered to have been selected by the board.

The selection policy should be set firmly and clearly long before the board encounters its first would-be censor. The librarian and trustees should know the arguments before they are presented. They also should know the answers. Faced with a self-assured librarian who has full backing from the board, most would-be censors will desist. A few determined ones will want to place the matter before the board itself. Here again, trustees who have a written policy to which to refer and arguments to back that policy may be able to reason with the critic. More important, however, good policy and arguments based on the public's right to read will persuade heretofore silent supporters of the library to come forward in a crisis and defeat the censors.

Freedom to Read Is the Public's Right

In broad definition, censorship is simply the suppression of ideas and information that certain persons, whether as individuals, groups, or in official capacities, find objectionable or dangerous. It is scarcely more complex than someone saying, "No, you cannot print that information, buy or read that magazine or book, or see that film—because I object to it!"

Censorship pressures historically have been brought to bear on works considered heretical, seditious, or obscene. At various times through the ages, each of these reasons has had its day. But there are reasons other than the traditional ones of religion, politics, and sex that cause censorship attacks on materials. During the 1970s, for example, civil rights and women's groups attacked alleged racism and sexism in library materials, particularly those for children. On the list of contested books was the (still frequently challenged) *Adventures of Huckleberry Finn*, for lowering black children's self-esteem, and *Little Women*, for its narrow portrayal of lifestyles for women. In the 80s the focus shifted to challenges revolving around materials believed to undermine or challenge "family values" or fundamentalist religious views. And, in the 90s, the censors have become obsessed with materials they perceive as condoning or informing about witchcraft, Satanism, or the occult, and any materials providing information about homosexuality.

In the final analysis, it is the trustee who stands between the library and those individuals and groups who believe they have been misrepresented in literature or who believe that the ideas contained in certain works are blasphemous, immoral, anti-American, or simply dangerous to their values and principles. The solution to offensive speech is more speech. Library users who perceive dangers in materials should be persuaded of the value of information about those dangers and encouraged to recognize that censorship is not a cure for social ills.

Library policies stand as evidence that the trustees have taken their responsibilities seriously, and that tax monies are being used in support of the library's public mission. Policies also attest to the trustee's leadership. It is only through well-drawn policies and procedures that trustees can achieve a greater public understanding of the role of the library in our society, and, in this way, secure for future generations the basic freedoms promised in the First Amendment to the United States Constitution.

Further Reading

Burress, Lee. *Battle of the Books: Literacy Censorship in the Public Schools, 1950 to 1985*. Metuchen, N.J.: Scarecrow, 1989. (Compiled results and commentary of many studies of school censorship conducted by Professor Lee Burress of the University of Wisconsin.)

Clarkson, Frederick and Skipp Porteous. *Challenging the Christian Right: The Activist's Handbook*, 2d ed. Great Barrington, Mass.:

Institute for First Amendment Studies, 1993. (A handbook of information arranged in a three-ring binder on right-of-center pressure groups and their tactics.)

Cornog, Martha, ed. *Libraries, Erotica, and Pornography*. Phoenix, Ariz.: Oryx, 1991. (A collection of essays on libraries and sexually oriented material. Winner, 1992 Eli M. Oboler Memorial Award.)

Culture Watch. Oakland: Data Center. (A monthly annotated bibliography on culture, art, and political affairs.)

Del Fattore, Joan. *What Johnny Shouldn't Read*. New Haven, Conn.: Yale Univ. Pr., 1992. (A report on textbook censorship cases and their residual effects on publishers and education—winner of 1994 Eli M. Oboler Memorial Award.)

Demac, Donna. *Liberty Denied: The Current Rise of Censorship in America*. 2d ed. New Brunswick, N.J.: Rutgers Univ. Pr., 1992. (A revised and expanded version of a 1988 work on trends in censorship.)

Green, Jonathan. *The Encyclopedia of Censorship*. New York: Facts on File, 1990. (An annotated reference on censorship throughout the ages.)

Heins, Marjorie. *Sex, Sin and Blasphemy: A Guide to America's Censorship Wars*. ACLU Arts Censorship Project, 1993. (A handbook on controversies involving the visual arts.)

Hentoff, Nat. *Free Speech for Me but Not for Thee: How the American Left and Right Relentlessly Censor Each Other*. New York: Harper Collins, 1993. (A study of how both sides of the political spectrum pay lip service to freedom of speech, but often support censorship of ideas with which they disagree.)

Intellectual Freedom Manual. 4th ed., Chicago: ALA, 1992. (Basic reference outlining the history and meaning of ALA intellectual freedom policies, including the Library Bill of Rights and interpretations. Essential reading.)

Marsh, Dave. *50 Ways to Fight Censorship*. New York: Thunders Mouth Press, 1991. (A guide and reference to fighting censorship, including addresses and phone numbers of anticensorship organizations and practical advice for activism.)

Newsletter on Intellectual Freedom. Chicago: Intellectual Freedom Committee, American Library Association. (A bimonthly newsletter reporting on current censorship incidents nationwide. Essential reading.)

Noble, William. *Book Banning in America: Who Bans Books and Why*. Middlebury, Vt.: Paul S. Eriksson, 1990. (An examination of current censorship trends.)

Pally, Marcia. *Sex & Sensibility: Reflections on Forbidden Mirrors and the Will to Censor*. New York: Ecco Pr., 1994. (Meditations on freedom of sexual expression and common arguments against it, including the antipornography feminist position that pictures of sex are harmful.)

Reichman, Henry. *Censorship and Selection: Issues and Answers for Schools*. 2d ed. Chicago: ALA, 1993. (An essential reference for school library media specialists and school board members on the special concerns of the school setting, and the censorship controversies which most frequently arise there.)

23 Trustees and Friends: A Natural Partnership

Sandy Dolnick

riends of the Library are by definition also Friends of the Trustees of the library—at least in the best of all possible worlds. Here you have both ends of a spectrum of support from the community, one a legal entity and one a volunteer organization, and both committed to making their library the very best institution they can.

Definition of Friends

The Friends of the Library represent the entire community and can be heterogeneous or homogeneous. They possess many talents because of their varied backgrounds, and can use their contacts in the community and a great deal of ingenuity to help the library. Many retired persons, as well as young professionals, are replacing the stereotypical club-women who once represented the entire membership of these groups. It is certainly to the benefit of the library to encourage all members of a community to become their Friends, and the trustees should be among the first to join. If a trustee isn't a Friend, who is?

Trustees can continue active work for the library in a Friends organization after their terms have expired. Moreover, prospective trustees emerge in a Friends group.

By volunteering their time, the Friends show the rest of the commu-

Sandy Dolnick is executive director, Friends of Libraries U.S.A.

nity that the library is an asset in their eyes, raising the library profile. Since they have a nonvested interest in what they are doing, their voice is clearly heard when the time comes to speak up to the county, city, and village officials. As Friends become more involved, they can't help but learn more about the actual workings of the library, and, in effect, can become "trustees in training." While there is certainly a difference in orientation between Friends and trustees, their roles can sometimes be reversed to energize their respective boards by injecting new ideas.

Friends originated in the early medieval libraries in cathedrals and universities as patrons who donated special collections to help in the development of those institutions. They gradually became institutionalized in the United States, with their greatest growth occurring in the 1950s because of the building of so many public libraries and their improvements with Library Services Construction Act (LSCA) funds. The 1980s have furthered their development because of several factors: the 1979 White House Conference; the effect of Proposition 13 (on property tax) in California, and the effect it had in the rest of the country; the general slowing down of the economy in the 1980s; and the involvement and development of Friends of the Libraries U.S.A. as a catalyst.

What is most interesting is that Friends of Libraries are not only a presence on the public library scene, but also in academic and special libraries. Every type of library—medical, legal, military, church, synagogue, architectural, private—has its own particular users, and these make up the nucleus of their group. In some cases, they can all participate together in a community celebration that highlights its library worlds.

Friends Are Assets to Trustees

Friends can make life much easier for trustees if they are seen as a means of outreach to the community. If communication is good between the two groups, trustees will find that Friends help in these areas as well:

1. Their most natural role is to disseminate their information about, and enthusiasm for, the library to the community.
2. They are barometers of public opinion and will be among the first to hear public reaction to events and policies concerning the library. It is important that the trustees have a line of communication set up so that they are aware of this.
3. Friends can support the policies of the board of trustees, and can play a major role in explaining and integrating a policy; however, they must be informed to do so.

4. Friends can also aid in organizing complementary activities to a new policy.
5. Supplementary funds raised by Friends are the most recognized form of support of the library.
6. Friends serve as a gadfly to move trustees to action, mirroring the community feeling.
7. Lack of tenure and their nonvested interest give Friends the ability to move quickly in a crisis, bypassing much red tape.

Types of Friends Activities

Friends activities fall under four headings, although each library may decide on a different emphasis. Few groups can maintain high activity levels in all areas as a general routine, and the profile changes as different needs arise.

Volunteers are, of course, the essence of Friends. The volunteer board calls on further volunteers to help at various events; community-minded citizens volunteer their help by supplying in-kind donations. Volunteers can supply as much or as little help in the library as is desired by the librarian, from helping at a children's story hour to helping at the check-out desk. Other tasks could include assistance with programs, displays, refreshments, reading shelves, clipping newspapers, genealogy research, and so forth. There is nothing that a volunteer can't do if properly trained and motivated.

Advocacy is one of the most significant ways that Friends aid their library. Just by being Friends they are announcing that they are advocates. With the judicious use of their numbers, Friends can influence budgets in favor of the library, not only on a local level but at state and national levels as well. While this influence can be a decisive factor in a crisis atmosphere, it can also be wielded annually with council members entertained at the library by their constituents who will later appear at the budget hearings to speak up for the library.

Fundraising is usually the primary function of the Friends, although the extent of such activity depends upon the community and the zeal of the group. Here imagination knows no limits: book sales raised to state-of-the-art affairs, auctions, movie previews, quilts and other handicrafts, calendars, hand-dipped strawberries, jellies, pies for Thanksgiving, book dedications—the list is endless. And not to be forgotten are the mammoth capital fundraising campaigns that galvanize the entire population.

Public relations are central to the Friends, and can best be viewed through the programs they present to the community. These programs display the various faces of the library, and in so doing encourage diverse groups of the population to become familiar with some aspect of the library service program. The Friends' publications, their membership brochure, their signs, and so on are all signals to the greater community that the Friends are a vital organization.

Friends and Trustee Conflicts

Ideally, there would be no conflict, but it is only realistic to recognize that where there are two highly motivated groups, both intent on doing the best they can, there may be some turf wars and some bruised feelings if there is not adequate communication and planning. Generally, the attitude should be that the trustees set the policy, the librarian carries it out, and the Friends support it. However, since humans are fallible, there will be some overlapping, usually meant in the very best spirit. If goals and objectives are clearly stated and routinely reviewed, these conflicts should be kept at a minimum. It should be noted, however, that disagreement can be healthy for the institution, if handled in such a way that some positive accord is reached.

Conflict can arise also between the staff and the Friends. For volunteers to enjoy their jobs and be productive, it is crucial for the staff to appreciate their efforts and to not feel threatened by their presence. Some prudent preparation before the volunteer begins work can usually help the staff. The volunteer also should go through an orientation of some kind to understand how his or her work fits into the program as a whole. More information on this subject can be found in the *Friends of Libraries Sourcebook*, published by ALA.

Organizing A Group

When a board of trustees or a librarian decides to organize a group, it should not be a spur-of-the-moment decision. There will be work involved and a time commitment. Choosing the right people to do the job can make all of the difference. It is also helpful to know that it is not necessary to reinvent the wheel when starting the effort. There is a great deal of help available. Most states now have a state Friends of the Library, and Friends of Libraries U.S.A. has produced a great deal of material for this very purpose, including several videotapes and many fact sheets, as well as a quarterly publication crammed with ideas used by groups of all sizes all over the United States. These, as well as many programs, provide a network with access for even the smallest groups at a minimum of expense.

The success of Friends of Libraries U.S.A. attests to the positive results of good Friends. Any library can benefit from this enthusiasm by developing the natural partnership between Friends and trustees.

States with Statewide Friends of the Library Groups

Alabama, Arizona, Arkansas, California, Colorado, Connecticut, District of Columbia, Florida, Georgia, Hawaii, Illinois, Indiana, Iowa, Kansas, Kentucky, Louisiana, Maine, Maryland, Massachusetts, Michigan, Minnesota, Mississippi, Nevada, New Hampshire, New Jersey, New Mexico, New York, North Carolina, Ohio, Oklahoma, Oregon, Pennsylvania, Rhode Island, South Carolina, Tennessee, Texas, Utah, Virginia, West Virginia, and Wisconsin.

For up-to-date information, contact Friends of Libraries U.S.A. FOLUSA, 1700 Walnut St., Suite 715, Philadelphia, Penna. 19103 (215-790-1674).

Further Reading

Dolnick, Sandy, ed. *Friends of Libraries Sourcebook*. 2d ed. Chicago: ALA, 1990.

Friends of Libraries U.S.A. News Update. Chicago: American Library Association, published quarterly with membership.

Information Kit, Friends of California Libraries. Sacramento, Calif.: Friends of California Libraries, 717 K. Street, Suite 300, 1990.

Sherman, Betty. *Operations Guide*, 4th ed. Friends of San Diego Public Library, San Diego, 1994.

Thompson, Charmain. *Winning Friends: A Handbook for Friends of the Library*. Jackson, Miss.: Friends of Mississippi Libraries, 1992.

Videos

Making Friends: Organizing Your Library's Friends Group. The Wilson Video Resource Collection, Bronx, N.Y.: Wilson, 1987.

Friends in Action. The Wilson Video Resource Collection, Bronx, N.Y.: Wilson, 1991.

Other materials available in the Friends of Libraries U.S.A.'s new member kits include *Friends Make a Difference*, success stories about various types of activities; fact sheets on a large number of areas of interest; sample copies of a constitution and bylaws; and the latest copy of the *News Update*. For a membership brochure write FOLUSA c/o ALA; 50 East Huron Street, Chicago, Ill. 60611.

24 Volunteers in the Library

Linda Bennett Wells

These Americans are a peculiar people. If in a local community a citizen becomes aware of a human need which is not being met, he thereupon discusses the situation with his neighbors. Suddenly a committee comes into existence. This committee thereupon begins to operate on behalf of the need. And, *mirabile visu*, a new community function is established. In the meantime, these citizens have performed this act without a single reference to a bureaucracy or to any official agency.

—Alexis de Tocqueville

n 1840 Alexis de Tocqueville identified what he felt was a unique characteristic of the American people: a willingness to work for something they believed in with no thought of monetary reward or of having someone else do it for them.

According to *The Dictionary of American History*, the library movement in America began with the establishment of the Harvard College Library, composed of three hundred volumes, a gift of the estate of the Reverend John Harvard. The Reverend Thomas Bray introduced parochial libraries in 1696, and by 1699 he had begun twenty colonial libraries. Although these libraries were designed for ministers only, they did serve as public libraries. Other volunteer-based libraries sprang up. It was not until 1833 that the first free public library, supported by public funds, was founded in New Hampshire.

From the 1870s on, a national network of volunteers was formed

Linda Bennett Wells is Library Services Manager (Public Service), Lewisville Public Library, Lewisville, Texas.

through the efforts of women's clubs across the country. In the early 1920s the Junior League was organized. Establishment and support of public libraries were prime interests of this and other women's groups.

During the 1940s and 1950s, the use of volunteers in libraries was actively discouraged by the profession, as librarians sought to clarify their own positions in the field. The attitude toward volunteers varied greatly depending on the community and its size and resources. In many small towns libraries had no professionally trained librarians and relied heavily on volunteers. By the 1960s a volunteer movement in school libraries was evident. But not until 1971 was approval of the use of library volunteers given by the American Library Association in its publication "Guidelines for Using Volunteers in Libraries." Volunteers were said to provide a "new outlook, a different concept."

Guiding Principles

Certain principles seems useful today in considering the use of volunteers in libraries.

Principle 1: *Every Library Can Benefit from Working with Volunteers*

The small one-person library, the large urban library system with a multitude of branches, and the specialized library—each can benefit from the time and experience of nonpaid staff. Volunteers bring with them a wealth of knowledge in special areas, as well as attitudes and ways of thinking which can widen the scope of any library. In addition, they have the time to give.

A combination of methods for locating good volunteers will insure the best results. Some libraries, such as the Fort Worth (Texas) Public Library, develop formal job descriptions and actively advertise for volunteers to fill certain needs. This is an excellent method for finding those people who can provide specific services. Other libraries call for volunteers in general, interviewing the respondents to see how they might help or what they have to offer in the way of new services.

In either case, the goal is the same: to find and to utilize skills and abilities that can enhance the services of the library. No matter how complete the staff, or how excellent, it can still benefit from association and help from others. Much of the rise in use and prestige of volunteers can be credited to library trustees, themselves volunteers and not infrequently responsible for the creation of the local library. Friends of the Library is also a volunteer group, and though often thought of as only fundraisers, Friends in many instances have initiated and may run a volunteer program.

Principle 2: *Not Every Library Ought to Use Volunteers*

In spite of the fact that every library can benefit from working with volunteers, not all libraries should have a volunteer program. There are many factors that will affect a decision on beginning a volunteer program, not the least of which is whether the board and director want one. A long list of excellent reasons for using volunteers may be entirely valid, but they may not strike a response in a particular situation. Volunteer programs are too complicated to be started by those who are not really interested or committed.

A lukewarm response on the part of the board and the director may be overcome if someone is available to act as volunteer coordinator and is really interested in the opportunity. Forcing the responsibility on someone, however, is apt to result in failure of the program, usually in the form of a long, slow death with participants becoming more and more disillusioned.

There are other factors that might preclude such a program, though most can be worked out. To be considered are insurance requirements, available space, training time on the part of the staff, political atmosphere, attitude of higher-ups such as governing authorities, and the availability of prospective volunteers. With a positive attitude and a little perspiration, most of these factors can be opportunities rather than problems.

Success in any volunteer program hinges on designing the program so that the needs of the library are met by volunteers who understand their roles and who also benefit from the association.

Principle 3: *Trustees Should Not Be Volunteers in the Library*

Since trustees hold an advisory, policymaking, or arbitration role, they will find it advantageous to keep themselves free of too close an association with the volunteers, just as they do with the paid staff.

If we assume that most volunteers will be used under the supervision of staff in ongoing tasks at the library, it is well to warn trustees not to interfere. However, there is room for volunteers assisting the library board in any events or programs it may sponsor, and a frequent volunteer job in smaller libraries is that of public relations, which must be related to the board as well as to the director. The board should know what tasks are assigned to volunteers, what controls are exercised, and what results are obtained.

The same rules should apply to the volunteer/trustee relationship as apply to the staff and trustee relationship. That is, any problems should go through channels, and the trustee should not try to solve the volunteers' problems outside the framework of established policy. Trustees may become volunteers, preferably not simultaneously with board service. One hopes that the experiences of one role will strengthen the individual's understanding and effectiveness when and if he or she assumes the other.

Principle 4: *Volunteer Programs Should Be Based on Written Policy*

Just as trustees work to provide a written framework for library services, so should they address the issue of volunteerism. The statement of goals and objectives may include mention of the program, or may merely state those goals toward which the library is working, whether or not they include the efforts of volunteers.

Any benefit package provided for volunteers should be clearly defined in writing. Most volunteer programs provide reimbursement for expenses incurred on behalf of the library (delivering books to the homebound, for example), and some pay transportation expenses in getting to and from the library.

Library policy and the volunteer plan should include job descriptions even if they are as general as: "Volunteers will work under the supervision of staff members in tasks assigned and fully described." Also included should be some statement about releasing a volunteer who is not reliable or who violates the library's standard for conduct and relations with the public. Using volunteers entails training them so that their supervision on a day-to-day basis does not burden the staff or cause extra work to correct mistakes.

All volunteers should receive an orientation which includes information about the library and its mission and services, rules, and regulations, including confidentiality (if there is a state law pertaining to confidentiality, this should be communicated); procedures for registering questions and comments; what to expect in the way of supervision and the details of any jobs assigned. Volunteers will grow in knowledge and skills, and their willingness to advance to more complex jobs should be noted and used.

Written policies and procedures, approved by the board, are essential so that harmony between volunteers and staff can be maintained. Volunteers need to know that they are auxiliary to the operation of the library, yet a kind of unpaid staff helping to make the library more effective and efficient.

Principle 5: *Volunteers Have a Right to Feel Good*

The one thing every volunteer should expect is to feel good about his or her involvement. Realistically, there will always be some who will not receive this benefit, but the library staff and board should constantly be aware of the volunteer's welfare. People volunteer for many reasons: out of altruism, for personal reasons, for enhancement of skills as a prelude to employment, and so on. The reason should not matter, except in seeing that the volunteers get what they want from the time spent. If volunteers feel that they are accomplishing personal goals, they are likely to be fulfilled and satisfied with themselves and with the library.

Although the needs of the volunteer do not supersede the needs of the library, every effort should be made to see that the volunteer has a feeling of accomplishment and appreciation. While trustees will not wish to interact on a regular basis, some kind of recognition from the board, such as a ceremony, reception, or certificate, would be appropriate.

Principle 6: *Differences between Staff and Volunteers Must Be Clear*

It is easy for volunteers to be critical of staff performance if the volunteers do not understand the job of staff and the perks which may be attached. In reverse, granting unusual perks to volunteers may disturb the staff. Avoiding the us-against-them-syndrome is a matter of quality training of both volunteers and staff.

General rules followed by the library should not be waived or bent for volunteers except by specific job descriptions. A frequent headache is the matter of punctuality. Staff may resent the shorter hours donated by volunteers, or volunteers may not accept staff direction when they feel unprepared or reluctant to perform a task. Clarity of assignment is a must.

Some volunteers do not accept staff authority. A chain of command, including how to lodge a complaint, is essential. Volunteers should expect to meet normal requirements for such activities as record keeping, handling of money, and taking of messages, and following library rules on the borrowing of materials.

Principle 7: *Almost Everyone Has Something to Offer*

Those libraries which utilize only volunteers whose skills fit preset job descriptions succeed in doing two things: they keep the inconvenience of volunteer programs to a minimum, insuring maximum time/cost benefit, and they forsake a myriad of possibilities that could happen when an unsought-for volunteer walks in. This is nowhere more evident than in the areas of special talents—music and art, for example—or specific knowledge. Imagine the benefit when a specialist such as a marine biologist volunteers a special knowledge that could help answer difficult cataloging questions. He or she might also conduct story hours, plan adult programming, or provide contacts who could. Other specialists could advise in acquisitions, provide materials for displays, suggest addresses for free mailing lists, and be included in the information referral file.

Some volunteers may have personal problems that limit their usefulness at a given time. Those going through a great deal of stress and having trouble handling it, those without transportation, and those with very limited availability may not be the best volunteers. Screening is necessary and will help the library avoid unproductive relationships.

Principle 8: *Every Volunteer Program Needs a Coordinator*

Volunteer programs must have a coordinator. In very large or active systems, this may be a staff member hired for that purpose. More commonly, it will be a staff member who is assigned the role. Less often, it will be a volunteer position.

No matter how widely spread the system, a program must have a basic homogeneity. There will be some systemwide standards or expectations. Beyond that there is much room for individuality, which is desirable. The volunteer coordinator's role is to establish the framework of the program, to assure that it is put into place and maintained, to develop skills in those working within the structure, and to handle problems as they arise. This can require varying amounts of time, depending upon the size of the system and the intricacy of the program. What is necessary is a coordinator who wishes to see the program succeed. Assigning an unwilling person to the task is the kiss of death to the program. No matter how faithfully the steps are carried out, a negative attitude will show through the most assiduous attention to duty.

The use of a volunteer as coordinator can be highly successful. Increasingly, there are available retired persons with administrative skills, time, and energy who can bring professionalism to the role of coordinator. When searching for such a person, the library should set job standards just as though the position were to be a paid one. Hospitals, social service agencies, educational institutions, library associations, and professional groups often use volunteers to coordinate a volunteer program. The experienced person who takes on this job probably has work experiences that fit comfortably into the structure of the staff.

Principle 9: *Volunteers and Volunteer Programs Should Be Evaluated*

Just as trustees, directors, and staff should be evaluated, so should volunteers and volunteer programs be evaluated. The best method is a combination of an ongoing assessment and a formal assessment. The evaluation will best serve as a tool of communication, one utilized by the coordinator and the volunteer.

It is important that the volunteer's immediate supervisor do the personal evaluation, since this will provide the most realistic basis for comment. Records should be maintained, and the coordinator should use them as a portion of the evaluation for the program as a whole.

Any evaluation requires understanding what is expected and should include forms designed for unbiased assessment. It is not enough to jot down personal opinion. Ratings should be given to all the factors affecting the performance of the volunteer, from attitudes through zip. Evaluators should be careful to decide well in advance what constitutes good performance and to include evaluation of the quality of supervision. Volunteers will appreciate knowing how they are doing, but will not expect an indepth, intense evaluation.

Principle 10: *Volunteers Are an Excellent Source of Good Public Relations*

A major function of the library board and its trustees is building good relations with the community, and a good volunteer program contributes. Volunteers performing satisfying work at the library can be a conduit to the community. However, if the volunteer experience is unsatisfactory, comments heard in the community can be negative. In a way, volunteers performing regularly in the library are a good sample of public opinion. They see the problems, note improvements, catch the spirit—all depending on the nature of their experiences.

In addition to word-of-mouth, volunteers are perfect for all the time-consuming little jobs of good public relations: writing news stories (under supervision), doing displays, artwork, making contacts to place information in bank statements, on grocery bags, and so forth, sending notices to church bulletins, taking flyers to places of distribution, setting up displays outside the library, giving book talks—the list is endless, and all these activities are among the first to go when staff time gets tight.

Principle 11: *As Society Changes so Do Opportunities for Attracting Volunteers*

Do you feel that attracting volunteers is too difficult because everyone is working now? Being aware of shifting political and social climates will enable the sharp librarian to create new opportunities. When the job market is down and when layoffs are rampant, many people are free to volunteer who are well trained and who could not have offered their services while they worked.

Problems with overcrowded jails can result in a plethora of minor offenders with sentences of community service. Libraries across the country are benefiting from these volunteers. Each one has a specific amount of time to serve, and each comes with some level of competency, often very high. To benefit, libraries will wish to contact the probation office nearest them to indicate interest and to investigate possibilities. One of the most basic questions to ask is, "What safeguards can you offer that someone dangerous to staff or patrons will not be assigned here?"

If these volunteers do not perform satisfactorily, they will be transferred by the probation office to another, more suitable agency, or their community service will be forfeited. If the library is dissatisfied for any reason it is very easy to dismiss the volunteer.

Conclusion

Every library needs to consider beginning a volunteer program. Some will actively plan for one, others not. Even the latter, however, will wish to say, "Not now," instead of "Never." Situations and people and needs change. Keeping all the possibilities active will assure the most effective library service possible.

Trustees considering the establishment of a volunteer program will wish to determine the need, speculate on the value of the program, develop policy, be sure that director and staff (even if not enthusiastic) will make the program work, assist in the recruitment of volunteers through trustees' connections in the community, insist on a plan for the program, build in evaluation, and provide for a reward system for the volunteers.

Remember, however, that though many volunteers bring capabilities that could fill paid jobs, they should not be used in this way. Libraries advance only when it is clear to the public that they require support and the ability to operate a professional service. Libraries need to insist on having adequate paid staff to which can be added the work of volunteers.

Further Reading

Bennett, Linda Leveque. *Volunteers in the School Media Center*. Englewood, Colo.: Libraries Unlimited, 1984.

Chadbourne, R. "Volunteers in the Library: Both Sides Must Give in Order to Get." *Wilson Library Bulletin* 67 (June 1993): 26–27.

Clarke, S. A. "A Strategy for Happy Endings." *Book Report* 11 (Nov./Dec. 1992): 14–15+.

Hedges, C., and S. Span. "Good Volunteer Management Helps Make the Difference." *Ohio Libraries* 4 (July/Aug. 1991): 20.

McCune, B. F. "The New Volunteerism: Making It Pay Off for Your Library." *American Libraries* 24 (Oct. 1993): 822–24.

Morris, B. J. "Organizing Volunteers." *Book Report 11* (Nov./Dec. 1992): 17.

Peterson, B. M. "Towards the Year 2000—Recruiting Volunteers for Today." *Colorado Libraries* 17 (June 1991): 5–6.

Smith, M. A. "Volunteerism." *Colorado Libraries* 17 (June 1991): 4–22.

Wakefield, B. J. "Court-ordered Volunteers." *Colorado Libraries* 7 (June 1991): 18.

25 Trustee Activities at the State, Regional, and National Levels

Virginia M. McCurdy

A revolution is occurring in the technology available for the communication of messages. The end of the twentieth century will surely be known as an era of information. In this environment of expanding technology, there is much debate on the question of the written word versus electronic delivery of information and how libraries can and should function in these changing times. There is no question, however, that libraries and library trustees are, and must continue to be, a vital part of society. President George Bush at the 1991 White House Conference said: "Our ability to stay ahead depends, in large part, on our ability to stay informed." As information becomes our country's most important resource and we move from printed to graphic and imagery forms of information, we must develop standards to control, use, exchange, and preserve these records. The opportunities for application are endless, and so are the issues yet to be resolved. Issues such as universal access, message control, cost, information overload, privacy, fairness, and effectiveness will continue to be debated as information technology develops in advance of the debate. Libraries are the very institutions to address these issues—both with trained professionals who have special education in technological policy applications, and as the last resort for people without resources or access to electronic aids. Libraries will also be vital for those segments of our population who are not quite ready for, or find no appeal in, cyberspace.

Virginia M. McCurdy is the chair of the DeKalb County Public Library System Board of Trustees, DeKalb County, Georgia, and the second vice president of the American Library Trustee Association.

To make sure that libraries are successful in meeting the needs of the people in the communities that they serve and across the nation as a whole, trustees must be hardworking, involved, and not afraid to get involved in the political arena. They must insure that information is available to all who need it while respecting and promoting the rights of free enterprise and the commercial information marketplace. Libraries must purposefully promote a proactive image of themselves to the communities that they serve if they are to sustain the public support and political clout they will need to survive and prosper as the nation makes its shift to an information economy. Trustees are in the unique position of being able to accomplish the goal for libraries, not only in their local communities but also on the state, regional and national level.

Most trustees of public libraries have a set of values based on the premise that libraries can make a positive difference in their communities. These values propel trustee actions, and the creating, articulating, and promoting of these values become the trustees' responsibility as library leaders. Proactive trustees reinforce the values of libraries by setting an example of the behavior they expect from others by spreading the word, publicly reinforcing, and measuring the performance of those acting on behalf of their institutions. As advocates for libraries, the trustees have the job to see that libraries deliver services, and that the public understands and appreciates those services.

Factors

Trustees are fortunate to have choices regarding the level of involvement they wish as they carry out their duties. Many choose to confine that involvement to the local level, while others seek to broaden their activities to the state, regional, and national levels. However, many trustees are unable to take part in activities outside their local community due to financial resources. It would be ideal if local libraries could pay travel and memberships, allowing their trustees to be active on state, regional, and national levels. Even though few libraries can do this for the entire board, a number of libraries pay the dues of their trustees in the state organization and at least one trustee's membership in the American Library Trustee Association. As trustee boards and library directors become more aware of having active and involved trustees on all levels, trustee boards will be more likely to fight for a reasonable share of available funding to help finance additional opportunities for trustee involvement outside the local area.

State Library Agencies and State Library Organizations

State library agencies vary greatly in operation, budget, and staff, so there is no uniform role in relation to trustees. Nevertheless, most state agencies regard fostering the work of trustees as an important responsibility and include some funding for that work in their state plan for library development. State library associations are often able and willing to help finance trustees in state roles, or in national roles that will in turn benefit the state functions. Many state library agencies play prominent roles in supporting trustee programs and training. Often it is the state library agency which maintains any statewide trustee mailing lists and is responsible for most cooperative efforts. This sometimes consists of newsletters that include trustee news and legislative advocacy information.

Trustees flourish at the state level when a strong state agency and a vigorous state library association recognize that informed and motivated trustees are an essential part of the ongoing process. A stable and active state trustee organization is of great benefit to trustees. It allows them opportunities for continuing education and for improving library services alongside trustees from neighboring communities across the state. Most states have a trustee division of the state library association. This division is likely in charge of programming for annual conferences and/or workshops and in most states is involved with a statewide lobbying effort such as "Library Day at the State Capitol." There are exceptions and a few states have associations that are separate. New York has a strong state association of library boards, with a state office in Albany. New York State Association of Library Boards (NYSALB) works with the state library agency on workshops, publications, and education efforts. California is another state with a strong state association, the California Association of Library Trustees and Commissioners. This group is heavily involved with trustee training.

Regional Associations

A section for trustees can be self-sustaining where a strong regional association of states exists. Currently there are six such groups in the United States. These organizations can be very effective in promoting general library service and librarianship within geographic areas. For example, the trustees and Friends of the Library section of the Southeastern Library Association have a biennial meeting and program, often worked out in cooperation with the public librarians' section. Continuity of trustees at this level benefits from the encouragement of library directors who are, themselves, active in the association.

National Involvement

Trustees with an interest on the national level are welcome to become involved with several strong and viable organizations. The oldest and best known is the American Library Trustee Association. As American Library Trustee Association (ALTA) members, trustees add their voices to the American Library Association—more than fifty-five thousand strong—in speaking out for national library legislation, in defending First Amendment rights, and in advocating the highest quality and information services for the people of the United States. Membership also includes eligibility for ALA's group insurance plans and credit card programs as well as discounts on ALA conference fees. The professional staffs of ALTA and ALA are available for consultation on such matters as intellectual freedom challenges, public awareness, automation, and fundraising.

The American Library Trustee Association has several focus areas in which they provide both opportunities and services for trustees. Legislation is one of the most active areas. ALTA works closely with the other divisions of the American Library Association in promoting legislation in the interest of better library service and trustees through association. The Library Services and Construction Act, the act creating the National Commission on Libraries and Information Science, as well as the bills authorizing and funding the White House Conferences on Libraries—all of which are the results of joint efforts.

ALTA is dedicated to providing its membership with the proper tools with which to do its job. A large investment of time and funding is devoted to literature. ALTA finds or develops and then distributes the best available published information in the fields of library policy, personnel, buildings, programs, and evaluation from the trustee point of view. On occasion, members are offered special discounts from ALA Graphics orders. ALTA publishes the *Trustee Voice* (formerly *The ALTA Newsletter*) to keep members informed of activities and developments important to trustees. *American Libraries*, the monthly membership publication of ALA, provides an overview of news and developments in library and information services across the United States. Fact sheets and other publications offering practical information are also available.

As a tool and as part of the networking efforts of ALTA, the production and participation in the exchange of audiovisual aids supporting good trusteeship are encouraged. At annual conferences and occasionally in regional settings, lively presentations, debates, dramatizations, and workshops on topics relevant to trustees are presented. Many are later packaged for replication at state or regional levels. ALTA officers and Speakers Bureau members have expertise in many areas of current library activity. They will travel, speak, and conduct workshops aimed at meeting trustee needs.

Recognition is a valuable part of trustee activity. This includes the public recognition of those individuals, businesses, and organizations that have been helpful to trusteeship and libraries, and recognition of actual trustees who have given high levels of their time and expertise. The American Library Association recognizes the important contribution of library trustees and annually awards citations to two trustees who have performed outstanding service. In addition, the ALTA Awards Committee identifies and helps local communities in giving due public recognition to major benefactors of libraries.

Many trustees belong to ALTA but have never attended a conference or a workshop sponsored by this trustee organization. The more dynamic trustee boards have developed the custom of local boards paying association dues. The next step is to manage funding for attendance at meetings so that full membership advantage can be realized and so that all members have equal opportunities for serving on committees as officers.

A second organization offering national activities for trustees is the White House Conference on Library and Information Services Taskforce (WHCLIST). This organization was established by resolution at the 1979 White House Conference and readopted at the 1991 White House Conference process. It continues to monitor the carrying out of recommendations of the first two conferences and is helping to plan for the third WHC. Trustees, library professionals, and lay members committed to insuring the best possible library services to all people have testified at local, state, and national hearings in support of libraries and library legislation. Membership is open to those who through their membership wish to be active in the conference process. WHCLIST is led by a steering committee elected at its annual meeting. Various committees and regional representatives also play in important part in the process.

WHCLIST is dedicated to partnerships at all levels. Public and private partnerships at local, state, and national levels are greatly encouraged and expanded to enable all types of libraries and information providers to work together to support literacy, productivity, and economic development efforts. Gathering ideas from diverse people at the grassroots level and applying their concerns and proposals to formulating solutions on policy and program issues which face the nation is an area where trustees can and do have important roles.

The resolutions of the WHC plus each state conference have offered solutions to help meet some of the challenges faced by Americans. However, these resolutions are not going to be passed on merit alone. Trustees must make themselves heard and understood. WHCLIST and ALTA are two groups working to insure that all trustees are aware of these needs, these resolutions, and the steps necessary to see them passed into law and/or funded as needed.

A strong example of the impact of The White House Conference is the effort to see that the Congress enacts legislation creating and funding the National Research and Education Network (NREN) to serve as an information "superhighway," allowing educational institutions, including libraries, to capitalize on the advantages of technology for resource sharing and the creation and exchange of information. This effort is dedicated to remembering that data are useless, while information is valuable.

One of the greatest benefits of being a library trustee in this fast-paced world is working with many other groups to reach the solutions to our challenges. Illiteracy, complex information technologies, economic development, social diversity, and the nurturing of our nation's young people are all problems. Libraries can help to solve these problems. As libraries seriously plan, their future leaders, i.e., trustees, must tell the library story and develop close relationships with funding decision makers. Telling the library story can chart the overall direction of a library, but it must be done strategically for maximum benefit. If the stories do not reach the decision makers, there is no success. Therefore, trustees have the opportunity to define the vision, as well as how to reach the decision makers. Trustees generally hold or have held positions on boards serving a variety of community agencies and activities, giving them unique networking and advocacy skills in reaching the correct audiences.

Other Opportunities for Trustees

A few states have library Political Action Committees (PACs). With federal, state, and local governments in financial crisis, the impact of an additional component in the political process that decides library budgets and policy must be considered in the light of some impressive data. In Connecticut political candidates sought the endorsement of the PAC. Strong bipartisan support was evident. The immediate benefits from the efforts of the library PAC were in the application of increased and new information revealed from the PAC process. Many candidates volunteered current or previous library associations as evidence of their identification as a library supporter and there was heightened media attention to the political dimension of library supporters.

Urban Libraries Council (ULC), which represents urban public libraries throughout the country, was founded in 1971 by a group of library trustees. Most of the executive board still consists of library trustees, as required by its bylaws. Their primary agenda is advocacy at the national level for legislation which provides support for urban public libraries.

A number of states and regions are now holding very specialized sessions, such as the Iowa Communications Network. This conference took advantage of its state's new fiber optic system and involved eighty-two sites statewide, with over 1,100 Iowa trustees and librarians. This may be a prime example of the conference of the future.

Funding is an important part of all that trustees are involved with on the state, regional, and national front. Recently several public library systems have launched significant fundraising, development, and public/private partnerships. Foundations are being created and all of these efforts afford trustees the opportunity to become involved in the fundraising efforts for libraries. The current national economic and political climate is conducive to making development for library trustees a real opportunity for the public good. As national projects on literacy, the information highway, and other special interests develop, there are many more opportunities for developing plans and projects which benefit an initial area and for serving as models for replication. Lobbying to prevent major library budget cuts or to increase funding from governmental sources—city, county, state, or national—is another manner in which trustees may play major roles in funding.

Trustees have given testimony before the National Commission on Libraries and Information Service (NCLIS) as well as before state and national lawmakers. Trustees fill the information gap. They can provide the information legislators need and can show cost-effectiveness. They can also be very adept at identifying key supporters and approaching them to provide information before legislative sessions begin.

The International Federation of Library Associations (IFLA) is an organization in which trustees, with a few exceptions, have had little involvement. However, as our society becomes more global in nature, there is every reason to believe that this group will give certain interested trustees an opportunity for involvement on a global level.

Further Reading

Board Member: A Continuing Information Service for Nonprofit Leaders. (1992–   ) Bimonthly. National Center for Nonprofit Boards.

Bergan, Helen. *Where the Money Is.* Alexandria, Va.: Bio Guide Press, 1992.

Cirino, Paul John. *Library Trustees: Saints or Sinners? The Business of Running a Library*. Jefferson, N.C.: McFarland & Co., 1991.

Lynch, Richard. *Lead! How Public and Nonprofit Managers Can Bring Out the Best in Themselves and Their Organizations*. San Francisco: Jossey-Bass, 1992.

Reed, Sally. *Saving Your Library: A Guide to Getting, Using and Keeping the Power You Need*. Jefferson, N.C.: McFarland & Co., 1992.

Trustee Facts File. Illinois Library Trustee Association. n.d. (twenty-four booklets covering practical aspects of trusteeship and the public library.)

26 Public Libraries and the Challenge of Preservation

Thomas W. Shaughnessy

ccording to a report issued a few years ago by the National Endowment for the Humanities, some seventy-six million volumes of important books and journals currently on the shelves of our nation's libraries are in danger of disintegrating. Many of these works will be lost unless action is taken within the next twenty to thirty years.

The problem does not involve all old books and manuscripts but principally those published *after* 1840. It was at this time that methods in the paper-manufacturing process changed. An acidic sizing compound was introduced into the process; as a result, most paper manufactured after this period contains within it the seeds of its own destruction. A cursory examination of later nineteenth- and early twentieth-century titles will reveal paper that is turning brown and becoming brittle. Pages of books in this condition are likely to break or crack when being turned.

What can be done to address this problem? Most preservation experts recommend two approaches: one for retrospective (older) collections and a different approach for current (and future) collections. With regard to the former, the *content* of important works which constitute the principal asset of our civilization must be preserved. While it may not be possible to preserve the physical book, it is possible to capture its content. The principal methods for doing this are microfilming the item's contents on film that meets archival standards; capturing its contents by electronically scanning texts and images and storing this

Thomas W. Shaughnessy is University Librarian, University of Minnesota, Twin Cities.

information in a computer-readable, digitized format; and finally, photo-copying the document onto acid-free paper. These sheets or pages might then be reassembled and bound as are other monographs and periodicals. Usually, the use that is expected to be made of the document will indicate the most appropriate preservation solution. While the text digitizing approach is appealing because of its potential for networked access and electronic distribution of the digitized document, obsolescent hardware and software could lead to significantly reduced access and possibly even to digitized collections becoming virtually inaccessible. Unlike the situation that applies in microfilming, national standards have not yet been agreed upon with respect to text and image digitizing. Until such standards are developed and followed, the use of this medium for long-term preservation will remain problematic.

Because the conditions under which book, periodical, microfilm, multimedia, and other collections are housed significantly affect their durability, they should be stored in a climate-controlled environment. A cool temperature (65° F.) is recommended, with humidity levels between 45 and 55 percent. Humidity levels above and below those recommended will significantly reduce the life span of paper. An environment that is too dry increases the brittleness of paper; one that is too moist can stimulate mold growth. If fluorescent lights are used in book stack areas, they should be fitted with ultraviolet light filters. Fluorescent lamps with a low ultraviolet emissions are available as well. It is also important that library collections be shielded from direct sunlight. Ultraviolet rays have been proven to bleach bindings and paper and to fade microfilm.

With regard to current and future collections, a climate-controlled environment is once again recommended. Increasingly, books that are oriented toward the library market are being printed on acid-free paper. Whenever possible, these editions should be purchased by libraries. For materials published on paper with acid content, decisions will need to be made concerning whether to deacidify these volumes in an attempt to preserve the documents as artifacts or to preserve their content by means of microfilming or other means. Unfortunately, there are very few options for large-scale deacidification of collections. Several companies which have been offering this service are no longer doing so.

For many public libraries, only certain collections should be considered for preservation because of the costs associated with this effort. These collections might include local histories, archival files and genealogies, rare books, and other special or unique collections. Grants from various foundations and agencies are sometimes available to assist libraries in addressing their preservation needs if the significance of these collections can clearly be demonstrated.

Naturally, the preservation challenge will fall most heavily on research libraries, those which are dedicated to the support of research and scholarship. Smaller libraries and historical societies may wish to cooperate with larger libraries in their respective regions in meeting this challenge. In some states, state library agencies are taking an active role in preservation planning and in coordinating preservation efforts. But even the smallest library can contribute to the process by educating its staff, its governing board, local officials, and library users about this issue. Library staff, in particular, need to become better informed about the proper handling of books, journals, other documents and media—steps which if implemented could contribute significantly to extending the life of these important, but fragile, communications media. Once the staff is sufficiently trained, informal programs to educate children and other library users might be initiated.

Lastly, most public libraries should consider developing a disaster action plan. The plan should spell out procedures for dealing with water-damaged or smoke-damaged library material. Addresses and phone numbers of local agencies which might assist in preserving library collections should be listed in the plan and updated at regular intervals. As is true with injuries to humans, prompt action is usually the key to the survival of library collections should disaster strike.

Because of the high costs of preserving library collections, it is recommended that a consortial approach be taken. Public libraries within a given locale or region should combine their expertise and resources and cooperatively address their preservation concerns. Greater progress is more likely to be achieved in this manner than by separate initiatives by individual libraries.

27 The Trustee in Tomorrow's World

Virgina G. Young

he library trustee may well find that the world of today provides sufficient challenges to test his or her effort and ingenuity, without trying to pierce the veil of the future. Rapid changes in technological equipment, in building design and function, in publication and reproduction of materials, in shifts of population, in amounts and methods of financing and grants, all pose a bewildering multiplicity of choices and decisions upon the lay trustee in the professional library world.

These problems, however, can be solved, as library boards are proving every day. Study and application, plus adaptability and willingness to learn, provide the trustee with the means of solving each new problem. Professional assistance is in ample supply from government and state agencies and through the American Library Association. Even if the difficult is not done immediately (and the impossible, of course, takes a little longer), it *can* be done.

It is not, therefore, the increasingly complex technological problems which provide the trustee's greatest challenge in the world of tomorrow. As the years of this century crowd by, human achievements in the technological field grow more and more dazzling. But it also becomes more apparent with every passing year that the viability of our civilization is not rooted in even the most sophisticated equipment or material, but in mutual understanding among nations, races, creeds, and individuals. If we have a world to live in tomorrow, it must be a world of person-to-person communication and interaction.

It is in helping to build this world that the library trustee finds an immediate challenge, an incomparable opportunity to serve. Libraries

192

exist by and for the human mind, and it is the human mind which bears the responsibility for what they are. No computerized mathematical projection can replace the far-reaching effect of vision prompted by concern.

The challenge of tomorrow's world for the library trustee, indeed, is rooted in the area of human concern—concern that the library shall offer total service, with particular thought for those disadvantaged economically or physically; concern for good and productive working relationships within and without the library walls; concern that the library and the community shall be mutual sources of service and support. The trustee who is dedicated to proving these concerns will find that the lesser problems of hardware and housekeeping will fall into their proper perspective. And that proper place is to serve the library, to furnish the everyday tools for the library's operation. No matter how complex the technological problems nor how grueling the challenge they present, their place is still subordinate to the areas of human concern embodied in the library. From chisel to stylus to pen to movable type, people and their libraries have pressed ever forward, discovering, inventing, and using new tools of learning.

The trustee in tomorrow's world will have a constructive role in the library's long story. Knowing that it is an individual who plans and operates machines (for people build computers, computers do not build people), tomorrow's trustee will regard technological complexity as merely another tool—another useful object to serve the library and the minds of people.

But even as today, tomorrow's trustee will need a sense of commitment. John W. Gardner, former secretary of Health, Education, and Welfare, has made the following statement which might be spoken directly to today's as well as tomorrow's trustee:

> We built this complex dynamic society, and we can make it serve our purposes. We designed this technological civilization, and we can manage it for our own benefit. If we can build organizations, we can make them serve the individual.
>
> To do this takes a commitment of mind and heart—as it always did. If we make this commitment, this society will more and more come to be what it was always meant to be: a fit place for the human being to grow and flourish.[1]

1. John W. Gardner, *No Easy Victories* (New York: Harper & Row, 1968).

1 The Trustee Orientation Program

Orientation sessions for new trustees should be conducted as part of the agenda of regular board meetings. They will be better with the participation of all trustees and can provide a useful review for other board members. They could appropriately be conducted as part of the library board's annual review of long-range plans for the library.

If the board agenda is crowded, portions of the orientation program might be given by the president or another qualified trustee in the librarian's office. It should be remembered that orientation is a continuing process and cannot be accomplished in one session.

Suggested outline:

I. Welcome of new members to the board
   A. Greetings and introductions.
   B. Statement by board president on the board and the role of the individual trustee.
II. Brief history of local library
   A. Suggested topics which may be presented either orally or in printed material.
      1. The library's beginning—the aims of the founders.
      2. The financial status with sources of income, including local, state, and/or federal grants.
      3. The library's goals and objectives.
      4. The plan for achieving these goals and objectives.
      5. A copy of the library budget.
      6. The library organization chart.
      7. List of personnel and the library pay scale.
      8. Written policies.
      9. Latest annual report.
      10. Agendas and minutes of a few previous meetings.
III. Responsibilities and duties
   A. Provide trustees with a copy of the local and state handbook

Prepared by the American Library Trustee Association, 1960; revised 1963, 1968, 1978.

for trustees. Refer to (1) state library law or local ordinances which set forth the legal basis of the library board, (2) Chapter 10 of Young's *The Library Trustee: A Practical Guidebook*, 5th edition.

  B. Clarify whether trustees are to be a policy-determining body for the library or an advisory board and what their responsibilities are for obtaining sufficient funds to meet library needs.

  C. Summarize the primary responsibilities.

    1. Make everyone in the community aware of the library.

    2. Secure adequate financial support.

    3. Hire a competent director when the position becomes vacant.

    4. Encourage continued growth and development of library staff.

IV. Organizations for trustees

  A. The importance of associations and conferences in bringing together trustees and librarians where common problems are discussed, solutions offered, and future plans made.

  B. Kinds of organizations.

    1. *Regional.* Explain your own state map of regions or districts. Discuss where regional meetings are usually held.

    2. *State.* Give purpose of organization. Discuss membership in state association, the dues, the divisions of state association with emphasis on trustee section and its executive board, and the meetings. Annual state library association meetings provide a fine opportunity for trustees to obtain a statewide view of library service, in addition to receiving information and stimulation. Many libraries pay trustees' expenses when they attend state or regional meetings.

    3. *National.* The American Library Association is the chief spokesman for the modern library movement in North America. It is an organization of libraries, librarians, trustees, Friends of the Library, publishers, and others interested in the promotion of library and librarianship.

      a. Encourage attendance at ALA annual conferences which are held each summer in various cities of the United States and Canada with special programs for trustees.

      b. Encourage membership in ALA and the American Library Trustee Association (ALTA), a division of ALA. Many libraries pay the dues for trustees.

      c. List the present officers of ALTA and some of the committees.

V. Tour of library
   A. Introduce trustees to staff when convenient and possible.
   B. Arrange for demonstrations of special services as appropriate and flexible.
VI. Reading list for trustees [see pp.238–41].
VII. Ongoing orientation
   A. In subsequent meetings schedule reviews of existing library policies and the library's philosophy of service.
   B. Ask the director to arrange for various staff members to meet with the board on occasion for discussions with them about their areas of responsibility, interests, and concerns.

2 Director Orientation

The attempt to establish good library board-director relations should start as soon as the director is hired. There are actions that board members can take to help establish such relations. At the same time, these actions should facilitate the new director's move to the area and into the position, help integrate her or him into the community, and help establish this person in the community consciousness as the head librarian.

What follows is a list of such actions. Board members might want to scan the list for ideas about how to welcome their directors.

1. Assemble and mail an information package containing some of the following items: one or two issues of each area newspaper; a map; a telephone directory; brochures and pamphlets containing facts on local businesses and industries, real estate, churches, schools, government agencies, tourist sites, cultural and recreational activities, history, climate and geography. Sources for these items might include the library, the chamber of commerce, banks and other businesses and the state Department of Culture, Recreation and Tourism.

2. Assemble and mail a package of materials pertaining to the library. Such a package might include, but would not be limited to, the following items: pertinent state and local laws; bylaws, civil service regulations; current and previous annual reports; current and previous budgets; minutes from the last three or four board meetings; plans of action, goals, objectives, and the timetable for their accomplishment; standards; all policy, regulations and procedural manuals; an organizational chart; job descriptions; a list of board members; a list of staff members complete with their job titles; a list of the members of the Friends group and other active library supporters; materials on the library's history; a publicity brochure on current facilities and operations; information on the health insurance and retirement program offered.

Prepared by the Louisiana State Library.

3. If the services of a public relations person are unavailable, write a news release, obtain a flattering photograph, and send the article and photograph to the newspapers. In addition to highlighting the new director's education and experience, highlight any unusual *positive* information about her or him. For example, if the librarian grew up in Thailand, or was once a welder, or sky dives as a hobby, emphasize such an interesting fact. Submission of the article should be timed so that its appearance will have maximum impact. The best time for the article to appear would probably be during the director's first week.

4. If there were not time for a formal library tour and staff introductions during the interview, greet the director the first morning, give the tour, and make the introductions. If no board member can be present, choose an appropriate staff member to do the honors.

5. Take the new director to lunch during her or his first week.

6. Arrange for the outgoing director or an appropriate staff member to work closely with the new director during the first month. Such an arrangement will allow the veteran worker to impart valuable information on the community's political climate; the library's role in the community; key opinion leaders and public officials; and current library policies, procedures, operations, and finances. Such a person might accompany the new director on visits to branches, introducing her or him to staff members and pointing out unique features of, or problems with, the facilities.

7. Arrange in conjunction with the Friends group an open house or reception to honor the new director. Invite to it everyone one needs to know to be an effective administrator. Such individuals might include local government authorities, as well as the superintendent of education, principals, teachers, business leaders, chamber of commerce representatives, and service club representatives.

8. Introduce the director at meetings of local business and civic organizations.

9. Schedule a series of visits during the director's first two months between her or him and individual board members. The character of the visits could vary depending upon the interests, capabilities, and personality of the board member involved. For example, a board member active in local politics might discuss with the director the political situation of the area. A board member might take the director on a tour of city hall or the school board office, introducing her or him to key individuals.

The senior board member, or the one most familiar with the workings of the board, might provide the new director with a history of the board's composition, philosophy, attitudes, and action. This person might also reiterate the board's ideas on what the director's duties and responsibilities should be. The board member most familiar with the day-to-day workings of the library might identify for the director the most active library supporters, discuss with her or him any major problems the library has recently faced, or solicit questions or comments from the director about the new job.

10. Express interest in the director not just as the professional who will be running the library but also as an individual. Ask about her or his family, pastimes, likes and dislikes. Ask whether she or he is comfortably settled. Mention cultural and social activities available as well as shopping areas, schools, churches, and modes of public transportation.

11. Remember that a reassuring, receptive attitude toward the librarian will help morale and performance during the first difficult weeks on the job. Listen to the librarian. Respond positively to her or his comments and suggestions. Reserve judgment. Do not interfere but be available in case problems arise. Establishing a rapport between board and director in the beginning will make it much likelier that the director will succeed in the new position.

3 Library Bill of Rights

The American Library Association affirms that all libraries are forums for information and ideas, and that the following basic polices should guide their services.

1. Books and other library resources should be provided for the interest, information, and enlightenment of all people of the community the library serves. Materials should not be excluded because of the origin, background, or views of those contributing to their creation.
2. Libraries should provide materials and information presenting all points of view on current and historical issues. Materials should not be prescribed or removed because of partisan or doctrinal disapproval.
3. Libraries should challenge censorship in the fulfillment of their responsibility to provide information and enlightenment.
4. Libraries should cooperate with all persons and groups concerned with resisting abridgment of free expression and free access to ideas.
5. A person's right to use a library should not be denied or abridged because of origin, age, background, or views.
6. Libraries which make exhibit spaces and meeting rooms available to the public they serve should make such facilities available on an equitable basis, regardless of the beliefs or affiliations of individuals or groups requesting their use.

By official action of the Council on February 3, 1951, the Library Bill of Rights shall be interpreted to apply to all materials and media of communication used or collected by libraries. Adopted June 18, 1948; amended February 2, 1961, June 27, 1967, and January 23, 1980, by the ALA Council.

4 Freedom to Read Statement

The freedom to read is essential to our democracy. It is continuously under attack. Private groups and public authorities in various parts of the country are working to remove books from sale, to censor textbooks, to label "controversial" books, to distribute lists of "objectionable" books or authors, and to purge libraries. These actions apparently rise from a view that our national tradition of free expression is no longer valid; that censorship and suppression are needed to avoid the subversion of politics and the corruption of morals. We, as citizens devoted to the use of books and as librarians and publishers responsible for disseminating them, wish to assert the public interest in the preservation of the freedom to read.

We are deeply concerned about these attempts at suppression. Most such attempts rest on a denial of the fundamental premise of democracy: that the ordinary citizen, by exercising critical judgment, will accept the good and reject the bad. The censors, public and private, assume that they should determine what is good and what is bad for their fellow-citizens.

We trust Americans to recognize propaganda, and to reject it. We do not believe they need the help of censors to assist them in this task. We do not believe they are prepared to sacrifice their heritage of a free press in order to be "protected" against what others think may be bad for them. We believe they still favor free enterprise in ideas and expression.

We are aware, of course, that books are not alone in being subjected to efforts at suppression. We are aware that these efforts are related to a larger pattern of pressure being brought against education, the press, films, radio, and television. The problem is not only one of actual censorship. The shadow of fear cast by these pressures leads, we suspect, to an even larger voluntary curtailment of expression by those who seek to avoid controversy.

Such pressure toward conformity is perhaps natural to a time of uneasy change and pervading fear. Especially when so many of our

Adopted June 25, 1953; revised January 28, 1972, January 16, 1991, by the ALA Council and the AAP Freedom to Read Committee.

apprehensions are directed against an ideology, the expression of a dissident idea becomes a thing feared in itself, and we tend to move against it as against a hostile deed, with suppression.

And yet suppression is never more dangerous than in such a time of social tension. Freedom has given the United States the elasticity to endure strain. Freedom keeps open the path of novel and creative solutions, and enables change to come by choice. Every silencing of a heresy, every enforcement of an orthodoxy; diminishes the toughness and resilience of our society and leaves it the less able to deal with stress.

Now as always in our history, books are among our greatest instruments of freedom. They are almost the only means for making generally available ideas or manners of expression that can initially command only a small audience. They are the natural medium for the new idea and the untried voice from which come the original contributions to social growth. They are essential to the extended discussion which serious thought requires, and to the accumulation of knowledge and ideas into organized collections.

We believe that free communication is essential to the preservation of a free society and a creative culture. We believe that these pressures toward conformity present the danger of limiting the range and variety of inquiry and expression on which our democracy and our culture depend. We believe that every American community must jealously guard the freedom to publish and to circulate, in order to preserve its own freedom to read. We believe that publishers and librarians have a profound responsibility to give validity to that freedom to read by making it possible for the readers to choose freely from a variety of offerings.

The freedom to read is guaranteed by the Constitution. Those with faith in free people will stand firm on these constitutional guarantees of essential rights and will exercise the responsibilities that accompany these rights.

We therefore affirm these propositions:

1. *It is in the public interest for publishers and librarians to make available the widest diversity of views and expressions, including those which are unorthodox or unpopular with the majority.*

   Creative thought is by definition new, and what is new is different. The bearer of every new thought is a rebel until that idea is refined and tested. Totalitarian systems attempt to maintain themselves in power by the ruthless suppression of any concept which challenges the established orthodoxy. The power of a democratic system to adapt to change is vastly strengthened by the freedom of its citizens to choose widely from among conflicting opinions offered freely to them. To stifle every nonconformist idea at birth would mark the end of the democratic process. Furthermore, only through the constant activity of weighing and selecting can the democratic mind attain the strength demanded by times like these. We need to know not only what we believe but why we believe it.

2. *Publishers, librarians, and booksellers do not need to endorse every idea or presentation contained in the books they make available. It would conflict with the public interest for them to establish their own political, moral, or aesthetic views as a standard for determining what books should be published or circulated.*

Publishers and librarians serve the educational process by helping to make available knowledge and ideas required for the growth of the mind and the increase of learning. They do not foster education by imposing as mentors the patterns of their own thought. The people should have the freedom to read and consider a broader range of ideas than those that may be held by any single librarian or publisher or government or church. It is wrong that what one can read should be confined to what another thinks proper.

3. *It is contrary to the public interest for publishers or librarians to determine the acceptability of a book on the basis of the personal history or political affiliations of the author.*

A book should be judged as a book. No art or literature can flourish if it is to be measured by the political views of private lives of its creators. No society of free people can flourish which draws up lists of writers to whom it will not listen, whatever they may have to say.

4. *There is no place in our society for efforts to coerce the taste of others, to confine adults to the reading matter deemed suitable for adolescents, or to inhibit the efforts of writers to achieve artistic expression.*

To some, much of modern literature is shocking. But is not much of life itself shocking? We cut off literature at the source if we prevent writers from dealing with the stuff of life. Parents and teachers have a responsibility to prepare the young to meet the diversity of experiences in life to which they will be exposed, as they have a responsibility to help them learn to think critically for themselves. These are affirmative responsibilities, not to be discharged simply by preventing them from reading works for which they are not yet prepared. In these matters taste differs, and taste cannot be legislated; nor can machinery be devised which will suit the demands of one group without limiting the freedom of others.

5. *It is not in the public interest to force a reader to accept with any book the prejudgment of a label characterizing the book or author as subversive or dangerous.*

The ideal of labeling presupposes the existence of individuals or groups with wisdom to determine by authority what is good or bad for the citizen. It presupposes that individuals must be directed in making up their minds about the ideas they examine. But Americans do not need others to do their thinking for them.

6. *It is the responsibility of publishers and librarians, as guardians of the people's freedom to read, to contest encroachments upon that freedom by individuals or groups seeking to impose their own standards or tastes upon the community at large.*

It is inevitable in the give and take of the democratic process that the political, the moral, or the aesthetic concepts of an individual or group will occasionally collide with those of another individual or group. In a free society individuals are free to determine for themselves what they wish to read, and each group is free to determine what it will recommend to its freely associated members. But no group has the right to take the law into its own hands, and to impose its own concept of politics or morality upon other members of a democratic society. Freedom is no freedom if it is accorded only to the accepted and the inoffensive.

7. *It is the responsibility of publishers and librarians to give full meaning to the freedom to read by providing books that enrich the quality and diversity of thought and expression. By the exercise of this affirmative responsibility, they can demonstrate that the answer to a bad book is a good one, the answer to a bad idea is a good one.*

The freedom to read is of little consequence when expended on the trivial; it is frustrated when the reader cannot obtain matter fit for the reader's purpose. What is needed is not only the absence of restraint, but the positive provision of opportunity for people to read the best that has been thought and said. Books are the major channel by which the intellectual inheritance is handed down, and the principal means of its testing and growth. The defense of their freedom and integrity, and the enlargement of their service to society, requires of all publishers and librarians the utmost of their faculties, and deserves of all citizens the fullest of their support.

We state these propositions neither lightly nor as easy generalizations. We here stake out a lofty claim for the value of books. We do so because we believe that they are good, possessed of enormous variety and usefulness, worthy of cherishing and keeping free. We realize that the application of these propositions may mean the dissemination of ideas and manners of expression that are repugnant to many persons. We do not state these propositions in the comfortable belief that what people read is unimportant. We believe rather that what people read is deeply important; that ideas can be dangerous; but that the suppression of ideas is fatal to a democratic society. Freedom itself is a dangerous way of life, but it is ours.

This statement was originally issued in May of 1953 by the Westchester Conference of the American Library Association and the American Book Publishers Council, which in 1970 consolidated with the American Educational Publishers Institute to become the Association of American Publishers.

A Joint Statement by:
American Library Association
Association of American Publishers

Subsequently Endorsed by:
American Booksellers Association
American Booksellers Foundation for Free Expression
American Civil Liberties Union
American Federation of Teachers AFL-CIO
Anti-Defamation League of B'nai B'rith
Association of American University Presses
Children's Book Council
Freedom to Read Foundation
International Reading Association
Thomas Jefferson Center for the Protection of Free Expression
National Association of College Stores
National Council of Teachers of English
P.E.N.—American Center
People for the American Way
Periodical and Book Association of America
Sex Information and Education Council of the U.S.
Society of Professional Journalists
Women's National Book Association
YWCA of the U.S.A.

5

Guidelines for a Library Policy

Elizabeth A. Kingseed

General Library Objectives

General library objectives to be considered should include:

1. Promote enlightened citizenship.
2. Enrich personal lives.
3. Encourage continuous self-education.
4. Seek to identify community needs.
5. Assume a leadership role in the community.
6. Support Library Bill of Rights and Freedom to Read Statement.
7. Assemble, preserve, and administer books and related materials.
8. Serve the community as a center of reliable information.
9. Provide free service to every resident in the community.

Services of the Library

The library provides books and materials for information, entertainment, intellectual development, and enrichment of the people of the community. The library should endeavor to:

1. Select, organize, and make available necessary books and materials.
2. Provide guidance and assistance to borrowers.
3. Initiate programs, exhibits, book lists, etc.
4. Cooperate with other community agencies and organizations.
5. Secure information beyond its own resources when requested.
6. Lend to other libraries upon request.
7. Provide special services to nonresidents, disadvantaged, blind, hospital patients, etc.
8. Maintain a balance in its services to various age groups.

Elizabeth A. Kingseed is former assistant state librarian, New Hampshire State Library.

9. Cooperate with, but not perform the functions of, school or other institutional libraries.
10. Provide service during hours which best meet the needs of the community.
11. Provide service outlets located at points of maximum interest.
12. Periodically review library service being offered.

Budget

The following points should be considered in a policy on budgets:

1. Preparation—who is responsible.
2. Scope—items to be included and percentages to be used for different categories.
3. Presentation—by whom and when.
4. Special budget for new construction or when capital improvements are needed.

Personnel

The main points of good personnel policy include the following:

1. A description of each job in the library, degree of responsibility, educational and other qualifications required, special abilities or skills required, and the salary scale attached to the job.
2. A regular salary scale, giving minimum and maximum salary or wages, amounts of increments, period between increments, etc.
3. Provision for provisional appointments with specified length of probation.
4. Comfortable working conditions—adequate heat, light, rest rooms, etc.
5. Vacation with pay.
6. Sick leave with pay.
7. A regular work week with specified number of hours.
8. Regular holidays granted other public employees in community.
9. Work breaks.
10. Social Security and fringe benefits available to other public employees—hospitalization, other insurance, pension plans, and Workers' Compensation coverage.
11. Tenure—protection against unfair discharge or demotion.
12. Attendance at library meetings—time off with pay and travel expenses.
13. Opportunities for further training with pay, if possible.

14. Resignation—amount of notice required and stipulation that resignation should be in writing.
15. Provision for hiring substitute librarians when needed.
16. Statement on responsibility of librarian for administration of library and responsibility of trustees for making library policy.

It is recommended that the policy carry the approval of the local government body to avoid misunderstandings over such matters as salaries and tenure.

Book Selection

1. Support of Library Bill of Rights and Freedom to Read Statement.
2. Who is responsible for selection.
3. Quality of books to be selected.
4. Scope, emphasis, and limits of collection.
5. Treatment of gifts.
6. Basis for withdrawals and disposal of discards.
7. Position on supplying textbooks, primers, and other materials related to school curriculum.

The best selection statement should reflect the philosophy and overall objectives of the library.

Cooperation or Networking with Other Libraries

A policy on cooperation should include statements on:

1. Recognition of need for cooperation.
2. Affiliation with Statewide Library Development Plan.
3. Kinds of libraries with which library should cooperate.
4. Areas of cooperation.

Public Relations

Some of the primary public relations goals of the library should be:

1. To inform the public of library objectives and services through the press, radio, TV, etc.
2. Recognition of part played by staff, trustees, and Friends of Library in public relations.
3. Participation by staff in community activities.
4. Responsibility of staff for making talks in the community.
5. To encourage use of the library.
6. To obtain citizen support for library development.

Gifts and Special Collections

Gifts can help promote the program of the library, but libraries have found it helpful to point to an established policy, especially when books and other articles are offered. A policy should include statements on:

1. Conditions under which gifts of books and other materials will be accepted.
2. Disposition of nonusable gifts.
3. Acceptance of personal property, art objects, portraits, etc.
4. Conditions under which gifts of money, real property, or stock will be accepted.
5. Shelving of special collections.
6. Use of special bookplates.
7. Acceptance of denominational literature.
8. Acceptance of historical materials and writings of local authors.
9. Storage of material not designated as an outright gift.
10. Encouragement of gifts for memorial purposes.

Relationships with Schools

The public library and the public school are companion educational agencies, but their responsibilities differ in scope and function. In writing a policy the library should:

1. Define the separate functions and objectives of the public library and the school library.
2. Determine ways of establishing cooperative relations with the school.
3. Provide for continuous joint planning between those responsible for school and public library service.
4. Provide a written contract if the library is to give full service to schools.

Use of Library by Groups

Libraries have found it useful to adopt a written policy stating:

1. Who may use the rooms and when.
2. Whether a fee will be charged, and if so, how much.
3. Whether janitor service will be provided.
4. Whether meetings are to be free to the public.
5. Whether smoking will be allowed.
6. What restrictions are needed for regularly scheduled meetings.
7. Whether refreshments may be served.

8. Whether library activities have priority.
9. Who is in charge of reservations.

Two Sample Policies

The preceding checklist suggests items which should be included in every library policy statement but adapted to suit local conditions and needs. Policy must express a true commitment of service and leadership.

Book Selection Policy[1]

The board of this library recognizing the pluralistic nature of this community and the varied backgrounds and needs of all citizens, regardless of race, creed, or political persuasion, declares as a matter of book selection policy that:

1. Books or library material selection is and shall be vested in the library director, and, under the librarian's direction, such members of the professional staff who are qualified by reason of education and training. Any book or library material so selected shall be held to be selected by the board.
2. Selection of books or other library material shall be made on the basis of their value of interest, information, and enlightenment of all people of the community. No book or library material shall be excluded because of the race, nationality, or the political or social views of the author.
3. This board believes that censorship is a purely individual matter and declares that while anyone is free to reject for oneself books which do not meet with the individual's approval, one cannot exercise this right of censorship to restrict the freedom to read of others.
4. This board defends the principles of the freedom to read and declares that whenever censorship is involved no book or library material shall be removed from the library save under the orders of a court of competent jurisdiction.
5. This board adopts and declares that it will adhere to and support:
   a. The Library Bill of Rights, and
   b. The Freedom to Read Statement adopted by the American Library Association,
   both of which are made a part hereof.

1. Developed by Alex Allain and Virgina G. Young.

Public Relations Policy[2]

In recognition of the _____ Library's responsibility to maintain continuing communication with present and potential users of the _____ Library's services and resources, so as to assure effective and maximum usage by all citizens, the Board of Trustees of the _____ Library adopts the following resolution as a matter of policy.

The objectives of the _____ Library's public relations program are:

- To promote community awareness of library service.
- To stimulate public interest in and usage of the _____ Library.
- To develop public understanding and support of the _____ Library and its role in the community.

The following means may be used to accomplish the foregoing objectives:

1. An annual plan of specific goals and activities shall be developed, sufficient funds shall be allocated to carry out the program, and the program shall be evaluated periodically.
2. Training sessions, workshops, and other aids shall be made available to library staff members to assure courteous, efficient, and friendly contact with library patrons and the general public.
3. Personal and informational group contacts shall be maintained with government officials, opinion leaders, service clubs, civic associations, and other community organizations by library staff and Board members.
4. Local media shall be utilized to keep the public aware of and informed about the _____ Library's resources and services.
5. Newsletters, brochures, and other promotional materials shall be produced and distributed through effective methods of reaching the public.
6. The _____ Library may sponsor programs, classes, exhibits, and other library-centered activities and shall cooperate with other groups in organizing these to fulfill the community's needs for educational, cultural, informational, or recreational opportunities.
7. The Library Director or a designated qualified staff member shall have the responsibility for coordinating the _____ Library's public relations and public information activities.

2. Reprinted from *Library Promotion Handbook* by Marian Edsall with permission from The Oryx Press.

6 Ethics Statement for Public Library Trustees

Trustees must promote a high level of library service while observing ethical standards.

Trustees must avoid situations in which personal interests might be served or financial benefits gained at the expense of library users, colleagues, or the institution.

It is incumbent upon any trustee to disqualify himself or herself immediately whenever the appearance of a conflict of interest exists.

Trustees must distinguish clearly in their actions and statements between their personal philosophies and attitudes and those of the institution, acknowledging the formal position of the board even if they personally disagree.

A trustee must respect the confidential nature of library business while being aware of and in compliance with applicable laws governing freedom of information.

Trustees must be prepared to support to the fullest the efforts of librarians in resisting censorship of library materials by groups or individuals.

Trustees who accept appointment to a library board are expected to perform all of the functions of library trustees.

This statement was developed by the ALTA-PLA Common Concerns Committee. It was adopted by both the ALTA and PLA boards. A number of local and system boards have included it in their policies.

7 Indemnification Statement

It should be considered mandatory that every library have an adequate level of insurance coverage. If any claim or action not covered by insurance of State Statute is instituted against a trustee, officer, employee, or volunteer of the _____ Library System arising out of an act or omission by a trustee, officer, employee, or volunteer acting in good faith for a purpose considered to be in the best interest of the System; or if any claim or action not covered by insurance of State Statute is instituted against a trustee, officer, employee, or volunteer allegedly arising out of an act or omission occurring within the scope of his/her duties as such a trustee, officer, employee, or volunteer; the System should at the request of the trustee, officer, employee, or volunteer:

   a. appear and defend against the claim or action; and

   b. pay or indemnify the trustee, officer, employee, or volunteer for a judgment and court costs, based on such claim or action; and

   c. pay or indemnify the trustee, officer, employee, or volunteer for a compromise or settlement of such claim or action, providing the settlement is approved by the Board of Trustees.

Decision as to whether the System shall retain its own attorney or reimburse the trustee, officer, employee, or volunteer expenses for their own legal counsel shall rest with the Board of Trustees and shall be determined by the nature of the claim or action.

For the purpose of this article, the term trustee, officer, employee, or volunteer shall include any former trustee, officer, employee, or volunteer of the System.

This statement was developed by the ALTA-PLA Common Concerns Committee. It was adopted by both the ALTA and PLA boards. A number of local and system boards have included it in their policies.

8 Budget Checklist

The Library Budget Buys Service

A. Personnel

1. *Salaries*	Current Year	Next Year
Professional	_____	_____
Clerical	_____	_____
Janitorial	_____	_____
Total salaries	_____	_____

1. Has the salary schedule been reviewed recently for increased cost-of-living adjustments?

2. How does the salary schedule compare to the schedules in libraries of similar size and population group?

3. Have provisions been made for any planned new positions on the staff?

4. Has the annual increment been added to this year's base salary in order to calculate the salary of each employee for next year?

5. Has provision been made for pensions and Social Security, and have the Social Security rate and salary base for next year been verified?

2. *Staff Hospitalization, Medical and Group Insurance* _____ _____

3. *Social Security Taxes* _____ _____

Prepared by the Library Development Bureau, Division of the State Library, Archives and History, New Jersey State Department of Education.

B. Books and Other Library Materials

	Current Year	Next Year
Books		
Magazines		
Newspapers		
Pamphlets		
Binding and Rebinding		
Recordings		
Film Strips		
Films		
8 mm		
16 mm		
Microfilm and Other Microform		
Art Prints		
Other		
(tapes, cassettes, videos, compact discs, etc.)		
Total materials		

1. Has the library in its written book selection policy included general guides as to the proportions of the book budgets to be spent for the various categories, including adult, juvenile, fiction, non-fiction, and reference titles; and have recent average prices in these separate categories been checked and provided for in the amount for next year?

2. Has provision been made in the book budget for the cost of pre-processing?

3. Will the book budget for next year allow purchase of a sufficient number of volumes and periodicals to comply with the requirements of the "Rules and Regulations for the Receipt of State Aid?"

4. Does the periodicals budget include subscriptions to professional journals?

C. Supplies

Library Supplies		
Janitorial Supplies		
Other		
Total supplies		

1. Are printed catalog cards and processing kits included in the amount for library supplies?

2. Has the amount for supplies been determined on the basis of planned ordering so as to take maximum savings through quantity discounts?

3. Does the library take advantage of the state discounts?

D. Building Maintenance

	Current Year	Next Year
Heat		
Light		
Water		
Telephone		
Insurance		
Repairs		
Maintenance Contracts		
Exterior and Grounds		
Rent		
Total building maintenance		

1. Does the insurance cover the building and contents, public liability, and the heating plant? Are there endorsements for extended coverage?

2. How recent is the estimate of the replacement cost of the building and contents, and does the insurance provide adequate coverage?

3. Does the amount for buildings provide for planned regular painting and roof and gutter inspection and repairs?

E. Furniture and Equipment

Shelving, Tables, Cabinets		
Office Machines		
Photocopy Machine		
Audiovisual Equipment		
Repairs		
Total Furniture		

1. What pieces of equipment should be replaced?

2. What new equipment is available for rental or purchase that would improve services?

F. Public Relations

	Current Year	Next Year
Printed Material		
Photographs		
Posters		
Exhibits and Displays		
National Library Week		
Children's Book Week		
Other		
Total public relations		

G. Conferences and Memberships

Staff participation in professional meetings (including travel expenses)

Trustee participation in professional meetings

Membership in the state association and the American Library Association (ALA)

    Total conferences

1. Does the conference budget provide a reasonable reimbursement of expenses and travel to encourage participation in professional meetings?

H. Capital Improvements

I. Miscellaneous

Contingency

1. Were there any emergencies this year which should be provided for in the budget for next year?

    Total library budget

9 Sample Bylaws

Article I: Name

This organization shall be called "The Board of Trustees of the _____ Library" existing by virtue of the provisions of Chapter _____ of the Laws of the State of _____, and exercising the powers and authority and assuming the responsibilities delegated to it under the said statute.

Article II: Officers

Section 1. The officers shall be a president, a vice president, a secretary, and a treasurer, elected from among the appointed trustees as the annual meeting of the board.

Section 2. A nominating committee shall be appointed by the president three months prior to the annual meeting who will present a slate of officers at the annual meeting. Additional nominations may be made from the floor.

Section 3. Officers shall serve a term of one year from the annual meeting at which they are elected and until their successors are duly elected.

Section 4. The president shall preside at all meetings of the board, authorize calls for any special meetings, appoint all committees, execute all documents authorized by the board, serve as an ex-officio voting member of all committees, and generally perform all duties associated with that office.

Section 5. The vice president, in the event of the absence or disability of the president, or of a vacancy in that office, shall assume and perform the duties and functions of the president.

Section 6. The secretary shall keep a true and accurate record of all meetings of the board, shall issue notice of all regular and special meetings, and shall perform such other duties as are generally associated with that office.

Section 7. The treasurer shall be the disbursing officer of the board, cosign all checks, and shall perform such duties as generally devolve upon the office. He shall be bonded in an amount as may be required by the resolution of the board. In the absence or inability of the treasurer, his duties shall be performed by such other members of the board as the board may designate.

Article III: Meetings

Section 1. The regular meetings shall be held each month, the date and hour to be set by the board at the annual meeting.

Section 2. The annual meeting, which shall be for the purpose of the election of officers and the adoption of an annual report, shall be held at the time of the regular meeting in ____(month)____ of each year.

Section 3. The order of business for regular meetings shall include, but not be limited to, the following items which shall be covered in the sequence shown so far as circumstances will permit:

a. Roll call or members
b. Disposition of minutes of previous regular meeting and any intervening special meeting
c. Director's financial report of the library
d. Action on bills
e. Progress and service report of director
f. Committee reports
g. Communications
h. Unfinished business
i. New business
j. Public presentation to, or discussion with, the board
k. Adjournment

Section 4. Special meetings may be called by the secretary at the direction of the president, or at the request of _____ members, for the transaction of business as stated in the call for the meeting.

Section 5. A quorum for the transaction of business at any meeting shall consist of _____ members of the board present in person.

Section 6. Conduct of meetings: Proceedings of all members shall be governed by *Robert's Rules of Order*.

Article IV: Library Director and Staff

The board shall appoint a qualified library director who shall be the executive and administrative officer of the library on behalf of the board and under its review and direction. The director shall recommend to the board the appointment and specify the duties of other employees and shall be held responsible for the proper direction and supervision of the staff, for the care and maintenance of library property, for an adequate and proper selection of books in keeping with the stated policy of the board, for the efficiency of library service to the public, and for its financial operation within the limitations of the budgeted appropriation. In the case of part-time or temporary employees, the director shall have interim authority to appoint without prior approval of the board provided that any such appointment shall be reported to the board at its next regular meeting.

Article V. Committees

Section 1. The president shall appoint committees of one or more members each for such specific purposes as the business of the board may require from time to time. The committee shall be considered to be discharged upon the completion of the purpose for which it was appointed and after the final report is made to the board.

Section 2. All committees shall make a progress report to the library board at each of its meetings.

Section 3. No committees will have other than advisory powers unless, by suitable action of the board, it is granted specific power to act.

Article VI: General

Section 1. An affirmative vote of the majority of all members of the board present at the time shall be necessary to approve any action before the board. The president may vote upon and may move or second a proposal before the board.

Section 2. The bylaws may be amended by the majority vote of all members of the board provided written notice of the proposed amendment shall have been mailed to all members at least ten days prior to the meeting at which such action is proposed to be taken.

Section 3. Any rule or resolution of the board, whether contained in these bylaws or otherwise, may be suspended temporarily in connection with business at hand, but such suspension, to be valid, may be taken only at a meeting at which two-thirds (_____) of all members of the board shall be present and two-thirds of those present shall so approve.

10 Evaluating the Library Director

The criteria for evaluation are grouped under general headings and pertain to the duties most library boards require of their library director. A rating range is provided for each criterion. In those areas where you feel that you do not have sufficient knowledge of the area to render a judgment, mark the item "Don't Know."

(Circle one number or the X)

	Poor		Good		Excellent	Don't Know
1. As technical advisor to the board:						
a. use of innovative methods of service delivery which have been studied and implemented only after they fit the needs of the institution and are proven to be cost-effective	1	2	3	4	5	X
b. maintenance of an adequate knowledge of the current state-of-the-art	1	2	3	4	5	X
c. encouragement of staff in maintaining an awareness of technological advances in the profession	1	2	3	4	5	X
2. Policy recommendation to the board:						
a. completes adequate staff work prior to presentation to the board	1	2	3	4	5	X

Developed by Virginia G. Young from criteria found in Nancy M. Bolt, *Evaluating the Library Director* (ALTA Publication no. 5; ALA, 1983).

	Poor		Good		Excellent	Don't Know

(Circle one number or the X)

b. recommends reasonable alternatives — 1 2 3 4 5 X

c. makes policy recommendations in advance rather than as a reaction to a problem — 1 2 3 4 5 X

d. makes policy recommendations only when necessary and appropriate to the efficient operation of the library — 1 2 3 4 5 X

3. Execution of board policies and decisions:

a. implements board decisions on a timely basis — 1 2 3 4 5 X

b. backs board policies and decisions rather than presenting them to staff in an apologetic or deprecatory manner — 1 2 3 4 5 X

4. Employment and supervision of staff:

a. emphasizes Equal Opportunity Employer and Affirmative Action hiring practices — 1 2 3 4 5 X

b. maintains positive relations with management and staff — 1 2 3 4 5 X

c. justifies the need for staff development funds, actively campaigns for them, and accounts for their use — 1 2 3 4 5 X

(Circle one number or the X)

	Poor		Good		Excellent	Don't Know
d. designs selection process to insure the selection of the most qualified person for the job	1	2	3	4	5	X
e. analyzes functions periodically with the objectives of combining, eliminating and/or creating new positions	1	2	3	4	5	X

5. Extending library services:

a. recommends priorities that implement the library's mission as defined by board policy	1	2	3	4	5	X
b. priorities reflect community needs	1	2	3	4	5	X
c. establishes priorities in advance rather than in response to a problem	1	2	3	4	5	X

6. Short- and long-range planning:

a. planning reflects board priorities	1	2	3	4	5	X
b. updates plans on a continuous basis reflecting changing circumstances	1	2	3	4	5	X
c. accomplishments reflect and relate to both short- and long-range plans	1	2	3	4	5	X
d. plans flexible enough to allow for unforeseen circumstances	1	2	3	4	5	X
e. provides adequate information to the board on the implementation, revision, etc., of short- and long-range planning	1	2	3	4	5	X

(Circle one number or the X)

	Poor		Good		Excellent	Don't Know

7. Public relations
   a. effectively communicates
      services of the library to
      the public   1   2   3   4   5   X
   b. establishes a proper and
      realistic balance between
      promotion of services and
      budget constraints   1   2   3   4   5   X
   c. analyzes circulation
      trends and in-house use
      and reacts appropriately
      to the results of such
      analysis   1   2   3   4   5   X

8. Community involvement
   a. director is active in
      community   1   2   3   4   5   X
   b. director is visible to large
      segments of the
      population   1   2   3   4   5   X
   c. director is available for
      speaking engagements in
      the community   1   2   3   4   5   X

9. Budgets and reports
   a. prepares regular reports
      embodying library's
      current progress and
      future needs   1   2   3   4   5   X
   b. prepares an annual
      budget in consultation
      with the board and gives
      a current report of
      expenditures against the
      budget at each meeting   1   2   3   4   5   X
   c. completes all staff work in
      a timely manner prior to
      budget presentation   1   2   3   4   5   X
   d. budget covers all
      necessary expenses   1   2   3   4   5   X

	Poor		Good		Excellent	Don't Know

e. allocations are made or
reserved for unanticipated
contingencies   1 2 3 4 5   X

f. funds are effectively
allocated   1 2 3 4 5   X

g. mid-course corrections are
minimized   1 2 3 4 5   X

10. Collection development
a. selects and orders (or
effectively delegates these
processes) all books and
other library materials   1 2 3 4 5   X

b. maintains an effective
program for determining
user needs and wants and
translating these needs
and wants into
acquisitions and services   1 2 3 4 5   X

c. has evolved a plan
enabling library to
respond to materials'
budget cuts   1 2 3 4 5   X

11. National and State
organization meetings
a. library represented and
director actively
participates in the
American Library
Association, state and
regional library
associations   1 2 3 4 5   X

b. director holds or has held
offices in professionsl
organizations   1 2 3 4 5   X

c. staff and director have
had articles published in
professional journals   1 2 3 4 5   X

(Circle one number or the X)

	Poor		Good		Excellent	Don't Know

12. General
    a. knows local and state
       laws and actively supports
       legislation in the state
       and nation

1 2 3 4   5   X

    b. utilizes services and
       consultants of the state
       library

1 2 3 4   5   X

    c. cooperates with the board
       to plan and carry out the
       library program

1 2 3 4   5   X

    d. reports regularly to
       library board, to local
       government officials, and
       the public

1 2 3 4   5   X

13. Maintenance and
    construction of facilities
    a. buildings and grounds are
       adequately maintained

1 2 3 4   5   X

    b. maintains an ongoing
       program that provides
       adequate information on
       the need for new or
       remodeled facilities

1 2 3 4   5   X

    c. new or remodeled
       facilities function
       appropriately and are
       aesthetically pleasing

1 2 3 4   5   X

    d. new or remodeled
       facilities are constructed
       within budget allocations

1 2 3 4   5   X

14. Miscellaneous rating factors
    a. difficult decisions are
       made and implemented
       rather than being
       deferred or ignored

1 2 3 4   5   X

		(Circle one number or the X)					Don't
		Poor		Good		Excellent	Know
b.	displays initiative rather than reacting to problems as they arise	1	2	3	4	5	X
c.	is objective in making necessary decisions and does not permit personal prejudices to intrude too often	1	2	3	4	5	X
d.	maintains consistency in decisions affecting public/ staff	1	2	3	4	5	X
e.	is open with the board and does not let a hidden agenda intrude	1	2	3	4	5	X
f.	sets an example for the staff through professional conduct, high principles, and a business-like approach	1	2	3	4	5	X
g.	attends all board meetings other than those at which his or her salary or tenure is discussed	1	2	3	4	5	X

15. Personality and behavior traits

		Poor		Good		Excellent	Don't Know
a.	has a cooperative attitude	1	2	3	4	5	X
b.	organizes work well	1	2	3	4	5	X
c.	takes initiative	1	2	3	4	5	X
d.	demonstrates creativity	1	2	3	4	5	X
e.	meets deadlines	1	2	3	4	5	X
f.	shows tact	1	2	3	4	5	X
g.	communicates well	1	2	3	4	5	X
h.	shows enthusiasm for work	1	2	3	4	5	X
i.	sets a professional example	1	2	3	4	5	X
j.	motivates staff	1	2	3	4	5	X
k.	is receptive to new ideas and suggestions	1	2	3	4	5	X
l.	makes good decisions	1	2	3	4	5	X

16. Comments:

A careful analysis of the results should be presented to the board and the director. Such results can be very useful in showing strengths, as well as highlighting areas that can be improved. Most often results are favorable, and it would be valuable for the director's files to contain a letter reflecting the board's evaluation.

11 Evaluation of Board Members

Following are two examples of trustee evaluation.

Trustee Scorecard

__ Have I attended at least one state library conference this year?

__ Do I know the library laws as they apply to my library?

__ Do I attend board meetings regularly?

__ Do I give a reasonable amount of time and thought to my job as a trustee?

__ Do I regularly read one library periodical?

__ Do I belong to any state or national library organization?

__ Have I studied and do I use for reference the State Handbook for Library Trustees?

__ Have I read *The Library Trustee* or *The Trustee of a Small Public Library* by Virginia G. Young?

__ Have I read issues of the state library association's journal?

__ Do I visit my library frequently enough to be thoroughly familiar with the services it offers?

__ Do I use every opportunity to inform civic groups and public officials of the services and needs of my library?

__ Do I know what services and aids are available to library boards from the state library?

__ Have I frequently contacted my senator or representative in the state legislature concerning library legislation?

__ Do I use the library for my personal reading and study?

__ Do I visit other libraries to inform myself of library practices?

__ Do I encourage and support my library director in efforts to provide good library service?

Developed by Missouri State Library.

__ Do I know how my library measures up to state and national standards?

__ Do I know whether or not and in what manner my library can participate in the use of federal funds?

__ Have I read *Planning and Role Setting for Public Libraries* and *Output Measures for Public Libraries?*

__ Am I thoroughly familiar with the policies adopted by my board, and do I study and review before voting "yes" or "no" at board meetings?

__ My score (5 points each question—100 point maximum)

Trustee Evaluation

1. *As I work with other board members*
   a. Do I attend most of the meetings and inform the librarian when I must be absent?
   b. Do I contribute effectively to the discussions from a reasoned and informed background?
   c. Is my attitude toward other board members fair, cooperative, and open?
   d. Am I willing to abide by the majority decision and support it publicly?
   e. Do I do an acceptable job in filling board offices and in undertaking committee assignments?

2. *As I relate to the director and staff*
   a. Do I understand and honor the dividing line between accepted trustee responsibilities (as set out in the literature) and the librarian's responsibility to administer?
   b. Is my attitude toward the librarian one of professional respect and encouragement?
   c. Do I refrain from initiating or entering into library-related discussions with staff except in board settings?
   d. Do I refrain from asking for special privileges or treatment?
   e. Do I encourage staff development?

3. *As I serve the community*
   a. Do I keep abreast of current library practices and possibilities through reading the literature, attending professional meetings, visiting other libraries, or other means?
   b. Do I understand and discharge my responsibilities to represent all segments of the community in an effort to provide the widest access and the best services possible? Am I open to innovation?
   c. Am I prepared to accept my responsibility to support the concept of intellectual freedom and to stand firmly in support of the librarian and the book selection policy, if an attack is mounted by an individual or a group?
   d. Do I discharge my responsibility to serve as a library advocate, both formally, to governmental bodies as appropriate, and informally, to the public at large?
   e. Do I discharge my responsibility to participate actively in tax elections and other fund-raising efforts?
   f. Is the public's perception of me such that my identification as a board member builds public respect for the library and enhances the library's image in the community?
   g. Do I avoid even the appearance of using my library connection as a means of self-aggrandizement?
   h. Am I zealous in presenting the library, the librarian and staff, and my fellow board members in a positive manner in my comments to individuals or groups in the community?

Developed by Linda Bennett Wells and Minnie-Lou Lynch, Allen Parish Libraries, Louisiana.

12 Rules for Volunteers

In the Daniel Boone Regional Library in Missouri, the Volunteer Friends of the public library is a division of the Friends of the Public Library, which has the primary function of raising money for the library. The volunteers assist in the daily operation of the library and may participate and belong to the Friends parent group. The Volunteer Friends program is directed by a paid staff member who serves as the volunteer coordinator and who reports to the director of the library.

The following material is taken from the Volunteer Friends of the Library Handbook *of the Daniel Boone Regional Library.*

Volunteers have always been important to the Daniel Boone Regional Library system. With the increasing cost of operations and regulations on temporary help, the library has felt the need to rely more heavily on its volunteers. The library plans to use volunteers to—

1. Accomplish one-time large projects that require above normal staffing levels.
2. Establish a pool of volunteer workers willing to be on call for tasks required to be performed on an intermittent basis.
3. Provide an ongoing source of assistance to library staff.
4. Provide assistance beyond the time that a staff member has to give to a project.
5. Develop a group of citizens, who, because of their involvement in the work of the library, can assist the library in interpreting its needs to the community and in improving the library's awareness of the informational needs of the community.

Rules for Volunteers

The Volunteer Friends are considered "staff" by the library and thus are subject to the following procedures and rules.

1. Sign in and out on the volunteer log sheet in the circulation department.
2. Use assigned storage space for handbags and coats.
3. Report to your area supervisor at the beginning of each work period.

4. If you are going to be late or absent from work for any reason, please notify your supervisor as far in advance as possible.
5. Wear your name tag for identification whenever you are working.
6. Wear appropriate clothing.
7. Do not smoke in public areas.
8. You may take 15-minute breaks in the staff lounge on the second floor.
9. Report any injury immediately. (In this library, volunteers are covered by Workers' Compensation insurance.)
10. Park your car in the last three rows of the west lot.
11. Work according to established procedures. If the volunteer develops a different method, discuss with the area supervisor to see if it is feasible to implement.
12. Practice professional ethics. Do not divulge confidential information to which you have access.
13. If you decide to terminate your service to the library, your resignation should be submitted to your supervisor in writing at least two weeks in advance. This will give the library time to find a replacement and to find out exactly where you are in the project on which you are working

Cardinal Rule: Never say "I don't know" to a patron. Always take the patron to a staff member who will be able to fill the patron's request.

13 Forming a Friends Group

Why Organize?

A need for Friends may arise in the community which has an inadequate building or book collection, limited services, insufficient or poorly paid staff, or insufficient funds for acquisition and upkeep. Where library size keeps pace with public demand, it may be that all citizens are not utilizing library facilities to the utmost, and a program to promote and extend library use is desirable.

Who Takes the Initiative?

An organized lay group, such as the American Association of University Women or a local service club, can inaugurate a Friends group through expansion of its existing committee on civic improvement or community affairs. Or the mayor, the librarian, or library trustees may invite public-spirited citizens to form a study group and initiate a Friends movement. An individual may provide the original impetus for any of these methods, or may simply call together, for a preorganizational meeting, like-minded citizens who require no sponsoring agent. The strongest Friends, however, are those who anticipate close cooperation with other community groups, including local government, and with the professional library staff.

What is the Preorganizational Meeting?

"When it is desired to form a permanent society, those interested in it should consult together before calling a meeting to organize the society."[1] This suggests an aura of smoke-filled rooms or a coffee klatch, but is eminently practical.

Prepared by the Friends of California Libraries, Inc.
1. *Robert's Rules of Order Revised*, pp. 284–291, details the steps to be taken in establishing an organization.

Essentially, a small group of people resolve, informally, "That a Friends of the Library of this City be formed to (accomplish certain stated aims)." This will be the statement you present to the public through newspapers and individual announcements that a Friends of the Library is forming.

Having stated, to yourselves, your reasons for forming, determine who should be invited to attend the organizational meeting, and where and when it should be held. Select a secretary pro tem and a chairman pro tem.

You may now appoint: (1) a bylaws committee which will prepare bylaws for approval at the organizational meeting, and (2) a nominating committee, instructed to draw up a slate of officers for presentation at the organizational meeting. You may also want to determine what other committees should be established. Instruct the secretary pro tem to send out notices stating time and place of the organizational meeting.[2]

Organizational Meeting: Who Comes and What Takes Place?

Invite the public at large, through newspaper stories and a poster or handbills in the library, schools, and community center. Write, quoting your resolution, to every organized group on the local chamber of commerce list, urging them to send one official representative and as many other members as can come. Include every club, league, guild, post, and parish. The library is the one public institution designed to be used by everyone, lifelong. Your membership must be open to all, and a Friends group which is inadvertently exclusive is weaker because of it.

At your organizational meeting, outline the purposes and the plans of the Friends group. If you have no Friends of California Libraries (FCL) Extension Committee speaker to do this, your chairman pro tem should speak, quoting statistics and established facts to show definite community need for a Friends group.

Follow immediately with the next procedural step: "Mr. Chairman?" "The chair recognizes Mrs. X." "I wish to make the following resolution: 'That it is the sense of this meeting that a Friends of the Library be formed to . . . etc.' " Discussion should follow, and the resolution, possibly amended, be put to the vote and passed.

If your bylaws committee has been appointed, the meeting then moves on to hear, debate, and adopt the bylaws. That done, procedure as

2. See "Sample Bylaws" and "Taxation & Incorporation" in *Friends of the Library Information Kit*, ed. by Lexie Nall (P.O. Box 455, Sierra Madre, California 91024: Friends of California Libraries, 1978).

specified in the bylaws must be followed, and the nominating committee may now be called on to place the slate of officers in nomination.

All those present who signed as members and are therefore qualified to vote, may then elect the officers and board. The chairman pro tem and secretary pro tem will turn over the gavel and pen, respectively, and the meeting can continue with the appointment of committees.

Just prior to entertaining the motion to adjourn to another date and place, the president can assert that he or she will expect proposals of action from each committee at the next meeting, and then Friends will be truly underway.

If you adhere to more formal procedure, you may do nothing more at your preorganizational meeting than state reasons for forming; appoint a secretary and chairman pro tem; and plan the organizational meeting.

Then, at your organizational meeting, you will (1) present the resolution that "a Friends . . . be formed to . . .," discuss it, and vote on it; (2) nominate and elect or appoint a chairman and committee to draft bylaws; (3) appoint a nominating committee; and (4) move that this meeting be adjourned to a future time and place at which officers will be elected, bylaws adopted, committees appointed, and minutes of the organizational meeting be read. The chair may request that all who are present sign up as charter members of the new Friends of the Library, and then entertain a motion for adjournment. You are launched.

Suggested Reading for Library Trustees

This brief list is intended to be a selective guide to various kinds of information useful to both new trustees and experienced ones. From it trustees may get an idea of the range of helpful materials available in the fields of trusteeship and librarianship.

For more information on topics suggested in these readings or on other topics of concern or interest, the trustee should consult the local library staff or the other agencies in the section Information Sources at the end of the list. Materials not available locally may be obtained on interlibrary loan from a neighboring library, the system headquarters, or the state library agency.

American Library Trustee Association. *Automating Your Library: A Planning Book.* Prepared by Kathleen Colson Mulroy and Elizabeth Steckman. Chicago: American Library Trustee Association, 1994.

A guide for librarians, school library media specialists, administrators and governing boards of all types of libraries that are planning for automation of cataloging, circulation and public access catalogs. Decision makers will be able to address key issues: whether to automate, what to automate, and how to automate.

Baughman, James C. *Policy Making for Public Library Trustees.* Foreword by Renée Rubin. Englewood, Colo.: Libraries Unlimited, 1993.

Twenty-five situations that call for library policies.

Bessler, Joanne M. *Putting SERVICE into Library Staff Training: A Patron-Centered Guide.* LAMA Occasional Papers, no. 2. Chicago: American Library Association, 1994.

This guide encourages mangers to identify and describe service ideals, to translate these ideals into realistic goals, and to lead new and experienced staff in fulfilling these ideals.

Bolt, Nancy M. *Evaluating the Library Director.* ALTA Publication, no. 5. Chicago: American Library Association, 1983.

Presents three methods of evaluating the library director and offers an approach to conducting the evaluation.

Bonnell, Pamela. *Fund Raising for the Small Library*. LAMA Small Libraries Publications, no. 8. Chicago: American Library Association, 1983.

This publication presents information helpful for determining need and for selecting and implementing a campaign method for fundraising.

Childers, Thomas A. and Nancy Van House. *What's Good? Describing Your Public Library's Effectiveness*. Chicago: American Library Association, 1993.

The core of this workbook is "A Model of Public Library Effectiveness," which is a table of sixty-one evaluative criteria. It includes a blank table for use in your library's own self-study.

Dahgren, Anders C. *Planning the Small Public Library Building*. LAMA Small Libraries Publications, no. 11. Chicago: American Library Association, 1985.

A source that touches on all the aspects of the library construction planning process.

Daubert, Madeline J. *Financial Management for Small and Medium-Sized Libraries*. Chicago: American Library Association, 1993.

This title covers financial management including explanations and examples for preparing the library's budget.

Geddes, Andrew and James A. Hess. *Securing a New Library Director*. ALTA Publications, no. 1. Chicago: American Library Association, 1979.

This practical paper provides helpful guidelines for library boards in their efforts to secure a library director.

Hill, Malcolm. *Budgeting and Financial Record Keeping in the Small Library*. 2d ed., #3. LAMA Small Libraries Publication. Chicago: American Library Association, 1992.

This booklet provides practical suggestions for the small library administration.

Ihrig, Alice B. *Decision Making for Public Libraries*. Library Professional Publications, 1989.

This book explores various issues that require sound trustee decision.

Ihrig, Alice B. *Library Trustees in State Organizations*. ALTA Publication, no. 4. Chicago: American Library Association, 1982.

Still pertinent, this title examines the strengths and functions of state trustee organization.

Kinny, Lisa F. *Lobby for Your Library: Know What Works*. Chicago: American Library Association, 1992.

This author provides "insider information" gleaned from her own career as a state senator.

Libraries for the Future: Planning Buildings that Work. Papers from the LAMA Library Buildings Preconference, June 27–28, 1991. Ed. Ron Martin. Chicago: American Library Association, 1992.

As the title suggests, this is a compilation of papers on various aspects of planning buildings for future libraries.

Lushington, Nolan. *Consultants and Library Boards.* ALTA Publication, no. 2. Chicago: American Library Association, 1981.

This guideline gives pointers on how to determine the need for a consultant and how to make effective use of consultants' services.

Manley, Will, and Richard Lee. *For Library Trustees Only: Living with Your Director.* Jefferson, N.C.: MacFarland, 1993.

The information for trustees is written with a sense of humor.

McClure, Charles, et at. *Planning and Role Setting for Public Libraries: A Manual Options and Procedures.* Chicago: American Library Association, 1987.

This publication provides a step-by-step planning program for public libraries.

Morris, John. *The Library Disaster Preparedness Handbook.* Chicago: American Library Association, 1986.

This publication offers a broad range of strategies of protection that are simple and inexpensive or sophisticated and costly.

Nelson, William G. *Selected Risks Pertaining to Library Operations: Their Control and Insurability.* Chicago: American Library Association, 1981.

This practical guide considers such risks as theft and mutilation of books and the vulnerability of the library and its staff to certain legal liabilities.

Prentice, Ann E. *Financial Planning for Libraries.* Metuchen, N.J.: Scarecrow, 1985.

The author explains financial planning techniques in addition to techniques for gathering data analyzing costs and controlling expenditures.

Rounds, Richard S. *Basic Budgeting Practices for Libraries.* 2d ed. Chicago: American Library Association, 1994.

The author explores budgeting across functions in the library and includes twelve steps in effective budgeting.

Rubin, Renée. *Avoiding Liability Risk: An Attorney's Advice to Library Trustees and Others.* Chicago: American Library Association, 1994.

In order to avoid being sued, the author points out areas of vulnerability to library board members, managers, and other in such positions.

Sheldon, Brooke. *Personnel Administration in the Small Public Library.* LAMA Small Libraries Publications, no. 5. Chicago: American Library Association, 1980.

This pamphlet expounds on the differences of the roles, responsibilities, and relationships of various library personnel, board, and volunteer groups.

Short, Jack. *Library Trustee Guidelines*. Avon, Conn.: Consultant Publications, 1994.

Covers many topics facing library trustees. Succinct discussion starters.

Swan, James. *Working Together: A How-to-Do-it Manual for Librarians*. New York: Neal-Schuman, 1992.

This book includes work sheets and summaries on the roles of trustees and librarians.

Water, Virginia A. *Output Measures for Public Library Service to Children: A Manual of Standardized Procedures*. Chicago: American Library Association, 1992.

A companion volume to *Planning and Role Setting*, the basic output measures can be used to reflect service to children fourteen years old and younger.

Weingand, Darlene E. *Administration of the Small Public Library*. 3rd ed. Chicago: American Library Association, 1992.

Aimed at library administrators, the author offers solutions to libraries faced with significant social and technological change.

Williams, Lorraine M. *The Library Trustee and the Public Librarian: Partners in Service*. Metuchen, N.J.: Scarecrow, 1993.

The emphasis of this book is on the relationship between the library board and library director in their distinct roles.

Young, Virginia G. *The Trustee of a Small Public Library*. 2d ed. LAMA Small Libraries Publication, no. 1. Chicago: American Library Association, 1992.

The work defines the role of a library trustee in relation to the library, the librarian, and the community.

Van House, Nancy, et al. *Output Measures for Public Libraries: A Manual of Standardized Procedures*. 2d ed. Chicago: American Library Association, 1987.

Describes a set of measures to assess common public library services.

Periodicals

Trustee Voice. The official publication of the American Library Trustee Association.

Index